# TEACHER LEADERSHIP IN PROFESSIONAL DEVELOPMENT SCHOOLS

# TEACHER LEADERSHIP IN PROFESSIONAL DEVELOPMENT SCHOOLS

EDITED BY

## JANA HUNZICKER

*Bradley University, Peoria, IL, USA*

United Kingdom – North America – Japan India – Malaysia – China

Emerald Publishing Limited
Howard House, Wagon Lane, Bingley BD16 1WA, UK

First edition 2018

Copyright © 2018 Emerald Publishing Limited

**Reprints and permissions service**
Contact: permissions@emeraldinsight.com

No part of this book may be reproduced, stored in a retrieval system, transmitted in any form or by any means electronic, mechanical, photocopying, recording or otherwise without either the prior written permission of the publisher or a licence permitting restricted copying issued in the UK by The Copyright Licensing Agency and in the USA by The Copyright Clearance Center. Any opinions expressed in the chapters are those of the authors. Whilst Emerald makes every effort to ensure the quality and accuracy of its content, Emerald makes no representation implied or otherwise, as to the chapters' suitability and application and disclaims any warranties, express or implied, to their use.

**British Library Cataloguing in Publication Data**
A catalogue record for this book is available from the British Library

ISBN: 978-1-78743-404-2 (Print)
ISBN: 978-1-78743-403-5 (Online)
ISBN: 978-1-78743-923-8 (Epub)

INVESTOR IN PEOPLE

# Contents

Foreword      *ix*
*Bruce E. Field*

Acknowledgements      *xiii*

Dedication      *xv*

List of Abbreviations      *xvii*

**Chapter 1    Professional Development Schools: An Overview and Brief History**
*Jana Hunzicker*      *1*

**Chapter 2    Teacher Leadership in Professional Development Schools: A Definition, Brief History, and Call for Further Study**
*Jana Hunzicker*      *19*

## Section I: Teacher Leadership and Student Learning

**Chapter 3    Collaborative Leadership in Meeting the Needs of English Learners in an Urban Elementary PDS**
*Nancy Dubetz, Maria Fella, Yokaira LaChapell and Jennifer Rivera*      *41*

**Chapter 4    De-Tracking Ninth Grade Algebra: A Teacher Leadership Success Story**
*Rhonda Baynes Jeffries*      *59*

**Chapter 5    Moving from Collaborative Teacher Inquiry to Leadership: Four Stories from Project Teacher Leadership**
*Clare Kruft and Diane Wood*      *75*

## Chapter 6  Teacher Leader Reflections: Teacher Leadership and Student Learning                99

A Courageous, Collegial Partnership
*Keri Haley and Christopher Urquhart*

From One to Many
*Nancy Cryder Jones*

Learning and Leading through Collaboration
*Jamie Silverman*

Questions for Further Reflection
*Jana Hunzicker*

## Chapter 7  Teacher Leadership and Student Learning
*Bernard J. Badiali*                107

### Section II: Definitions, Structures, and Cultures that Promote Teacher Leadership

## Chapter 8  Teacher Leader Identities and Influences as Defined by Liaisons-in-Residence
*Jennifer L. Snow, Sarah Anderson, Carolyn Cort, Sherry Dismuke and A. J. Zenkert*                121

## Chapter 9  Lab School Teacher Leaders as Learners and Change Agents
*Margaret Hudson and Jayne Hellenberg*                141

## Chapter 10  National Board Certified Teachers as Bridges for Teacher Candidates Entering the Profession
*Anna M. Quinzio-Zafran and Elizabeth A. Wilkins*                161

## Chapter 11  Teacher Leader Reflections: Definitions, Structures, and Cultures that Promote Teacher Leadership                181

Total Teacher Leaders
*Ashley Bennett*

Quiet Opportunity
*P. Erin Lichtenstein*

Bridges
*Suzanna Nelson*

The Best PDS Perk
*Azaria Cunningham*

Questions for Further Reflection
*Jana Hunzicker*

**Chapter 12  Definitions, Structures, and Cultures that Promote Teacher Leadership: Making Sense of Section Two**
*Michael N. Cosenza*     191

### Section III: Teacher Leader Preparation and Development

**Chapter 13  Cultivating Teacher Candidates' Passions into Leadership for Tomorrow: The Gift that Keeps on Giving**
*Vail Matsumoto, Jon Yoshioka and Lori Fulton*     201

**Chapter 14  Developing Teacher Leaders Using a Distributed Leadership Model: Five Signature Features of a School–University Partnership**
*Brianne W. Morettini, Kathryn McGinn Luet, Lisa J. Vernon-Dotson, Nina Nagib and Sharada Krishnamurthy*     217

**Chapter 15  Growing our Own: Fostering Teacher Leadership in K-12 Science Teachers through School–University Partnerships**
*Zareen G. Rahman, Mika Munakata, Emily Klein, Monica Taylor and Kristen Trabona*     235

**Chapter 16  Developing Leadership Capacity in PDS Master Teachers**
*Somer Lewis, Amy Garrett Dikkers, Lynn Sikma and Katie Fink*     255

**Chapter 17  Teacher Leader Reflections: Teacher Leader Preparation and Development**     269

Knowing and Being Known
*Mark Meacham*

Tools for Successful Leadership
*Stefanie D. Livers*

Lost Voices
*Francisco J. Ocasio*

Questions for Further Reflection
*Jana Hunzicker*

**Chapter 18 Teacher Leader Preparation and Development in PDS: Themes and Recommendations**
*Rebecca West Burns*     *277*

More Questions for Reflection and Discussion     289

Tables, Illustrations, and Figures     295

About the Contributors     297

Index     303

# Foreword

Professional development schools (PDSs) excel in preparing new teachers, supporting practicing teachers in their professional growth, and engaging stakeholders in carefully crafted examinations of issues that directly shape schools. At their very best, PDSs bridge the gap between the two very different cultures of the P-12 and university worlds and, in doing so, positively boost student learning.

That said, the road to a successful PDS partnership is rarely, if ever, smooth, and those who embark on this path typically have to overcome roadblocks that remind them every day just how difficult a task it is to produce a meaningful and productive school–university partnership. These roadblocks often appear in the form of questions. For example, PDS collaborations that rely on grants have often asked, "What happens when the money runs out?" while those that have limited to no funding at all ask, "How can we sustain this partnership over time?"; other frequently asked questions include, "Can not-yet-tenured university faculty really afford to spend their time in schools in the face of tenure and promotion requirements?"; "How much buy in (and from whom) do we need to make this a successful venture?"; "Can we do this without the full support of administrators at the university, district, and/or school levels?"; and, assuming the partnership does indeed have such administrative support, "What happens when the administrators change?" These last few questions about leadership have been pervasive in the PDS world for quite some time, with it now very well understood that crafting and sustaining a successful PDS partnership is next to impossible if you do not have committed support from your dean, superintendent, or principal. And, since individuals in these particular roles seem to change rather quickly and consistently over time, it truly is critical to ask, "What happens when the administrators change?"

The contributors to *Teacher Leadership in Professional Development Schools* understand this last point – that successful PDSs require support from above. However, they also believe that top-down leadership, while critical, is not the only form of leadership necessary to build and sustain PDSs. In fact, they argue without fail that PDSs are the perfect venue for a different kind of leadership to emerge – the leadership of teachers. As Jana Hunzicker relates in her two opening chapters, the concept of teacher leadership has gained traction in American schools in the last 10–15 years, a time when, perhaps not coincidentally, PDSs have also taken flight. What those two simultaneous events have produced are a new set of questions that Hunzicker and her PDS colleagues pose in this volume. In three carefully crafted sections – each featuring three or four chapters contributed by teacher leaders and scholars from across the United States, three to four personal reflections written by practicing and/or former P-12 teacher leaders, and a synthesis chapter written by a leading expert in the field – PDS practitioners ask, "How can teacher leadership positively shape student learning?"; "What kinds of PDS-embedded structures can be put in place to promote teacher leadership?"; and "How do we prepare and develop teachers to be teacher leaders in the first place?"

What emerges in the pages that follow, as teacher leaders from ten universities and their P-12 school partners address these questions through the sharing of their work, is a powerful image of teachers taking on roles that heretofore were considered off-limits. Or, as one set of contributors put it, involvement in their particular teacher leader project "provided an opportunity for teachers to be treated as the professionals that they are." This long-overdue recognition is one of many lessons to be learned from *Teacher Leadership in Professional Development Schools*, lessons that will serve all educators well, not just those involved in PDSs. Foremost among these lessons is that students must be our collective and primary focus and that teacher leaders have an obligation (one writer said "the courage") to do what's right for students – even if what we do for them flies in the face of conventional practice.

Another lesson from these pages is that teacher leaders can be powerful advocates for turning around what has been a significant weakness of the teaching profession – a collective failure to consistently share the results of our work with others within the profession and with the broader communities we serve. Teachers, and particularly teachers in PDSs, are engaged in remarkable initiatives that significantly benefit their students; yet they typically keep the results of their work, intentionally or unintentionally, to themselves. The end result is that the broader public is kept in the dark about the positive programs taking place in schools, which leads all too often to those involved in the crafting of education policy doing so with limited – and in some cases inaccurate – information. As seen time and again in these pages, teacher leaders can have a major impact on public policy through the simple act of sharing what's going on in their schools with their school colleagues; teacher candidates; school boards; teachers and administrators in other area schools; and state, regional, and national organizations focused on educational practice.

Teacher leaders can also help schools craft – and stick to – specific goals that meet the unique needs of their individual schools. When the National Association for Professional Development Schools released its Nine Required Essentials of a PDS in 2008, it intentionally began the list with the expectation that PDSs must have "a comprehensive mission that is broader in its outreach and scope than the mission of any [one] partner." In other words, PDSs are created not for spurious reasons or simply for the sake of coming together, but instead for specific goals and missions. Examples to be found in these pages include helping English Language Learners grow while simultaneously helping their teachers understand the needs of this specific group of students, enhancing the knowledge base and teaching skills of science teachers, providing students not typically given the opportunity to engage in higher level math classes the chance to do just that, and requiring teacher candidates to develop Professional Growth Plans from day one so that they are prepared not only to teach but also to lead. Each of these projects succeeded because a teacher leader, or a group of teacher leaders, took the initiative to introduce and promote an agenda that they believed was important to student success.

In addition to offering these types of lessons, *Teacher Leadership in Professional Development Schools* makes it clear that, while there are multiple paths to becoming a teacher leader, some intentional and others accidental, most of those paths involve individuals stepping out of their comfort zones and accepting challenges not traditionally ascribed to teachers. This can create some awkward situations, as when an instructional coach is told by a school principal that, "You will not come into my school and bother my teachers," or when another instructional coach learned that her writing observations in a notebook made teachers nervous, or when a new teacher leader realized that she was now privy to information about colleagues that normally would not be available to her. But, as is clear in many of the stories shared in this volume, the role of teacher leader is a long-overdue and positive addition to the world of education. Who, other than teachers, are better positioned to know their students' and their community's needs? Who has a more direct impact on those students – and their families? Who has the proverbial boots on the ground? And who is better positioned to help the other teachers in their schools grow "as the professionals that they are"?

The value of *Teacher Leadership in Professional Development Schools* is enhanced by the fact that all of the contributors are affiliated with PDSs that have, over a very long span of time, dedicated themselves to promoting school–university partnerships for the benefit of teaching and learning. It was refreshing – and reassuring – to see the names of these institutions and to know that the work they have been engaged in over time has continued and has produced such positive results. It was also refreshing to read the reflections offered by the P-12 teacher leaders who engaged in this work, and, finally, to know that the synthesis chapters come from three exceptionally well-qualified and enthusiastically engaged PDS scholars. Jana Hunzicker is to be commended for bringing together this impressive collection of PDS advocates and for challenging them to examine – and to share – their work.

Bruce E. Field<br>
Georgia Southern University

# Acknowledgements

This book would not have been possible without the support and assistance of many. I especially wish to thank Zoe Morris and Kimberley Chadwick for adeptly ushering me through the proposal and editorial management processes, Rebecca West Burns for critiquing my original proposal and offering suggestions that significantly improved the project, and Bruce Field for reading the book's introductory chapters–and later the entire book–and providing invaluable feedback.

I also wish to thank the book's 49 contributors. Thank you to Bruce Field for writing the book's foreword, to Bernard Badiali, Michael Cosenza, and Rebecca West Burns for writing the synthesis chapters for each section, to the 33 authors who wrote scholarly chapters related to their teacher leadership and PDS work. And most of all, thank you to the 11 teacher leaders who wrote personal reflections about their leadership successes, insights, and challenges. Just as teacher leadership is almost always collaborative, the creation of this book was truly a team effort!

Jana Hunzicker
Bradley University

To America's teacher leaders, past, present, and future.

# List of Abbreviations

| | |
|---|---|
| AACTE | American Association of Colleges for Teacher Education |
| AAT | Architecture of Accomplished Teaching |
| AFT | American Federation of Teachers |
| ASCD | Association for Supervision and Curriculum Development |
| BCPS | Baltimore County Public Schools |
| CAB | Community Advisory Board |
| CAEP | Council for the Accreditation of Educator Preparation |
| CFG | Critical friends group |
| CIP | Continuous improvement plan |
| CP | College prep |
| CCSSO | Council of Chief State School Officers |
| CTQ | Center for Teaching Quality |
| CV | Curriculum vitae |
| DC | District coordinator |
| DRA | Developmental Reading Assessment |
| EL | English learner |
| ELL | English language learner |
| ELA | English/Language Arts |
| ELAS | English Language Arts Standards |
| ENL | English as a New Language |
| EPP | Education preparation providers |
| IEP | Individualized Education Program |
| IIRP | International Institute for Restorative Practices |
| IRB | Institutional Review Board |
| K-8 | Kindergarten through eighth grade |
| K-12 | Kindergarten through twelfth grade |
| LOG | Learning objective goals |
| MAP | Measures of Academic Progress |
| MEdT | Master of Education in Teaching |
| MSU | Montclair State University |
| MSUNER | Montclair State University Network for Educational Renewal |

| | |
|---|---|
| MTA | Master teacher associate |
| NAPDS | National Association for Professional Development Schools |
| NBCT | National Board Certified Teacher |
| NBPTS | National Board for Professional Teaching Standards |
| NCATE | National Council for Accreditation of Teacher Education |
| NEA | National Education Association |
| NNER | National Network for Educational Renewal |
| NYC | New York City |
| NYSESLAT | New York State English as a Second Language Achievement Test |
| P-12 | Pre-school through twelfth grade |
| P-20 | Pre-school through post-graduate school |
| PDS | Professional development schools |
| PK-12 | Pre-kindergarten through twelfth grade |
| PLC | Professional learning community |
| PLS | Professional learning series |
| POL | Promise of leadership |
| PTO | Parent and Teacher Organization |
| SBS | Side By Side |
| SEC | Supervisory effectiveness continuum |
| SEF | Science Education Fellowship |
| SMED | Department of Secondary and Middle School Education |
| STEM | Science, technology, engineering, mathematics |
| TC | Teacher candidate |
| TESOL | Teachers of English to Speakers of Other Languages |
| TIG | Teacher Impact Grants |
| TLEC | Teacher Leadership Exploratory Consortium |
| TLC | Teacher Leader Competencies |
| TLMS | Teacher Leader Model Standards |
| ToM | Targets of Measurement |
| TPP | Teacher Preparation Program |
| TQP | Teacher Quality Partnership |
| TU | Towson University |
| UHM | University of Hawai'i at Mānoa |
| UNCW | University of North Carolina Wilmington |
| UNLV | University of Nevada, Las Vegas |
| US | United States |
| UW | University of Wyoming |
| WCE | Watson College of Education |
| WPU | William Paterson University |

Chapter 1

# Professional Development Schools: An Overview and Brief History

Jana Hunzicker

## Abstract

Professional development schools (PDSs) are a specific type of school–university partnership designed to support teacher preparation, professional development, inquiry and research, and student learning. Active teacher engagement in PDS work over the past three decades has led to the emergence of teacher leader practice and development as a serendipitous outcome of PDS partnerships. Emphasizing teacher leadership throughout, this chapter provides an overview of PDSs, including a definition and core purposes, benefits of continuous learning for all PDS stakeholders, and the complexities of PDS work before offering a brief history of PDS in the United States.

*Keywords*: Professional development schools; history of professional development schools; school–university partnerships; history of education in the United States; laboratory schools

Professional development schools (PDSs), a specific type of school–university partnership, were established in the 1990s to bolster the preparation of preservice teachers by placing them in authentic classroom settings from where they could learn with and from experienced classroom teachers (Rutter, 2006; Teitel, 1997). To support classroom teachers charged with mentorship and supervision, partnering colleges and universities provided professional development and other forms of support aimed at enhancing teaching and leadership of experienced teachers (Teitel, 1997). Shaped primarily to address school reform and increase teacher professionalization (Holmes Group, 1986, 1990), the parallel work of John Goodlad and the National Network for Educational Renewal (NNER) expanded the PDS vision to include teacher leadership (Neapolitan & Levine, 2011).

As it turned out, the Holmes Group's (1986, 1990) core PDS purposes of teacher preparation, professional development, inquiry and research, and student learning have defined the PDS mission nationwide for the past three decades. Moreover, active teacher engagement in PDS work has led to the emergence of teacher leader practice and development as a serendipitous outcome of PDS partnerships (Cosenza, 2013; Teitel, 2004). Emphasizing teacher leadership throughout, this chapter provides an overview of PDSs, including a definition and core purposes, benefits of continuous learning for all PDS stakeholders, and the complexities of PDS work before offering a brief history of PDS in the United States.

## Definition and Core Purposes of Professional Development Schools

Teitel (2004) described PDSs as "a cornerstone of serious attempts to simultaneously improve teacher education and public schools." (p. 401). Carpenter and Sherretz (2012) wrote, "PDS partnerships support professional and student learning through the use of an inquiry-oriented approach to teaching." (p. 89). While school–university partnerships admirably focus on teacher preparation and other "special projects or school directed community or business partnerships that only peripherally connect to the PDS," (Rutter, 2006, p. 11). PDSs do even more. The "widely accepted cornerstones of the PDS initiative" (Field, 2014, p. 133) that distinguish PDSs from other school–university partnerships are teacher preparation, professional development, inquiry and research, and student learning (Ferrara, 2014; Neapolitan & Levine, 2011; Teitel, 2004). In the 2008 position article titled "What it Means to be a Professional Development School," the National Association for Professional Development Schools (NAPDS) articulated the definition and core purposes of PDSs as follows:

> Unique and particularly intense school–university collaborations, PDSs were designed to accomplish a four-fold agenda: preparing future educators, providing

current educators with ongoing professional development, encouraging joint school–university faculty investigation of education-related issues, and promoting the learning of P-12 students. (p. 1)

From a broader perspective, PDSs exist to promote innovation and to create sustainable practices in the service of teacher preparation, professional development, inquiry and research, and student learning (Neapolitan & Levine, 2011). Toward these ends, collaborative partnerships between school and university are essential. Ferrara (2014) explained:

> Understanding the teaching/learning cycle and the critical impact that teachers have on student success has been the mission of PDSs for almost two decades. This mission has helped professionals serving preK-12 students, as well as those preparing teacher candidates, recognize that working in isolation is no longer a viable solution to the complex problems of student learning and teacher quality. (p. 12)

Mutual sharing of human, informational, and fiscal resources also promotes innovation and supports the sustainability of PDS partnerships. Berkeley (2006) wrote, "The primary intent is for school partners and university partners to become resources of first resort to one another, contacting one another for a variety of reasons." (p. 157).

## Continuous Learning of all PDS Stakeholders

Through collaboration and sharing, PDSs offer mutual benefits to school and university. The greatest benefit is the opportunity to support continuous learning of all PDS stakeholders. Ferrara (2014) stated, "PDSs create environments where preservice teachers, practicing teachers, college faculty, and preK-12 students come together under one roof to engage the process of learning." (p. 11). Through the ongoing process of learning via practice, professional development, and inquiry, school–university partners create a level playing field where reciprocal learning is valued (Miller, 2015; NAPDS, 2008). Hartzler-Miller (2006) wrote, "PDSs create the conditions for de-legitimizing traditional power structures by bringing university faculty into K-12 classrooms and teachers onto college campus [sic] as serious professionals, consultants, co-researchers, instructors, and leaders in their field." (p. 171). Moreover, responsibility for learning is shared, creating opportunities for teachers to emerge as leaders. Carpenter and Sherretz (2012) elaborated:

> Accountability for learning in PDS is no longer the sole responsibility of the principal. In a learning community, a teacher's role expands from one's classroom to the entire school…such a context empowers teachers; specifically, teachers begin to take on more responsibility to mentor or coach each other and advocate for their profession and students. (p. 98)

From a university perspective, PDS work is "a place in academia that 'keeps it real'." (Hartzler-Miller, 2006, p. 165). In PDS partnerships, P-12 teachers benefit from the theoretical knowledge provided by university faculty, and university faculty benefit from the practitioner knowledge of P-12 teachers.

## Complexities of PDS Work

A recent concern about quality teacher preparation and increased accountability for teacher certification and licensure has created a renewed interest in PDSs (Howey, 2011). Yet even in ideal circumstances, PDS work is challenging. Berkeley (2006) described the "added-on complexities" of PDS leadership as "the rigorous demands of those at levels even higher than themselves – institutional leaders, community leaders, political leaders, and citizen leaders." (p. 151). One such complexity is perpetual tension between innovation and standards. PDS work focused on innovation tends to be nonhierarchical, voluntary, internally controlled, and responsive to local conditions (Neapolitan & Levine, 2011). Such conditions foster creativity but may possibly lack substance and/or resources. However, PDS work focused on standards or other external parameters, such as a grant, which may be limited to specific initiatives, groups, or activities or distract PDSs from their mission (Miller, 2015). Teitel (2004) elaborated:

> When PDS becomes "just another thing" required by the people higher up, the opportunities for PDSs to transform and improve schools and teacher education institutions are lost. Leadership and participants at all levels – at the PDS, state, or municipal levels – need to consciously address ways to retain the underlying vision and vitality of PDS. (p. 404)

A second complexity is the provisional status of many PDSs, which often results from limited institutional support. Neapolitan and Levine (2011) explained:

> With few exceptions, the PDS has...not been able to make the changes in the basic structure, financing, roles, and relationships of the partners involved, and therefore have not been institutionalized...Primarily driven by universities, they have been unevenly implemented. Few districts, again with some exceptions, have made the basic commitment necessary to sustaining them. (p. 320)

Institutional supports such as time, funding, and recognition for participation in PDS efforts are necessary to sustain PDSs indefinitely (Ferrara, 2014; Field, 2014). In addition, state funding, governance, and accountability systems are needed to sustain widespread PDS work (Neapolitan & Levine, 2011).

A third complexity faced by today's PDSs is low advocacy. Field (2014) identified several "things that PDS practitioners currently are not doing very well," (p. 138) including the need to clarify the mission of PDS work, pursuing the PDS mission in day-to-day efforts, and advocating for PDSs "with measureable data demonstrating the impact of PDS collaborations." (pp. 138–139). Yet the empirical research base on PDSs remains thin. Ferrara (2014) stated:

> Historically, PDSs examine those factors that affect student learning, such as teacher effectiveness, implementation of research-based practices, or ways in which schools transform as a result of partnership work. However, a clear link between these inputs and student achievement has not been made in most PDS settings. (p. 21)

Hartzler-Miller (2006) concurred, "Without solid conceptual frameworks for interpreting, explaining, and visioning PDS work, our PDS partnerships are like houses made of straw, vulnerable to constant shifts in political winds." (p. 165).

A fourth and final complexity of PDS work is staying true to the fourfold PDS mission. Miller (2015) identified mission creep as "the biggest threat to school–university partnerships," (p. 28) since it hinders the conditions that support teacher leadership. Because successful PDS work requires buy-in from all stakeholders (Field, 2014), teacher leadership is integral to the success of PDSs. Moreover, as individual stakeholders come and go, the PDS mission is more likely to remain in focus when a significant number of teacher leaders are engaged in PDS work. Clark (1999) wrote, "A partnership that has as its purpose the creation of a partnership – rather than the accomplishment of some ultimate goal – is inevitably doomed to early failure. Continuous, critical examination of the reasons for a partnership is the only prevention for this possible malady." (p. 168). If successful PDS partnerships are to be sustained over time, complexities such as these must be addressed.

## A Brief History of Professional Development Schools

The notion of school–university partnerships dates back to the 1820s, when model schools were first used by state teacher colleges as practice settings for future teachers (Hausfather, 2000). By the late 1800s, model schools were common across the United States; and after John Dewey opened the first laboratory school in 1896, model schools expanded their mission to include Dewey's concept of "putting theory into practice in an experimental setting." (Hausfather, 2000, p. 32). Sustained through continuing partnerships with teacher colleges, model schools became widely known as laboratory schools in the early 1900s (Hausfather, 2000). "Consciously modeled after the teaching hospital, laboratory schools emphasized systematic research, joint faculty appointments with the university, and careful attention to preservice teacher education." (Hausfather, 2000, p. 32). The number of laboratory schools nationwide peaked in 1964 before steadily declining in the 1980s (Hausfather, 2000). Hausfather (2000) expounded:

> As the number of students enrolling in teacher education programs increased, student teaching moved to the plentiful public school classrooms in communities surrounding colleges and universities. Teacher education professors spent more time in these public school placements, creating a widening gap between the college education faculty and the laboratory school. (p. 34)

Thus, laboratory schools set the early stage for a new school-university partnership model: the PDS. But more events were to unravel before PDSs made their debut.

## From Sputnik to "A Nation Prepared"

In 1957, the world's first artificial Earth satellite, Sputnik, was launched by the Soviet Union, which led to the curriculum of American schools – and those who taught it – being doubted by many. Rutter (2006) explained:

> Schools were blamed because we had not produced the requisite scientists and engineers to win that first step in the space race. Suddenly math and science were front and center in our curriculum, and professionals in those fields were brought in to design relevant "teacher-proof" curriculum to ensure we would not fall further behind. (p. 289)

In the 1960s and 1970s, as school curricula across the United States were being revised and reformed in response to Sputnik, educators began to recognize a lack of collaboration between the nation's teacher preparation programs and P-12 schools (Neapolitan & Levine, 2011). Then, in 1983, the notorious report "A Nation at Risk: The Imperative for Educational Reform" by the National Commission on Excellence in Education called into serious question the quality of instruction taking place in our P-12 schools and communicated misgivings about the competence of America's teaching force (Rutter, 2011).

In response to "A Nation at Risk," several reports offered recommendations for reform. In 1985, the Ford Foundation's Academy for Education Development's "Teacher Development in Schools" report called for ongoing professional development and differentiated roles and responsibilities for teachers (Rutter, 2011). In 1986, the Carnegie Task Force on Teaching as a Profession's "A Nation Prepared: Teachers for the 21st Century" report promoted higher professional standards, mastery certification, increased accountability, and greater decision-making authority for teachers (Rutter, 2011). "A Nation Prepared" also envisioned the creation of university teaching centers and clinical schools to support teacher education programs, signaling the nation's readiness for PDSs (Rutter, 2011). Indeed, the term *professional development school* was coined by the Holmes Group the same year (Teitel, 2004).

## Launch of the PDS Movement

In 1986, "Tomorrow's Teachers: A Report of the Holmes Group" was the first response to "A Nation at Risk," which connected teacher professionalization to the desired outcome of student learning and achievement through its vision of professional learning communities and leadership opportunities for teachers (Rutter, 2011). The report outlined five goals:

1. To make the education of teachers intellectually more solid.
2. To recognize differences in teachers' knowledge, skill, and commitment, in their education, certification, and work.
3. To create standards of entry to the profession – examinations and educational requirements – that are professionally relevant and intellectually defensible.
4. To connect our own institutions to schools.
5. To make schools better places for teachers to work, and to learn (Holmes Group, 1986, p. 4).

Similar to the Carnegie Task Force, the Holmes Group envisioned collaboration between schools and universities to support teacher preparation, but expanded the vision of school–university partnerships to include inquiry-based research and professional learning (Rutter, 2011).

In 1990, the Holmes Group (later re-named the Holmes Partnership) released a second report, "Tomorrow's Schools: Principles for the Design of Professional Development Schools," which further articulated the group's vision for PDSs based on six principles: (1) teaching and learning for understanding; (2) creating a learning community; (3) teaching and learning for understanding for everybody's children; (4) continuing learning by teachers, teacher educators, and administrators; (5) thoughtful long-term inquiry into teaching and learning; and (6) inventing a new institution (Holmes, 1990, p. 7). Together, "Tomorrow's Teachers" and Tomorrow's Schools" initiated what came to be known as the PDS movement. Neapolitan and Levine (2011) explained:

> The Holmes Partnership bears distinction as the organization that defined the PDS as a school–university partnership for the specific purpose of training future teachers and supporting the ongoing professional development of experienced educators within collaboratively designed clinical settings focused on the needs of P-12 students. (p. 315)

By the time "Tomorrow's Schools" was published, the PDS movement had already begun. "In a parallel major reform initiative, John Goodlad and his colleagues advocated centers of pedagogy and formed the NNER." (Howey, 2011, p. 326). The NNER was founded in 1990 to create a school–university partnership structure that would strengthen teacher preparation, promote teacher professionalism, and ultimately, increase student learning and achievement (Rutter, 2011). Based on the premise that "professional education and the renewal of schools must work in tandem to effect systemic change in the education system at large," (Neapolitan & Levine, 2011, p. 307) the NNER articulated four areas of school–university collaboration very similar to the fourfold PDS mission: teacher preparation, professional development, curriculum development, and research/inquiry. The NNER emphasized professional development focused "on leadership development at every level of the career, from teacher candidates to school and university faculty, to school, district, and university administrators." (Neapolitan & Levine, 2011, p. 317). The NNER's vision for P-20 leadership development was an important first step toward the expansion of teacher leadership in American schools nationwide.

In a detailed history of the early PDS movement, Rutter (2011) identified teacher professionalism and school reform as two consistently offered recommendations in the reports that followed "A Nation at Risk": teaching should be professionalized similar to medicine and law, and schools should be restructured "to accommodate the new roles and status of teaching professionals." (p. 303). Around the same time, Howey (2011) wrote, "The emphasis was on moving from teachers as members of a guild to teachers as professionals, prepared in a parallel manner to other professionals, and especially the clinical type of preparation that occurs in teaching hospitals." (p. 327). By 1990, this notion of PDSs had been embraced by many education scholars and practitioners across the United States (Carpenter & Sherretz, 2012; Neapolitan & Levine, 2011; Rutter, 2011).

## The Early Years of PDS

The first PDSs were loosely defined. Teitel (2004) recalled, "In their first decade – the late 1980s and early 1990s – much of the focus of PDSs' energies was on starting up the partnerships and making them work." (p. 407). Although PDS partnerships were supported by professional organizations such as the National Education Association (NEA) and the American Federation of Teachers (AFT) (Carpenter & Sherretz, 2012), developing strong and sustainable partnerships required effort and perseverance. Teitel (2004) elaborated:

> Early PDSs struggled for support, resources and recognition, and at the same time functioned with high levels of autonomy, often outside of the scrutiny, and sometimes not even on the radar screen of school districts or larger university teacher education programs. (p. 403)

Despite these start-up challenges, PDS enthusiasm and energy remained high as the Holmes Group and the NNER worked to keep their visions alive.

In 1995, the Holmes Group released a third report, "Tomorrow's Schools of Education: A Report of the Holmes Group," which devoted an entire chapter to articulating the importance of PDSs as integral to P-12 and school of education reform. "Tomorrow's Schools" outlined seven goals:

1. To make education schools accountable to the profession and to the public for the trustworthy performance of their graduates at beginning and advanced levels of practice
2. To make research, development, and demonstration of quality learning in real schools and communities a primary mission of education schools
3. To connect professional schools of education with professionals directly responsible for elementary and secondary education at local, state, regional, and national levels to coalesce around higher standards
4. To recognize interdependence and commonality of purpose in preparing educators for various roles in schools, roles that call for teamwork and common understanding of learner-centered education in the 21st century
5. To provide leadership in making education schools better places for professional study and learning
6. To center our work on professional knowledge and skill for educators who serve children and youth
7. To contribute to the development of state and local policies that give all youngsters the opportunity to learn from highly qualified educators (Holmes Group, 1995, pp. 12–15)

The detailed vision of PDSs and the roles of university partners described in "Tomorrow's Schools of Education" provided the much-needed definition for aspiring and newly formed PDS partnerships. Soon, the promise of PDS had grown prominent enough to evoke financial incentives from the federal government. For example, in 1998, the Teacher Quality Enhancement Partnership Grant program was launched by the United States Department of Education, providing competitive matching fund grants to support partnerships between teacher preparation programs and high-need schools for the purpose of improving the clinical preparation of teachers (McCann, n.d.).

## The Creation of PDS Standards, Structures, and Networks

During the 2000s, the PDS movement continued to flourish. In March 2000, the Holmes Partnership and the University of South Carolina's College of Education launched the PDS National Conference in Columbia, South Carolina (Field, 2014), an important first step in creating a nationwide PDS network "focused solely on issues related to PDSs." (Ferrara, 2014, p. 15). Around the same time, the National Council for Accreditation of Teacher Education (NCATE) joined with PDS practitioners and researchers from across the United States to develop "a set of guidelines that provided a theoretical framework, offered technical support, and operationalized practices." (Ferrara, 2014, p. 13). Published in 2001, the NCATE PDS standards articulated PDSs as "innovative institutions formed through partnerships between professional education programs and P-12 schools" (para 1) that prepare new teachers, support faculty development, improve instructional practice, and enhance student achievement. The NCATE PDS standards outline five defining characteristics of PDSs: I. Learning Community; II. Accountability and Quality Assurance; III. Collaboration; IV. Equity and Diversity; and V. Structures, Resources, and Roles (NCATE, 2001, para 2).

The NCATE PDS standards were "extremely influential in shaping and solidifying the PDS movement" (Teitel, 2004, p. 406) because they "brought together the teacher quality agenda of the 1990s and the overarching vision of effecting change in P-12 education through school–university partnerships." (Neapolitan & Levine, 2011, p. 316). Although they were not (and still are not) required for accreditation of teacher preparation programs, the NCATE PDS standards provided the much-needed structure for colleges and universities engaged in or thinking about initiating PDS relationships. Following publication of the NCATE PDS standards, individuals, institutions, and some states operationalized them through policy and practice. One example is Teitel's (2003) PDS

Standards Student Learning Pyramid (p. xviii). Moreover, states that have required PDS involvement as part of the teacher preparation process include Maryland, Louisiana, Florida, and West Virginia (Neapolitan & Levine, 2011; Teitel, 2004).

In 2005, as interest in PDS work continued to grow, the NAPDS was founded (Field, 2014). Ferrara (2014) described the NAPDS as "the premier professional organization for all things PDS," elaborating that "its website, newsletter, peer-reviewed journal, and an annual national conference are the lifeline for PDS educators." (p. 15). The publication of the NCATE PDS standards in 2001 and the founding of the NAPDS in 2005 signaled that PDSs had reached a national level of common practice in teacher preparation. In 2006, Rutter wrote, "The PDS movement has grown beyond being just a reform movement. It is now nearly the norm, the way many of us commonly view teaching and learning." (p. 12).

Despite standards and a national professional network, PDSs remained widely interpreted in the mid-2000s. Field (2014) explained, "The term PDS had come to be used in a variety of ways and, in particular, seemed to be used routinely to describe any school–university relationship that engaged in the preparation of new teachers." (p. 132). Therefore in 2008, the NAPDS articulated "nine required essentials of a PDS" (p. 2) to distinguish PDSs from other school–university partnerships (see Figure 1).

The NAPDS Nine Essentials were written to "set the philosophy for the PDS" and "provide direct guidance on some of the logistics and

1. A comprehensive mission that is broader in its outreach and scope than the mission of any partner and that furthers the education profession and its responsibility to advance equity within schools and, by potential extension, the broader community;
2. A school–university culture committed to the preparation of future educators that embraces their active engagement in the school community;
3. Ongoing and reciprocal professional development for all participants guided by need;
4. A shared commitment to innovative and reflective practice by all participants;
5. Engagement in and public sharing of the results of deliberate investigations of practice by respective participants;
6. An articulation agreement developed by the respective participants delineating the roles and responsibilities of all involved;
7. A structure that allows all participants a forum for ongoing governance, reflection, and collaboration;
8. Work by college/university faculty and P-12 faculty in formal roles across institutional settings; and
9. Dedicated and shared resources and formal rewards and recognition structures.

Figure 1: Nine Essentials of a Professional Development School (NAPDS, 2008, pp. 2–3).

structures of the PDS relationship" (Neapolitan & Levine, 2011, p. 310) while still leaving room for interpretation and customization. Field (2014) stated as follows:

> The NAPDS made the case that while all PDS relationships must have collaborative missions, not all PDS missions must be the same...Similarly, while all PDS relationships must have formal written agreements in place, the content of those agreements will vary considerably from place to place, as will the roles created to support each PDS, the reward structures designed to recognize PDS work, the ways in which the "sharing of resources" is implemented from site to site, and a whole host of subtle nuances that acknowledge the uniqueness and individuality of each PDS relationship. (p. 134)

The PDS standards, structures, and networks created in the 2000s brought together all of the pieces needed for PDSs to achieve the original vision of the Holmes Group. Moreover, these standards, structures, and networks primed PDSs to engage deeply in pursuit of the four core areas of PDS work: teacher preparation, professional development, research and inquiry, and student learning (NAPDS, 2008).

## Professional Development Schools Today

Today, as PDSs continue to flourish across the United States, the call to remain strong is louder than ever. In 2010, NCATE's Report of the Blue Ribbon Panel on Clinical Preparation and Partnerships for Improved Student Learning recognized PDSs as exemplary models for teacher preparation. In support of PDSs and other school–university partnerships, the report argued that

> ...teacher education programs must work in close partnership with school districts to redesign teacher preparation to better serve prospective teachers and the students they teach. Partnerships should include shared decision making and oversight on candidate selection and completion by school districts and teacher education programs. (NCATE, 2010, p. ii)

Significantly, NCATE's (2010) Blue Ribbon Report envisioned teacher leadership outcomes such as "advancing shared responsibility for teacher preparation; supporting the development of complex teaching skills; and ensuring that all teachers will know how to work closely with colleagues, students, and community." (p. ii). The statement concluded that "[Clinical preparation partnerships] will be a crucial step towards empowering teachers to meet the urgent needs of schools and the challenges of 21st century classrooms." (p. ii). Neapolitan and Levine (2011) wrote that the report is "testimony to the significance of PDS work done over the last two decades." (p. 323).

In 2012, the American Association of Colleges for Teacher Education (AACTE) reinforced the work of the Blue Ribbon Panel by publishing a position statement on the clinical preparation of teachers that advocated for school–university partnerships; full-year student teaching; rigorous, high-quality performance assessments for preservice and practicing teachers; consistency and collaboration across states in regard to certification, licensure, and hiring; teacher residency programs; and incentives for "schools to serve as clinical settings for teacher candidates by subsidizing mentor teachers, substitutes for teacher–candidate pull out sessions, and postgraduate residents." (American Association of Colleges for Teacher Education, 2012, p. 2). The position taken by AACTE was intended to ensure that new teachers are "ready to teach the moment they set foot into a classroom." (Abdul-Alim, 2014, para 1).

In 2013, the Council for the Accreditation of Educator Preparation (CAEP) replaced NCATE as the national body for accrediting teacher preparation programs and continues to recognize and promote PDSs and other school–university partnerships as integral to teacher preparation. CAEP Standard 2: Clinical Partnerships and Practice (2013) states that "…effective partnerships and high-quality clinical practice are central to [teacher] preparation so that candidates develop the knowledge, skills, and professional dispositions necessary to demonstrate positive impact on all P-12 students' learning and development" (para 1). The language of CAEP Standard 2 supports school–university partnerships by stating that partners will "co-construct mutually beneficial P-12 school and community arrangements…" (para 2.1). The standard supports teacher leadership by stating that partners will "co-select, prepare, evaluate, support, and retain high-quality clinical educators, both provider- and school-based, who demonstrate a positive impact on candidates' development and P-12 student learning and development" (para 2.2).

Since 2010, the Blue Ribbon Panel, the AACTE, and CAEP have all recognized the importance of pairing school–university partnerships and teacher leadership roles and responsibilities in order to realize their visions. Moreover, professional and financial support for this important work remains steady. The NNER (2017) and the NAPDS (2017) continue to provide information, networking, and consulting for P-12 and higher education and federal grant programs continue to emphasize the importance of school–university partnerships. In 2008, the Teacher Quality Enhancement Partnership Grant program was changed to Teacher Quality Partnership (TQP) with continued emphasis on "the quality of current and future teachers through better preparation, recruitment, and professional development." (McCann, n.d., para 2) The most recent TQP call for proposals continues to emphasize the importance of school–university partnerships for purposes of clinical preparation, promoting in particular federal support for model teaching residency programs and/ or year-long student teaching experiences within the context of school–university partnerships (AACTE, 2012; United States Department of Education, 2016).

## Conclusion

Emphasizing teacher leadership throughout, this chapter has provided an overview of PDSs, including a definition and core purposes, benefits of continuous learning for all PDS stakeholders, the complexities of PDS work, and a brief history of PDS in the United States. With an understanding of PDS established, chapter two defines teacher leadership in PDSs and other school–university partnerships, introduces distributed leadership theory, and provides a brief history of teacher leadership in the United States before asserting several characteristics that render PDSs and other school-university partnerships ideal settings for studying teacher leadership.

## References

Abdul-Alim, J. (2014, March 3). Experts: New teachers can't hide behind steep learning curve. *Diverse Issues in Education*. Retrieved from http://diverseeducation.com/article/61018/

American Association of Colleges for Teacher Education. (2012). *Where we stand: Clinical preparation of teachers*. Retrieved from https://secure.aacte.org/apps/rl/res_get.php?fid=482&ref=rl

Berkeley, T. R. (2006). Interweaving, interwoven: Perspective on PDS leadership from the university with the school. In J. E. Neapolitan & T. R. Berkeley (Eds.), *Where do we go from here? Issues in the sustainability of professional development school partnerships* (pp. 149–164). New York, NY: Peter Lang Publishing, Inc.

Carpenter, B. D., & Sherretz, C. E. (2012). Professional development school partnerships: An instrument for teacher leadership. *School–University Partnerships, 5*(1), 89–101.

Clark, R. W. (1999). School–university partnerships and professional development schools. *Peabody Journal of Education, 74*(3–4), 164–177.

Cosenza, M. N. (2013). Teacher leadership development in PDSs: Perceptions of 22 veteran teachers. *School–University Partnerships, 6*(1), 47–58.

Council for the Accreditation of Educator Preparation. (2013). *CAEP standards.* Retrieved from http://caepnet.org/standards/standards/standard2/

Ferrara, J. (2014). Historical context of the PDS movement. In J. Ferrara (Ed.), *Professional development schools: Creative solutions for educators* (pp. 9–26). Plymouth: Rowman & Littlefield.

Field, B. E. (2014). A national perspective on the current state of PDSs. In J. Ferrara (Ed.), *Professional development schools: Creative solutions for educators* (pp. 129–142). Plymouth: Rowman & Littlefield.

Hartzler-Miller, C. (2006). Response on future directions: Leadership. In J. E. Neapolitan & T. R. Berkeley (Eds.), *Where do we go from here? Issues in the sustainability of professional development school partnerships* (pp. 165–176). New York, NY: Peter Lang Publishing, Inc.

Hausfather, S. (2000). Laboratory schools to professional-development schools: The fall and rise of field experiences in teacher education. *The Educational Forum, 65*(1), 31–39. Retrieved from https://blogs.maryville.edu/shausfather/vita/lab-schools-to-pds/

Holmes Group. (1986). *Tomorrow's teachers: A report of the Holmes Group.* East Lansing, MI: Holmes Group.

Holmes Group. (1990). *Tomorrow's schools: A report of the Holmes Group.* East Lansing, MI: Holmes Group.

Holmes Group. (1995). *Tomorrow's schools of education: A report of the Holmes Group.* East Lansing, MI: Holmes Group.

Howey, K. R. (2011). Response to section I: What's needed now. *Yearbook of the National Society for the Study of Education, 110*(2), 325–336.

McCann, C. (n.d.). Teacher Quality Partnership Grants. Retrieved from http://www.edcentral.org/edcyclopedia/teacher-quality-partnership-grants/

Miller, L. (2015). School–university partnerships and teacher leadership: Doing it right. *Educational Forum, 79*(1), 24–29.

National Association for Professional Development Schools. (2008). *What it means to be a professional development school.* Retrieved from http://napds.org/9%20Essentials/statement.pdf

National Association for Professional Development Schools. (2017). *Home.* Retrieved from http://napds.org/

National Council for Accreditation of Teacher Education. (2001). *Standards for professional development schools.* Retrieved from http://www.ncate.org/ProfessionalDevelopmentSchools/tabid/497/Default.aspx

National Council for Accreditation of Teacher Education. (2010). *Transforming teacher education through clinical practice: A national strategy to prepare effective teachers* (Report of the Blue Ribbon Panel on Clinical Preparation and Partnerships for Improved Student Learning). Retrieved from http://www.ncate.org/LinkClick.aspx?fileticket=zzeiB1OoqPk%3D&tabid=7

National Network for Educational Renewal. (2017). *Mission statement.* Retrieved from http://www.nnerpartnerships.org/about-us/mission-statement/

Neapolitan, J. E., & Levine, M. (2011). Approaches to professional development schools. *Yearbook of the National Society for the Study of Education, 110*(2), 306–324.

Rutter, A. (2006). The evolution of the PDS research landscape. In J. E. Neapolitan & T. R. Berkeley (Eds.), *Where do we go from here? Issues in the sustainability of professional development school partnerships* (pp. 3–16). New York, NY: Peter Lang Publishing, Inc.

Rutter, A. (2011). Purpose and vision of professional development schools. *Yearbook of the National Society for the Study of Education, 110*(2), 289–305.

Teitel, L. (1997). Professional development schools and the transformation of teacher leadership. *Teacher Education Quarterly, 24*(1), 9–22.

Teitel, L. (2003). *The professional development schools handbook: Starting, sustaining, and assessing partnerships that improve student learning.* Thousand Oaks, CA: Corwin Press, Inc.

Teitel, L. (2004). Two decades of professional development school development in the United States. What have we learned? Where do we go from here? *Journal of In-service Education, 30*(3), 401–416.

United States Department of Education. (2016, May 23). *Programs: Teacher Quality Partnership Grant Program.* Retrieved from http://www2.ed.gov/programs/tqpartnership/index.html

Chapter 2

# Teacher Leadership in Professional Development Schools: A Definition, Brief History, and Call for Further Study

*Jana Hunzicker*

### Abstract

In today's educational climate of data, differentiation, and accountability, teacher leadership is essential; and professional development schools (PDSs) offer distinctive settings for teacher leader practice and development. Building on chapter one, this chapter defines teacher leadership in PDSs, introduces distributed leadership theory, and provides a brief history of teacher leadership in the United States before asserting several characteristics that render PDSs ideal settings for studying teacher leadership. Instead of asking why we should study teacher leadership in PDSs and other school–university partnerships, a better question might be, why wouldn't we?

*Keywords:* Professional development schools; teacher leadership; history of teacher leadership in the United States; history of education in the United States; school–university partnerships

In today's educational climate of data, differentiation, and accountability, teacher leadership is essential (Curtis, 2013; Hargreaves, 2014; Superville, 2015). At the classroom and school levels, teacher leaders model exemplary teaching (Cosenza, 2013; Portner, 2008), promote effective instruction (Campbell & Malkus, 2011; Carlough, 2016), and facilitate school improvement efforts (Gordon, 2004; Teach Plus, 2014). At the district, state, and national levels, teacher leaders share best practices (Fairman & Mackenzie, 2012), influence educational policy (Soglin, Hunt, & Reilly, 2016), and advocate for the teaching profession (Coggins & McGovern, 2014). Teacher leaders are a powerful force in today's schools because teachers are respected as instructional experts (Carver, 2016; Danielson, 2006). Teachers know students well and are committed to student learning (Cannata, McCrory, Sykes, Anagnostopoulos, & Frank, 2010), and their tendency to lead collaboratively creates a sense of shared responsibility that supports student learning and builds instructional capacity schoolwide (Mangin & Stoelinga, 2008; Smulyan, 2016; Vernon-Dotson & Floyd, 2012).

Professional development schools (PDSs) offer distinctive settings for teacher leader practice and development (Carpenter & Sherretz, 2012; Miller, 2015; Teitel, 1997), especially around the core PDS purposes of teacher preparation, professional development, inquiry and research, and student learning (Holmes Group, 1986, 1990). In PDSs and other school–university partnerships (hereafter referred to simply as PDSs), opportunities abound for teachers to assume leadership roles such as mentor, committee chair, professional developer, instructional coach, and action researcher (Teitel, 1997; Ferrara, 2014). Cosenza (2010) found that PDS opportunities for teachers to engage in collaboration and mentoring outside their classrooms supported their emergence as teacher leaders and increased teacher leader capacity schoolwide. PDS settings also provide an ideal context for teacher leader preparation. Snow-Gerono, Dana, and Silva (2001) found that first-year teachers who had completed yearlong internships in a PDS setting were more focused on student learning and more likely to demonstrate emerging teacher leader behaviors, such as offering support to colleagues, than first-year teachers who were not PDS-prepared.

Burns, Yendol-Hoppey, Nolan, and Badiali (2013) wrote, "The possibility for real change occurs when universities learn from the field, and the field learns from universities." (p. 26). Given that PDSs provide a fertile environment for practicing and developing teacher leaders, a closer look at teacher leadership in these settings is necessary. Building on chapter one, this chapter defines teacher leadership in PDS, introduces distributed leadership theory, and provides a brief history of teacher leadership in the United States before asserting several characteristics that render PDSs and other school–university partnerships ideal settings for studying teacher leadership.

## Definitions and Descriptions of Teacher Leadership

Over the past 40 years, numerous definitions and descriptions of teacher leadership have been asserted, but no single definition has been commonly accepted (Cosenza, 2015). Due to the conceptual diversity surrounding teacher leadership, Wenner and Campbell (2016) suggested that scholars explicitly define teacher leadership within their particular context of study. In response, this section considers several definitions and descriptions of teacher leadership before articulating a definition of teacher leadership in PDSs.

### *Formal, Informal, and Hybrid Teacher Leadership*

Conceptions of teacher leadership are grounded in instructional leadership. From an instructional perspective, teacher leadership can be classified into three broad models: (1) the *teacher leadership model,* which formalizes instructional leadership roles and responsibilities with recognition and compensation such as titles, release time, and stipends; (2) the *multiple leadership roles model,* which informally distributes instructional leadership roles and responsibilities across many teachers although each teacher leader's official title and position remains classroom teacher; and (3) the *every teacher a leader model,* which informally involves all teachers in collaborative efforts toward instructional improvement and school reform without assigning specific roles and responsibilities (Gordon, 2004). These broad instructional models of teacher leadership also have been conceptualized as formal and informal teacher leadership. Usually holding an official title, formal teacher leaders work full time outside their classrooms to support changes in teaching practice and to coordinate school- and district-wide reform efforts (Lord, Cress, & Miller, 2008; Manno & Firestone, 2008). Informal teacher leaders teach full time and accept school- and district-wide leadership responsibilities in addition to their classroom teaching duties (Danielson, 2006; Watt, Huerta, & Mills, 2009).

Between formal and informal teacher leadership, Margolis and Huggins (2012) used the term *hybrid teacher leader* to describe teachers "whose official schedule includes both teaching K-12 students and leading teachers in some capacity, most often as a 'coach'." (p. 954). Like informal teacher leaders, hybrid teacher leaders engage in responsibilities such as providing professional development, facilitating collaboration, creating common assessments, observing and modeling teaching, writing curriculum, and sharing lesson plans and resources (Barnwell, 2015;

Margolis & Huggins, 2012). Zeichner (2010) extends the concept of hybrid teacher leadership to "bring[ing] together school and university-based teacher educators and practitioner and academic knowledge in new ways to enhance the learning of prospective teachers." (p. 486).

In recent years, informal and hybrid teacher leadership have emerged as prevailing teacher leadership models (Wenner & Campbell, 2016). Vernon-Dotson and Floyd (2012) described informal/hybrid teacher leaders as "teachers who go above and beyond their job description of teaching in their isolated classroom ... to take action on school-wide issues and model teacher leadership for their colleagues." (p. 40). Margolis and Huggins (2012) stated, "Teachers in these roles provide the increasingly crucial function of supplying frontline support to teachers while maintaining the integrity of school, district, and state efforts to align curriculum and instruction." (p. 955). Cosenza (2013) wrote, "This type of emergent leadership characterizes the highest level of professionalism in education." (p. 48).

## Deep Commitment to Students

Whether formal, informal, or hybrid, teacher leadership is characterized by teachers working together on behalf of students. Silva, Gimbert, and Nolan (2000) described teacher leadership as "ultimately based on doing what is right by children." (p. 799). Lieberman and Friedrich (2007) articulated it as "working collaboratively" and "making a commitment to students." (p. 44). Katzenmeyer and Moller (2009) wrote that teacher leaders "identify with and contribute to a community of teacher learners and leaders." (p. 6). Because of their deep commitment to students, teacher leaders are well positioned to influence student learning and achievement schoolwide through roles such as mentor, instructional coach, role model, and committee member. Vernon-Dotson and Floyd (2012) explained, "... teachers are the closest to school problems, experts on school issues, and a valuable resource in problem solving and decision making regarding what is best for students, teaching, and learning." (p. 39). Carver (2016) asserted, "With their close connection to the classroom, teacher leaders have natural credibility with their peers." (p. 160).

## Teacher Leaders as Boundary Spanners

Because teacher leaders collaborate beyond their classrooms to affect schoolwide change, they have been referred to as boundary spanners

(Miller, 2015; Teitel, 1997; Zeichner, 2010). Clark (1999) elaborated, "Although a single, charismatic individual may have considerable influence on a partnership, the presence of one leader, no matter how effective, is insufficient in the long run. Leaders are required in various roles in higher education and the schools." (p. 169). Burns & Badiali (2015) documented a PDS model in which teachers who had successfully served as classroom-level student–teacher mentors could apply to serve in the boundary-spanning role of novice supervisor for several student teachers. Zeichner (2010) described a boundary-spanning *teacher-in-residence* program in which experienced urban teachers worked, taught, and served in all aspects of their partner university's teacher education program and participated in ongoing teacher leadership seminars for two years before returning to their classroom teaching positions in the public school system. Teacher leaders in PDSs and other school–university partnerships also have opportunities to influence PDS stakeholders across institutions. One study found that 73% of teachers who participated in collaborative leadership projects with a partner university went on to assume school- or district-level teacher leadership roles (Vernon-Dotson & Floyd, 2012).

### *Teacher Leadership as a Process, Strategy, and Stance*

In their seminal review of teacher leadership studies, conducted between 1980 and 2004, York-Barr and Duke (2004) defined teacher leadership as "the process by which teachers, individually or collectively, influence their colleagues, principals, and other members of school communities to improve teaching and learning practices with the aim of increased student learning and achievement." (pp. 287–288). Soglin et al. (2016) described teacher leadership as "a powerful strategy to promote collaborative efforts and effective teaching practices that lead to improved decision-making through distributed leadership at the school, district, and state levels." (p. 2). Others describe teacher leadership as a stance, or worldview (Poekert, Alexandrou, & Shannon, 2016; Smulyan, 2016). Smulyan (2016) found that, regardless of leadership role or position, teacher leaders share three common assumptions: (1) Teaching is a profession, (2) Teaching is a political act, and (3) Teaching is a collaborative process.

Taken together, teacher leadership can be viewed as a process, a strategy, *and* a stance. Teacher leadership is a process because teachers' individual and collective efforts impact teaching and learning gradually, over time (Carver, 2016; Hunzicker, 2012). Teacher leadership is a strategy because impacting teaching and learning requires knowledge and skill, careful planning, and intentional decision-making (Danielson, 2006; Soglin et al., 2016). Teacher leadership is a stance because it is motivated by deep commitment to students and to the teaching profession (Coggins & McGovern, 2014; Huang, 2016), and acted upon through vision and perseverance (Frost, 2012; Smulyan, 2016).

### Teacher Leadership in PDSs and Other School–University Partnerships

Frost (2012) conceptualized teacher leadership as "the *process* whereby a teacher can clarify [his or her] *values*, develop a personal vision of improved practice, and then act *strategically* to set in motion a *process* where colleagues are drawn into activities such as self-evaluation and innovation." (p. 211, italics added for emphasis). In this way, teacher leadership in PDSs can be defined as a strategic, process-oriented stance motivated by deep concern for students and activated through formal, informal, and hybrid leadership roles that span the boundaries of school, university, and community. With a definition established, teacher leadership in PDSs and other school–university partnerships can be further elucidated with a closer look at distributed leadership theory.

## Distributed Leadership Theory

In 2004, York-Barr and Duke wrote, "The concept of teacher leadership suggests that teachers rightly and importantly hold a central position in the ways schools operate and in the core functions of teaching and learning." (p. 255). Two years later, Fulmer and Basile (2006) observed, "In schools today... it is becoming evident that leadership is not the function of one individual, but rather it is distributed across the school with a variety of players giving and taking across the organization." (p. 128). Indeed, between 1980 and 2004, theoretical frameworks frequently used to study teacher leadership included participative leadership (Leithwood & Duke, 1999), organizational leadership (Ogawa & Bossert, 1995), parallel leadership (Crowther, Kaagen, Ferguson, & Hahn, 2002), and distributed leadership (Spillane. Halverson, & Diamond, 2001, 2004). Between 2004 and 2013, distributed leadership theory stood out as the theory used most often to frame teacher leadership studies (Wenner & Campbell, 2016). Because distributed leadership theory has been used extensively in recent years to study teacher leadership, it is described in some detail here as one approach to understanding teacher leadership in PDSs.

First conceptualized by Engestrom (1999) and later by Spillane et al. (2001), distributed leadership theory rests on "the notion that leadership is often exercised informally, rather than embodied in an assigned role." (Hartzler-Miller, 2006, p. 170). Similar to other inclusive leadership theories, distributed leadership theory recognizes the plentiful but often subtle contributions of teacher leaders in service to students, schools, and the teaching profession. York-Barr and Duke (2004) explained, "These models presume that leadership must emerge from many individuals within an organization and is not simply vested in a handful of formally recognized leaders." (p. 288).

According to distributed leadership theory, leadership is socially distributed when leadership tasks are stretched across leaders and followers (Spillane, Halverson, & Diamond, 2004). Leadership can be stretched across time, activity, or perspective. For example,

- Grade-level teams of teachers analyze state test scores in preparation for a schoolwide meeting to establish instructional priorities (time).
- A mentor teacher regularly observes a first-year teacher and the two meet afterward to debrief the observation (activity).
- A teacher chairs a districtwide committee comprising one teacher representative from each school (perspective).

Distributed leadership can also be stretched over situations, including organizational structures such as meeting times and deadlines; language-based tools such as meeting agendas and school improvement plans; and demographic considerations such as race, class, and gender (Spillane et al., 2004). Because distributed leadership involves dynamic interaction among leaders, followers, and situations working toward a specific goal or around a specific task, leadership becomes a product of all participants' knowledge, beliefs, and behaviors "in and through particular social, cultural, and material contexts." (Spillane et al., 2004, p. 10).

Distributed leadership theory also considers how leadership is stretched from leaders with positional authority (e.g., principals and formal teacher leaders) to informal leaders (e.g., informal and hybrid teacher leaders) to followers (e.g., colleagues, parents, students, etc.) (Spillane et al., 2004). This focus on so many different actors makes it possible for leaders to influence as well as to be influenced by social and situational factors (Spillane et al., 2004). For example, a new teacher who is asked to demonstrate an innovative teaching strategy for more experienced colleagues may feel intimidated, even when she knows the strategy well. This teacher is influenced by social and situational factors. A different teacher may occasionally share teaching materials with grade level colleagues, which eventually leads to the grade-level team co-planning together. This teacher is influential over social and situational factors. In this way, the impact of distributed leadership is usually significant because "a group of leaders working together to enact a particular task leads to the evolution of a leadership practice that is potentially more than the sum of each individual's practice," (Spillane et al., 2004, pp. 18–19) a concept Covey (1989) referred to as synergy.

Spillane et al. (2004) summarized, "Without a rich understanding of how leaders go about their work, and why leaders do and think what they do, it is difficult to help school leaders think about and revise their practice." (p. 8). Distributed leadership theory is particularly useful to the study of teacher leadership because it is designed to explore both the subtleties and the complexities of teacher leadership, including formal, informal, and hybrid teacher leadership; teacher leaders as boundary-spanners; and teacher leadership as a process, strategy, and stance. Moreover, PDSs exemplify one context in which distributed leadership may occur.

## A Brief History of Teacher Leadership

In the United States, modern conceptions of teacher leadership arose from the instructional leadership movement, which emerged in the 1980s in response to two influential reports: "A Nation at Risk: The Imperative for Educational Reform" by the National Commission on Excellence in Education in 1983 (Hallinger & Murphy, 1985; Leithwood & Montgomery, 1982) and "A Nation Prepared: Teachers for the 21st Century" by the Carnegie Task Force on Teaching as a Profession in 1986 (Frost, 2012). Just like the PDS reform movement, teacher leadership came to the forefront as part of the nationwide effort to increase teacher professionalism (York-Barr & Duke, 2004). Calling for "a reinvigoration of the teaching profession in the USA…teacher leadership was seen to be the key lever for this invigoration." (Frost, 2012, p. 209).

In the early 1980s, teacher leadership was conceptualized primarily within small-scale projects and specific contexts (Little, 2003, as cited in Wenner & Campbell, 2016). By the late 1980s, in response to "A Nation at Risk," teacher leadership roles and responsibilities shifted to schoolwide reform (Wenner & Campbell, 2016). Influenced by the National Network for Educational Renewal's vision for teacher leadership development at all career stages (Neapolitan & Levine, 2011), reform efforts in the late 1980s and early 1990s actively engaged teachers in activities to increase teacher quality and improve teaching conditions, including performance-based compensation systems, career ladders, teacher mentoring programs, site-based decision-making, and *professional development schools* (emphasis added) (York-Barr & Duke, 2004).

Pragmatic reasons for actively engaging teachers in school reform efforts included "additional person power," "consideration of employee perspectives," and "greater ownership and commitment to organizational goals." (York-Barr & Duke, 2004, p. 258). Moreover, teacher expertise became recognized as a valuable asset during this time. Lieberman (2013) explained:

> During the 1980s and 1990s, it was becoming clear that teachers who assumed leadership roles had to deal not only with the role they were playing but also the organizational and cultural influences of their work. The focus was on individuals with the idea that teachers could be empowered by taking leadership, which would move teaching and teachers toward a "real" profession. (p. 169)

In 1987, the National Board for Professional Teaching Standards (NBPTS) was convened in response to "A Nation Prepared" to develop a national, voluntary teacher certification system based on "high and rigorous standards for what accomplished teachers should know and be able to do." (National Board for Professional Teaching Standards [NBPTS], 2017, para 1) In 1995, the first National Board Certified Teachers (NBCTs) were certified, opening the door for many new leadership opportunities for NBCTs.

By the early 1990s, school restructuring efforts such as Theodore Sizer's Essential Schools movement engaged teachers across the United States in revisioning teaching and learning in middle and high schools (Fox, 2009). In a 1992 article titled "The Move toward Transformational Leadership," Leithwood wrote, "At the reins of today's new schools will be not one but many leaders who believe in creating the conditions that enable staffs to find their own directions." (p. 8). Benefits of teacher leadership documented between 1980 and 2004 included attracting and retaining talented teachers, motivating and rewarding established teachers, ensuring meaningful and ongoing professional development, improving teacher morale, and increasing student learning and achievement (York-Barr & Duke, 2004). However, the late 1990s brought widespread concern that America's schools were not adequately preparing students in comparison to educational systems in other nations (Klein, 2015).

In 2002, the "No Child Left Behind Act" was signed into law under President George W. Bush. Along with "No Child Left Behind" came significant accountability measures for both students and teachers. Klein (2015) explained:

> ["No Child Left Behind"] significantly increased the federal role in holding schools responsible for the academic progress of all students. And it put a special focus on ensuring that states and schools boost the performance of certain groups of students, such as English-language learners, students in special education, and poor and minority children, whose achievement, on average, trails their peers. States did not have to comply with the new requirements, but if they didn't, they risked losing federal Title I money (What is NCLB? para 1).

"No Child Left Behind" also required states to ensure that all teachers were "highly qualified," defined as holding a bachelor's degree in their assigned content area(s) and state certification, especially in hard-to-staff, high-need schools (Klein, 2015).

In terms of teacher leadership, the "No Child Left Behind" legislation expanded schools' efforts to actively engage teachers in school reform. Margolis and Huggins (2012) stated:

> Pre-No Child Left Behind, many teachers were released from teaching time (or received extra pay) to perform duties to help the school. However, these activities were primarily administrative...Efforts that were made to utilize teachers as instructional leaders remained informal and often suffered from a lack of sanctioned space within the school system. (pp. 956–957)

Following "No Child Left Behind," the focus of teacher leadership shifted to school accountability. In response, schools quickly mobilized teacher leaders to engage in a variety of instructional leadership roles and responsibilities aimed at increasing student achievement (Margolis & Huggins, 2012).

York-Barr and Duke (2004) observed that between 1980 and 2004, the notion of teacher leadership evolved from formal teacher leadership roles (e.g., department chair and union representative) to instructional leaders (e.g., mentor, curriculum developer, and workshop leader) to schoolwide reform participants (e.g., leadership team representative and data analysis coach), reflecting "an increased understanding that promoting instructional improvement requires an organizational culture that supports collaboration and continuous learning and that recognizes teachers as primary creators and re-creators of school culture." (p. 260). Parallel to the PDS movement, the nationwide trend to actively engage teachers in school reform efforts began shifting the culture of America's schools to collaborative environments where teaching, learning, and inquiry on behalf of student learning became the norm.

## Teacher Leadership Today

Teacher leadership today "has become an increasingly popular topic among educational policymakers and influential educational organizations as an important component of school reform." (Wenner & Campbell, 2016, p. 2). Since the mid-2000s, teacher leadership in the United States has increased in stature due to a variety of large-scale initiatives. In 2008, a group of concerned educators from across the country convened "to examine the current research and thinking about the critical leadership roles that teachers play in contributing to student and school success." (Teacher Leader Model Standards [TLMS], 2012, Preface, para 2) An outcome of this effort was the formation of the Teacher Leadership Exploratory Consortium, and in 2012 the first nationally recognized standards for teacher leadership were published. The Teacher Leader Model Standards (TLMS, 2012) consist of seven domains designed to "codify, promote, and support teacher leadership as a vehicle for transforming schools to meet the needs of $21^{st}$-century learners" (Standards Overview, para 1). Within each domain, four to eight functions further elaborate the purposes and processes of teacher leadership (see Figure 1).

In January 2014, the National Education Association, the Center for Teaching Quality (CTQ), and the NBPTS launched the national Teacher Leadership Initiative "to define the foundational competencies of teacher leadership, [develop] relevant experiences and supports to help teachers cultivate those competencies, and [mobilize] teachers to be leaders within their profession." (Wenner & Campbell, 2016, p. 2). Out of this initiative, 8 overarching and 12 pathway-specific Teacher Leadership Competencies

- Domain I: Fostering a collaborative culture to support educator development and student learning
- Domain II: Accessing and using research to improve practice and student learning
- Domain III: Promoting professional learning for continuous improvement
- Domain IV: Facilitating improvements in instruction and student learning
- Domain V: Promoting the use of assessments and data for school and district improvement
- Domain VI: Improving outreach and collaboration with families and community
- Domain VII: Advocating for student learning and the profession

Figure 1.  TLMS (2012) Seven Domains.

were articulated "to inspire teachers to realize their potential and help their colleagues do the same" (p. 9) (Center for Teaching Quality, National Board for Professional Teaching Standards, & National Education Association, 2014, p. 3) (see Figure 2).

In March 2014, the United States Department of Education and the NBPTS jointly launched Teach to Lead, a nationwide professional development, networking, and grant program designed "to advance student outcomes by expanding opportunities for teacher leadership, particularly those that allow teachers to stay in the classroom." (United States Department of Education, 2015, para 1) Recent Teach to Lead projects include building school–university–community partnerships to create a community school with a healthcare clinic in Michigan and developing a year-long induction and mentoring program to retain new teachers in Rhode Island (United States Department of Education, 2015).

In May 2016, the United States Department of Education, the Association for Supervision and Curriculum Development (ASCD), and the NBPTS jointly launched the Teacher Impact Grants program "to develop, expand and evaluate promising practices and programs that can transform the academic trajectory of students." (United States Department of Education, 2016, para 1) In a press release announcing the new grants, an ASCD spokesperson stated, "These Teacher Impact Grants will provide teacher leaders across the nation opportunities to develop, expand and evaluate innovative and ambitious projects focused on making their schools and classrooms more effective communities of learning" (para 3).

Federal and privately funded programs such as these demonstrate the United States' continuing interest in school reform, with America's teacher leaders at the forefront. Not as high profile, but no less significant are teacher leadership efforts and initiatives at the school and district levels, particularly in PDSs.

Overarching Competencies

- Reflective practice
- Personal effectiveness
- Interpersonal effectiveness
- Communication
- Continuing learning and education
- Group processes
- Adult learning
- Technological facility

Instructional Leadership

- Coaching/mentoring
- Facilitating collaborative relationships
- Community awareness, engagement, and advocacy

Policy Leadership

- Policy implementation
- Policy advocacy
- Policy-making
- Policy engagement and relationships

Association Leadership

- Organizational effeciveness: Leading with vision
- Organizational effectiveness: Leading with skill
- Organizing and advocacy
- Building capacity of others
- Learning community and workplace culture

Figure 2. Teacher Leadership Competencies (Center for Teaching Quality et al., 2014).

## Why Study Teacher Leadership in PDSs?

In 2004, Spillane et al. (2004) reasoned, "If expertise is distributed, then the school rather than the individual leader may be the most appropriate unit for thinking about the development of leadership expertise." (p. 29). Around the same time, York-Barr and Duke (2004) wrote, "…informal means of leadership are becoming more recognized in contexts such as professional development schools." (p. 287). Indeed, several characteristics render PDSs ideal settings for studying teacher leadership.

First, PDSs distinctively prioritize teacher learning and leadership. In support of teacher learning, Clark (1999) wrote that PDSs offer "strong leadership endowed with the ability to see through fads and simplistic solutions." (p. 169). Ferrara (2014) noted that PDSs provide "opportunities for stakeholders' reflection, mechanisms for collaboration, enriched school culture, opportunities for inquiry, creation of professional learning laboratories, participation in professional development activities, and improved practice." (p. 17). Regarding teacher leadership, Teitel (1997) explained that PDS work distinctively requires teachers to assume leadership roles related to teacher preparation, inquiry and professional development, diverse student populations, and collaborative decision-making. Miller (2015) identified three characteristics of school–university partnerships that are supportive of teacher leadership: (1) the connection between leadership, learning, and learning to lead; (2) firm values and established practices that "provide a moral compass for emerging teacher leaders"; and (3) "spaces for teachers to try on new leadership roles and experiment with new ideas." (p. 29).

Second, PDSs model innovation and best instructional practices. Snow-Gerono et al. (2001) described PDSs as "existing exemplars of practice." (p. 35). Lecos et al. (2000) found that opportunities to serve as PDS mentor teachers and site coordinators resulted in teacher feelings of empowerment, pride, and career satisfaction, as well as increased confidence and professional growth. Miller (2015) articulated that effective school–university partnerships support teacher leadership by:

- Eliminating hierarchies, giving equal voice to all members, and establishing reciprocal relationships.
- Reading texts together, developing theories from practice, and using theory to inform practice.
- Creating collaborative agendas and flexible structures for collegial learning, responding to teacher needs and interests as opposed to policy and administrative directives, and creating a common language for learning.
- Providing spaces to play with ideas, trying out and reflecting on new practices, and providing and receiving feedback.
- Crossing institutional boundaries between schools and universities to provide spaces for authentic teacher leadership (pp. 24–25).

Ferrara (2014) explained, "... analyzing their practice, attending conferences, conducting research, mentoring student teachers, or developing curricula as part of their PDS involvement... not only improve[s] teacher competence but, perhaps more important, improve[s] the school." (p. 23).

Third, PDSs support the pursuit and dissemination of educational research and other scholarly work. Carpenter and Sherretz (2012) described PDSs as places of inquiry and innovation where "PDS partners develop new approaches for examining and improving...practices through integrating partners' expertise and knowledge." (p. 91). Gillenwaters (2009) stated, "Co-constructed relationships among communities, schools, and universities have the potential...to contribute to a new cultural model capable of transforming K-12 urban schools." (p. 12). Teitel (1997) articulated that "several compelling reasons to study leadership in PDSs" is based on the conviction that PDSs are established "learning laboratories," are "fertile areas for emerging leadership," and "require leaders to function in multidimensional inter-organizational settings... where the traditional boundaries around a school are blurred." (p. 10).

To summarize, PDSs prioritize teacher learning and leadership, model innovation and best instructional practices, and support the pursuit and dissemination of educational research and other scholarly work. Instead of asking why we should study teacher leadership in PDSs and other school–university partnerships, a better question might be, why wouldn't we?

## References

Barnwell, P. (2015, February 18). Why schools need more 'hybrid' teaching roles. Retrieved from http://www.edweek.org/tm/articles/2015/02/18/why-schools-need-more-hybrid-teaching-roles.html?r=751929773

Burns, R. W., & Badiali, B. J. (2015). When supervision is conflated with evaluation: Teacher candidates' perceptions of their novice supervisor. *Action in Teacher Education, 37*(4), 418–437.

Burns, R. W., Yendol-Hoppey, D., Nolan, J. F., & Badiali, B. J. (2013). Let's learn together. *Phi Delta Kappan, 94*(7), 26.

Campbell, P. F., & Malkus, N. N. (2011). The impact of elementary mathematics coaches on student achievement. *Elementary School Journal, 111*(3), 430–454.

Cannata, M., McCrory, R., Sykes, G., Anagnostopoulos, D., & Frank, K. A. (2010). Exploring the influence of National Board Certified Teachers in their schools and beyond. *Educational Administration Quarterly, 46*(4), 463–490.

Carlough, S. (2016). Making space for the struggle: Teacher leadership as mentoring. *Schools: Studies in Education, 13*(1), 29–45.

Carpenter, B. D., & Sherretz, C. E. (2012). Professional development school partnerships: An instrument for teacher leadership. *School–University Partnerships, 5*(1), 89–101.

Carver, C. L. (2016). Transforming identities: The transition from teacher to leader during teacher leader preparation. *Journal of Research on Leadership Education, 11*(2), 158–180.

Center for Teaching Quality, National Board for Professional Teaching Standards, & National Education Association (2014). *The Teacher Leadership Competencies*. Retrieved from http://www.nbpts.org/sites/default/files/teacher_leadership_competencies_final.pdf

Clark, R. W. (1999). School–university partnerships and professional development schools. *Peabody Journal of Education, 74*(3–4), 164–177.

Coggins, C., & McGovern, K. (2014). Five goals for teacher leadership. *Phi Delta Kappan, 95*(7), 15–21.

Cosenza, M. N. (2010). The impact of professional development schools on teacher leadership. Ph.D. thesis. Retrieved from ProQuest LLC (ED521937). https://search.proquest.com/docview/763418294

Cosenza, M. N. (2013). Teacher leadership development in PDSs: Perceptions of 22 veteran teachers. *School–University Partnerships, 6*(1), 47–58.

Cosenza, M. N. (2015). Defining teacher leadership: Affirming the Teacher Leader Model Standards. *Issues in Teacher Education, 24*(2), 79–99.

Covey, S. R. (1989). *The 7 habits of highly effective people: Powerful lessons in personal change*. New York, NY: Simon & Schuster.

Crowther, F., Kaagen, S. S., Ferguson, M., & Hann, L. (2002). *Developing teacher leaders: How teacher leadership enhances school success*. Thousand Oaks, CA: Corwin Press.

Curtis, R. (2013). *Finding a new way: Leveraging teacher leadership to meet unprecedented demands*. Washington, D.C.: The Aspen Institute. Retrieved from http://files.eric.ed.gov/fulltext/ED541444.pdf

Danielson, C. (2006). *Teacher leadership that strengthens professional practice*. Alexandria, VA: ASCD.

Engestrom, Y. (1999). Activity theory and individual and social transformation. In Y. Engestrom, R. Miettinen, & R. L. Punamaki (Eds.), *Perspectives on activity theory* (pp. 19–38). Cambridge: MA: Cambridge University Press.

Fairman, J. C., & Mackenzie, S. V. (2012). Spheres of teacher leadership action for learning. *Professional Development in Education, 32*(2), 229–246.

Ferrara, J. (2014). Historical context of the PDS movement. In J. Ferrara (Ed.), *Professional development schools: Creative solutions for educators* (pp. 9–26). Plymouth: Rowman & Littlefield.

Fox, M. (2009, October 22). Theodore R. Sizer, leading education-reform advocate, dies at 77. *The New York Times*. Retrieved from http://www.nytimes.com/2009/10/23/education/23sizer.html

Frost, D. (2012). From professional development to system change: Teacher leadership and innovation. *Professional Development in Education, 38*(2), 205–227.

Fulmer, C. L., & Basile, C. G. (2006). Investigating distributed leadership in professional development schools: Implications for principals, schools, and school districts. In J. E. Neapolitan & T. R. Berkeley (Eds.), *Where do we go from here? Issues in the sustainability of professional development school partnerships* (pp. 127–148). New York, NY: Peter Lang Publishing, Inc.

Gillenwaters, J. N. (2009). *Co-constructing community, school, university partnerships for urban school transformation*. Ph.D. thesis. Retrieved from ProQuest, LLC (ED532847). https://search.proquest.com/docview/304998567

Gordon, S. P. (2004). *Professional development for school improvement: Empowering learning communities*. Boston, MA: Allyn & Bacon, Inc.

Hallinger, P., & Murphy, J. (1985). Assessing the instructional leadership behavior of principals. *Elementary School Journal, 86*(2), 217–248.

Hargreaves, A. (2014). Foreword: Six sources of change in professional development. In L. E. Martin, S. Kragler, D. J. Quatroche, & K. L. Bauserman (Eds.), *Handbook of professional development in education: Successful models and practices, preK-12* (pp. x–xix). New York, NY: The Guilford Press.

Hartzler-Miller, C. (2006). Response on future directions: Leadership. In J. E. Neapolitan & T. R. Berkeley (Eds.), *Where do we go from here? Issues in the sustainability of professional development school partnerships* (pp. 165–176). New York, NY: Peter Lang Publishing, Inc.

Holmes Group. (1986). *Tomorrow's teachers: A report of the Holmes Group*. East Lansing, MI: Holmes Group.

Holmes Group. (1990). *Tomorrow's schools: A report of the Holmes Group*. East Lansing, MI: Holmes Group.

Huang, T. (2016). Linking the private and public: Teacher leadership and teacher education in the reflexive modernity. *European Journal of Teacher Education, 39*(2), 222–237.

Hunzicker, J. (2012). Professional development and job-embedded collaboration: How teachers learn to exercise leadership. *Professional Development in Education, 38*(2), 267–290.

Katzenmeyer, M. H., & Moller, G. V. (2009). *Awakening the Sleeping Giant: Helping Teachers Develop as Leaders* (3rd ed.). Thousand Oaks, CA: Corwin Press.

Klein, A. (2015, April 10). No child left behind: An overview. *Education Week*. Retrieved from http://www.edweek.org/ew/section/multimedia/no-child-left-behind-overview-definition-summary.html

Lecos, M. A., Evans, C., Leahy, C., Liess, E., & Lucas, T. (2000). Empowering teacher leadership in professional development schools. *Teaching and Change, 8*(1), 98–113.

Leithwood, K. A. (1992). The move toward transformational leadership. *Educational Leadership, 49*(5), 8–12. Retrieved from http://www.ascd.org/ASCD/pdf/journals/ed_lead/el_199202_leithwood.pdf

Leithwood, K., & Duke, D. L. (1999). A century's quest to understand school leadership. In K. S. Louis & J. Murphy (Eds.), *Handbook of research on educational administration* (2nd ed., pp. 45–72). San Francisco, CA: Jossey-Bass.

Leithwood, K., & Montgomery, D. (1982). The role of the elementary principal in program improvement. *Review of Educational Research, 52*(3), 309–339.

Lieberman, A. (2013). Teacher leadership: An introduction. *The New Educator, 9*, 169–172.

Lieberman, A., & Friedrich, L. (2007). Teachers, writers, leaders. *Educational Leadership, 65*(1), 42–47.

Lord, B., Cress, K., & Miller, B. (2008). Teacher leadership in support of large-scale mathematics and science education reform. In M. M. Mangin & S. R. Stoelinga (Eds.), *Effective teacher leadership: Using research to inform and reform* (pp. 55–76). New York, NY: Teachers College Press.

Mangin, M. M., & Stoelinga, S. R. (2008). Teacher leadership: What it is and why it matters. In M. M. Mangin & S. R. Stoelinga (Eds.), *Effective teacher leadership: Using research to inform and reform* (pp. 1–9). New York, NY: Teachers College Press.

Manno, C. M., & Firestone, W. A. (2008). How teacher leaders with different subject knowledge interact with teachers. In M. M. Mangin & S. R. Stoelinga (Eds.), *Effective teacher leadership: Using research to inform and reform* (pp. 36–54). New York, NY: Teachers College Press.

Margolis, J., & Huggins, K. S. (2012). Distributed but undefined: New teacher leader roles to change schools. *Journal of School Leadership, 22*, 953–981.

Miller, L. (2015). School–university partnerships and teacher leadership: Doing it right. *Educational Forum, 79*(1), 24–29.

National Board for Professional Teaching Standards. (2017). *Mission and History*. Retrieved from http://www.nbpts.org/mission-history

Neapolitan, J. E., & Levine, M. (2011). Approaches to professional development schools. *Yearbook of the National Society for the Study of Education, 110*(2), 306–324.

Ogawa, R. T., & Bossert, S. T. (1995). Leadership as an organizational quality. *Educational Administration Quarterly, 31*, 224–243.

Poekert, P., Alexandrou, A., & Shannon, D. (2016). How teachers become leaders: An internationally validated theoretical model of teacher leadership development. *Research in Post-Compulsory Education, 21*(4), 307–329.

Portner, H. (2008, October 1). Are you an informal teacher-leader? Retrieved from http://www.teachers.net/gazette/OCT08/portner/

Silva, D. Y., Gimbert, B., & Nolan, J. (2000). Sliding the doors: Locking and unlocking possibilities for teacher leadership. *Teachers College Record, 102*(4), 779–804.

Smulyan, L. (2016). Stepping into their power: The development of a teacher leadership stance. *Schools: Studies in Education, 13*(1), 8–28.

Snow-Gerono, J. L., Dana, N. F., & Silva, D. Y. (2001). Where are they now? Former PDS interns emerge as first-year teacher leaders. *Professional Educator, 24*(1), 35–48.

Soglin, A., Hunt, E., & Reilly, P. (2016). *Illinois P-20 Council teacher leadership report: P-20 Teacher and Leadership Effectiveness Committee*. Illinois State University Center for the Study of Education Policy. Retrieved from https://education.illinoisstate.edu/csep/Wallace%20TL%20Report%20Layout%20FINAL.pdf

Spillane, J. P., Halverson, R., & Diamond, J. B. (2001). Investigating school leadership practice: A distributed perspective. *Educational Researcher, 30*(3), 23–28.

Spillane, J. P., Halverson, R., & Diamond, J. B. (2004). Towards a theory of leadership practice: A distributed perspective. *Journal of Curriculum Studies, 36*(1), 3–34.

Superville, D. R. (2015, January 21). School districts turn to teachers to lead: Rising demands push principals to tap teacher talent. *Education Week.* Retrieved from http://www.edweek.org/ew/articles/2015/01/21/school-districts-turn-to-teachers-to-lead.html#

Teach Plus. (2014). Turnaround teacher teams (T3) initiative. Retrieved from http://www.teachplus.org/programs/t3-initiative

Teacher Leader Model Standards. (2012). Home. Retrieved from http://teacherleaderstandards.org/index.php

Teitel, L. (1997). Professional development schools and the transformation of teacher leadership. *Teacher Education Quarterly, 24*(1), 9–22.

Vernon-Dotson, L. J., & Floyd, L. O. (2012). Building leadership capacity via school partnerships and teacher teams. *The Clearing House, 85,* 38–49.

Watt, K. M., Huerta, J., & Mills, S. J. (2009). Advancement via individual determination (AVID) professional development as a predictor of teacher leadership in the United States. *Professional Development in Education, 36*(4), 1–16.

Wenner, J. A., & Campbell, T. (2016). The theoretical and empirical basis of teacher leadership: A review of the literature. *Review of Educational Research, 86*(2), 1–38. doi:10.3102/0034654316653478

York-Barr, J., & Duke, K. (2004). What do we know about teacher leadership? Findings from two decades of scholarship. *Review of Educational Research, 74*(3), 255–316.

United States Department of Education. (2015, July 27). *Fact sheet: Teach to Lead* [Archived information]. Retrieved from http://www.ed.gov/news/press-releases/fact-sheet-teach-lead

United States Department of Education. (2016, May 3). *U.S. Department of Education collaborates with ASCD and National Board for Professional Teaching Standards to provide grants that support teacher leadership projects* [Press release]. Retrieved from http://www.ed.gov/news/press-releases/us-department-education-collaborates-ascd-and-national-board-professional-teaching-standards-provide-grants-support-teacher-leadership-projects

Zeichner, K. (2010). Rethinking the connections between campus courses and field experiences in college and university-based teacher education. *Educacao, Santa Maria, 35*(3), 479–501.

# Section I

**Teacher Leadership and Student Learning**

Chapter 3

# Collaborative Leadership in Meeting the Needs of English Learners in an Urban Elementary PDS

*Nancy Dubetz, Maria Fella, Yokaira LaChapell and Jennifer Rivera*

### Abstract

In this chapter, the authors describe collaborative efforts of three teacher leaders and a college professional development school (PDS) liaison to ensure that preservice candidates and practicing teachers can effectively meet the needs of English learners (ELs). The chapter includes an introduction to the PDS's history and mission, an overview of research on effective practices that promote ELs' learning, a description of teacher leadership in the PDS context, examples of professional learning opportunities to help preservice candidates and practicing teachers ensure that ELs are academically successful, and a discussion of how data are being used to evaluate the impact of this work on both teachers and students.

*Keywords:* Professional development schools; English learners; teacher leadership; professional development; student achievement; Teacher Leader Model Standards

Over 9% of all school-age children in public schools in the United States are English learners (ELs). These students are being educated in schools in all types of communities: urban, suburban, and rural (National Center for Educational Statistics, 2017). To ensure ELs' educational needs are met, state and federal policies have included the academic achievement of ELs as a criterion for measuring school effectiveness. Given the number of ELs in public schools and the importance of their success in school accountability measures, it would seem obvious that all teachers should be prepared to educate these students. However, states and school districts report that lack of expertise among mainstream teachers and inadequate accountability for teaching ELs in the current teacher evaluation structures present significant challenges (United States Department of Education, 2012).

The need to prepare educators to be effective teachers of ELs is a particularly high priority in urban school districts such as New York City (NYC) where immigrant families are concentrated. There are over 150,000 ELs in the NYC public schools, and 61% have been in the school system for fewer than three years (New York City Department of Education, 2016). Ensuring that ELs can access grade level content poses a challenge for classroom teachers because these students need targeted support that takes into account their language needs as well as their academic needs (deJong & Harper, 2005).

In this chapter, we describe the collaborative efforts of three teacher leaders and a college liaison in an urban professional development school (PDS) to meet the needs of ELs. We describe how our collaboration is shaping teacher preparation and professional development to ensure that our PDS's large population of ELs develop the English language skills needed to be academically successful. Three of the authors, Yokaira, Maria, and Jennifer, are experienced teachers of ELs, and the fourth, Nancy, is the college-based PDS liaison with expertise in effective practices for multilingual learners. Yokaira, Maria, and Jennifer are certified as English as New Language (ENL) teachers and/or as bilingual teachers. Yokaira is a kindergarten ENL teacher, Maria is an ENL coordinator and teacher who pushes in to other teachers' classrooms, and Jennifer is a literacy specialist and teacher who also pushes into classrooms to work directly with teachers and students. All three have served as cooperating teachers to student teachers at the PDS within the past five years. Nancy has served as the college liaison for the PDS since 2001.

We begin our story by introducing our PDS history and mission to provide a profile of our teaching and learning context. This is followed by an overview of research on effective practices that promote ELs' learning, and a discussion of how we conceptualize teacher leadership in a PDS context. We then describe the professional learning opportunities we created for preservice candidates and practicing teachers in order to improve ELs' learning, share how this work is impacting adults in the PDS, and present our plan for using student learning data to evaluate the impact of our efforts on ELs. As we describe our work, we illustrate how qualities of teacher leadership are revealed and developed in the PDS context. We conclude with reflections on how this work has impacted our professional lives.

## The Lehman/Public School 291 PDS Partnership

Lehman College is part of the public university system in NYC, and Public School (PS) 291 is a public K-5 school located in a working class community of primarily Latino families in the Bronx. Lehman's School of Education and PS 291 formalized their PDS partnership in 2001. An important PDS goal that has guided our teacher preparation, professional development, and research efforts has been to improve instruction for ELs. In the 2016–2017 school year, 24.5% of the students at PS 291 were designated as ELs or former ELs. These students were clustered in ten classrooms, two per grade level. Eight classes contained ELs learning alongside English speaking peers, and two were bilingual classes of all ELs. In grades four and five, math and English/language arts are departmentalized so that teachers taught two classes of children each day; one in the morning and another in the afternoon.

The Lehman/PS 291 PDS has a long history of collaborating to meet the needs of ELs. To prepare teachers to be effective with ELs, partners have (1) organized after-school programs where preservice candidates taught young ELs under the supervision of college instructors, (2) supported a study group of bilingual teachers and student teachers, (3) hired school faculty with expertise in teaching ELs to serve as adjunct professors in college programs, and (4) provided student teaching experiences for programs in early childhood, Teachers of English to Speakers of Other Languages and bilingual education. In our most recent work aimed at improving instruction of ELs in the PDS, we identified specific practices for teaching ELs that have been shown to positively impact their learning, and to design professional learning opportunities for preservice candidates and practicing teachers.

## Research-Based Teaching Practice for Ensuring Els' Academic Success

To prepare teacher candidates and practicing teachers in the PDS to meet the needs of ELs, we use a set of core teaching practices identified by Dubetz and Collett (2016). Based on criteria adapted from practice-based teacher education (McDonald, Kazemi, & Kavanagh, 2013), the practices identified are (1) commonly recognized by second language and bilingual educators as effective in teaching ELs and used with high frequency, (2) adaptable to different classroom contexts (i.e., different grade levels, content areas and program types including bilingual and English-medium classrooms), (3) appropriate for individuals who are at the early stages of learning to teach, and (4) proven to positively impact ELs' learning, and help novices "see" how a core teaching practice could be enacted to promote English language development and content learning. The five core practices for teaching ELs are as follows:

1. Engaging ELs in learning academic language by frontloading academic language instruction.
2. Making grade level content comprehensible for ELs.
3. Using ELs' cultural and linguistic resources to support new learning.
4. Promoting oral language development to enhance literacy development and academic learning.
5. Using culturally and linguistically responsive forms of assessment to analyze learning and provide feedback (Dubetz & Collett, 2016).

Later in the chapter, we illustrate how we used these practices to prepare preservice candidates and engage PDS faculty in professional learning to improve practice and promote ELs' achievement.

## Teacher Leadership in the PDS Context

PDSs are places where student learning improves as a result of school–university collaboration. There is compelling evidence to support that PDSs can improve both the quality of teaching and the quality of student learning (Cave & Brown, 2010; Houston, Hollis, Clay, Ligons, & Roff, 1999; Klinger, Ahwee, van Garderen, & Hernandez, 2004; Marchant, 2002; Teitel, 2001). Research also suggests that a positive relationship exists between professional development in PDSs and student achievement (Marchant, 2002), and that PDS work can be particularly supportive of ELs' learning (Cave & Brown, 2010).

We believe that the role of teacher leaders is central to improve teaching and learning in a PDS, and we have adopted Wenner and Campbell's (2017) definition of a teacher leader as an individual who continues to teach children while also working outside the classroom with colleagues. Yokaira is a classroom teacher, and although Jennifer and Maria are no longer responsible for their own classrooms, they spend the good part of each day pushing in to classrooms to provide differentiated instruction to groups of learners. Maria provides ENL instruction and Jennifer teaches reading.

## Aligning the Teacher Leader Model Standards to PDS Functions

To describe the work of teacher leaders in our PDS, we draw upon the Teacher Leader Model Standards (TLMS) developed by the Teacher Leadership Exploratory Consortium (2012). The Office of Leadership in the NYC Department of Education has developed a library of resources for promoting leadership, and the TLMS is one of these resources. The TLMS is divided into seven domains, and in this chapter, we illustrate how our work to improve learning for our ELs reflects the standards of teacher leadership in five of the seven domains:

1. Domain I: Fostering a Collaborative Culture to Support Educator Development and Student Learning.
2. Domain II: Accessing and Using Research to Improve Practice and Student Learning.
3. Domain III: Promoting Professional Learning for Continuous Improvement.
4. Domain IV: Facilitating Improvements in Instruction and Student Learning.
5. Domain V: Use of Assessments and Data for School and District Improvement.

The TLMS focuses on leadership within a school community, but we argue that the PDS work for teacher leaders extends beyond the school walls to include efforts to prepare preservice candidates, some of whom will learn to teach in the PDS and others who will never visit the PDS but will benefit from PDS expertise. PDSs have four functions: teacher preparation, professional development of school and college faculty, collaborative inquiry, and promoting student learning (Holmes Group, 1986, 1990). The TLMS standards offer a starting point for exploring how teacher leadership is embedded in each of these functions.

Teacher learning is an important function of a PDS. In a PDS, teacher leaders must be able to promote a culture of learning that simultaneously promotes adult learning for both preservice candidates and practicing teachers. This requires embedding structures within a PDS where preservice candidates and practicing teachers work together to meet shared goals. The skills needed to undertake this PDS work effectively are those outlined in Domains I and III of the TLMS.

Teacher leaders in a PDS must keep abreast of the latest research and know how to expose educators at different stages of professional learning to the latest research on teaching effectiveness and student learning (TLMS Domain II). PDS partnerships are uniquely positioned to capitalize on inquiry-based collaborations between K-12 schools and institutions of higher education to research critical issues in education and study best practice in systematic ways (TLMS Domain II).

Perhaps the most important function of a PDS is to improve student learning. In a PDS, all educators including preservice candidates, higher education faculty, and school faculty must learn how to design appropriate forms of assessment and know how to interpret student learning data. Teacher leaders in a PDS must also be able to help others learn how to use these data to improve instruction. TLMS Domain IV and Domain V outline a set of expectations for an effective teacher leader that point to improved instruction and student learning. These expectations are as important to effective teachers preparing new teachers as they are to supporting practicing teachers.

## Promoting Pre-Service Candidate Learning Through Mentoring

Because PDSs have a dual mission of preparing new teachers and supporting practicing teachers, they offer unique spaces for teacher leaders to engage in the activities outlined in the TLMS across preservice preparation and professional development. At PS 291, teachers assume a variety of leadership roles to support adult learning and improve student learning. These include two roles identified by Harrison and Killian (2007): mentoring and serving as learning facilitators. In a PDS context, where members are committed to teacher learning, mentoring pre-service candidates offers an opportunity for teachers to use their leadership skills to prepare the next generation of educators. Maria, Yokaira, and Jennifer first became involved in PDS work by hosting pre-service candidates in their classrooms to undertake fieldwork and complete student teaching. All three teachers had ELs in their classrooms, so an important part of their work was helping novices learn to be effective teachers of ELs. In the following section, we offer examples of how Yokaira and Jennifer apply and further develop their leadership skills by mentoring preservice candidates to assist them in becoming effective teachers of ELs. We also illustrate how their mentoring practices reflect qualities identified in the TLMS.

## Helping PreService Candidates Understand the Factors that Affect ELs' Learning

Yokaira feels responsible for ensuring that preservice candidates gain an understanding of the complexity and challenges teachers face as they strive to develop ELs' academic skills and content knowledge while advancing their English language proficiency. ELs are all acquiring a new language, but the rate at which each develops proficiency varies from student to student depending on various factors that include the students' first language, willingness to take risks, home support, socioeconomic status, motivation, age, and background knowledge. As an experienced ENL teacher, Yokaira knows how these factors affect student learning, and she believes her role in working with preservice candidates is to help them develop an understanding of how these factors should guide practice. As a teacher leader who understands how adults learn (TLMS Domain I), Yokaira talks with preservice candidates when they first arrive in her classroom to gain an understanding of their own strengths and needs. In collaboration with Nancy, she then creates learning opportunities that are mutually beneficial for ELs and those candidates who are learning to teach. Preservice candidates observe as Yokaira models best teaching practices for preservice candidates and provides opportunities for them to teach. For example, she works with candidates from Nancy's teaching methods class to plan curriculum-based, developmentally appropriate lessons that they implement with small groups of ELs using the core teaching practices described earlier in the chapter. In this way, Yokaira's ELs benefit from research-based, small group instruction and the preservice candidates benefit from having opportunities to deepen their knowledge of best practices (TLMS, Domains II & IV).

## Using a Gradual Release Model to Mentor Student Teachers

As a bilingual teacher for ten years, Jennifer has developed a repertoire of best practices that support ELs in learning language, content, and developing critical thinking skills. This knowledge informs her practice as a mentor to student teachers. To build a climate of trust and critical reflection (TLMS Domain V), Jennifer uses a gradual release model with her student teachers that involves planning, teaching, and observation.

Many of the units in the first grade language arts curriculum require that ELs have the prior knowledge and academic language needed to understand the content. Many include nonfiction texts on academic topics such as the human body and astronomy. In the planning stage of the gradual release model, Jennifer and her student teacher begin by discussing what they want to achieve. As they plan a lesson, Jennifer introduces her student teacher to specific research-based practices that support ELs' learning of academic content and language. For example, they discuss how to develop both content and language objectives for a lesson. They plan ways to frontload key vocabulary and use visual images to represent the vocabulary as an instructional scaffold for ELs. Jennifer shows her student teacher how to develop strategic groupings for small group discussions and turn and talks that maximize ELs' participation, which is critical to promoting the oral language proficiency needed to read and write in English.

After they plan the lesson together, Jennifer models how to implement the lesson while the student teacher takes focused notes. Following the lesson, they reflect on the lesson, focusing on levels and types of EL participation. Over time, Jennifer transfers responsibility to the student teacher who begins teaching the lesson while Jennifer observes. During these lessons, she will participate if needed by addressing student misconceptions that her novice student teacher might not recognize or know how to address. Following the lessons, they reflect on what practices were most effective in promoting ELs' learning, and Jennifer offers constructive feedback. By using the gradual release model, Jennifer works collaboratively with her student teacher to build ownership and actions that support student learning, an important function of the work of teacher leaders (TLMS Domains I & IV).

## Teacher Leaders Shaping the Preservice Teacher Education Curriculum

In the process of regularly evaluating PDS work, college and school partners develop shared perspectives about the knowledge and skills novices need to teach in urban classrooms. Teachers like Yokaira and Maria model best practices, but can only mentor a small number of preservice candidates at the PDS. To share their expertise with larger numbers of preservice candidates, Maria and Yokaira volunteered to have their instruction professionally videotaped. They were videotaped teaching math and literacy to illustrate best practices in teaching ELs in mainstream classrooms. These locally relevant videos of teaching practice realistically portrayed the kinds of instruction that effectively address linguistic diversity in urban classrooms (TLMS Domain IV).

Nancy edited the videos, selecting 3- to 8-minute samples of teaching that aligned with the core teaching practices described earlier in the chapter. These samples were organized into a series of online modules that are accessible to all students in Lehman College's School of Education. They serve as resources for preservice teaching methods' courses and are used to help candidates prepare for a state certification examination where they must demonstrate their knowledge of ELs and instructional methods that support their learning. The online modules allow us to share Yokaira's and Maria's expertise with a large number of preservice candidates unable to visit the PDS. By collaborating with Nancy in this important work, Yokaira and Maria helped to bridge the theory–practice divide for teacher candidates by demonstrating how research-based practices can be enacted in real classrooms (TLMS Domain II). The videos also serve as a resource for practicing teachers.

## Teacher Leaders as Learning Facilitators for Practicing Teachers

Harrison and Killian (2007) point out that "when teachers learn with and from one another, they can focus on what most directly improves student learning. Their professional learning becomes more relevant, focused on teachers' classroom work, and aligned to fill gaps in student learning." (p. 75). As learning facilitators, teacher leaders help shape professional learning for themselves and their colleagues by undertaking a variety of functions outlined in the TLMS.

One skill set for teacher leaders in TLMS Domain 2 is to assist colleagues in to access and use research in order to select appropriate strategies to improve student learning. In September 2016, school administrators invited the four authors to collaboratively plan and implement two professional learning series focused on improving instruction for ELs as well as classroom support for teaching ELs.

### *Professional Learning Series on Core Practices for all PDS Faculty*

Both college and school authors contributed their expertise equally to prepare professional learning series that aligned core teaching practices to local curriculum and student needs. The team met weekly during a common planning period arranged by school administrators. We began by reviewing the core teaching practices for ELs and came to consensus on which ones we wanted to emphasize based on staff needs. We then discussed how to present the core practices to teachers with different levels of experience and professional knowledge regarding ELs. Yokaira and Maria incorporated segments of their videotaped lessons to illustrate specific practices, and they drafted detailed graphic lesson plans to provide colleagues with an understanding of how particular practices were used across a lesson.

The first professional learning series was organized into six sessions of approximately 90 minutes each. Sessions one and two were designed to introduce the entire school faculty to the core practices and raise awareness of the challenges of learning in a new language. In the following four sessions, faculty were divided between upper grades and lower grades, and the core practices were explored in more detail through examples of practice specific to the grade range. Sessions 3 and 4 offered a deeper investigation of strategies that promote oral language development, and the focus of sessions 5 and 6 was helping teachers learn ways to adapt classroom-based assessments to measure learning for ELs at different language proficiency levels. Through this professional learning, we sought to develop a collective wisdom among all teachers and administrators about how to meet the needs of ELs (TLMS Domain I).

In preparing for a session, Nancy would draft an outline of how a core teaching practice might be introduced, and then the team would meet and modify it, integrating video segments of Yokaira's and Maria's instruction and adding interactive activities that would maximize participation. In this process, we drew heavily upon Yokaira's, Jennifer's, and Maria's insider knowledge of the school staff to make decisions about the content and structure of interactive activities around the core practices. Yokaira and Maria decided which video segments we would use to illustrate the core practices. We then decided who would take the lead in facilitating different parts of each session. Following each session, the team would come together, review evaluation feedback, and use it to inform planning for the next one. This experience afforded us the opportunity to deepen our own understandings of how to increase the capacity of colleagues to implement best practices that would ultimately improve student learning (TLMS Domain III).

### *Professional Learning Series on the NYSESLAT for Classroom Teachers of ELs*

The first series of professional learning sessions was followed by a two-session series, which focused on how teachers could integrate practices to address the kinds of reading, writing, speaking, and listening assessed by the New York State English as a Second Language Achievement Test (NYSESLAT). The NYSESLAT annually assesses the English language development of every EL enrolled in grades K-12, and is fully aligned with the state's English Language Arts standards (ELAS). Besides providing information about each EL's proficiency level in the four language modalities, the test measures and tracks students' proficiency using five levels of language development: Entering, Emerging, Transitioning, Expanding, and Commanding.

Tasks on the NYSESLAT are designed to assess the degree to which ELs are developing the English language proficiency needed to meet the linguistic demands for the ELAS. These linguistic demands are articulated as Targets of Measurement (ToMs), which describe what a student should be able to do at each grade level band. The NYSESLAT is administered in six grade level bands from K-12. The four bands covering the elementary grades are: kindergarten, grades 1–2, grades 3–5, and grades 5–6. An example of a ToM for the third and fourth grade band is that students can use grade appropriate language to describe or convey relevant details and narrate a story or process in sequence (ToM.S.3–4.2).

Because only ELs are tested using the NYSESLAT, the second professional learning series targeted only the 10 teachers with ELs in their classes. Teachers in this group ranged from first-year teachers to experienced teachers. Using their deep understanding of state language proficiency standards and the tasks used to measure them, Jennifer and Maria took the lead in organizing this series. They organized the sessions in ways to engage colleagues in reflective dialog around their student work through the lens of standards-based criteria (TLMS Domain IV). Nancy participated in the role of learner and small group facilitator, and Yokaira participated as a member of the kindergarten grade band group of teachers.

In the first session of the NYSESLAT professional learning series, Jennifer and Maria provided teachers with the grade level ToMs for speaking and the rubric used to score students' spoken proficiency. Teachers were grouped by grade bands to explore together what was expected of ELs and how they would be scored. They then created criteria charts for the ELs in their classrooms using the language from the ToMs and discussed related implications for their teaching. In the second part of the session, teachers reviewed the ToMs for the listening and reading modalities and discussed what ELs in their grade level band are expected to do related to listening and reading. Teachers reviewed sample questions and discussed ways of incorporating questioning into their daily instruction.

The focus of the second session was to explore collaboratively how student writing is assessed on the NYSESLAT. As part of the preparation for this session, teachers administered an extended constructed response assessment to their EL students. For this assessment, students were asked to write a two-paragraph response to a prompt. The session began with an activity in which teachers reviewed the writing ToMs for their grade level band along with the NYESLAT writing assessment rubric. They discussed their observations in groups, and were then given student writing samples to analyze and discuss using the rubric. Maria facilitated a reflective debriefing of this activity, and the teacher teams then scored the samples of their own students' writing. Using the results, they identified areas within each classroom that needed attention and used the information to guide targeted small group instruction in writing. Professional learning opportunities like these are critical to developing teacher expertise, and organizing these experiences required an ability to plan for professional learning that is team based, job-embedded, and aligned with school goals (TLMS Domain III).

### *Facilitating Teacher Learning in the Classroom*

To build on the professional learning series, we supported teachers in their classrooms. Maria helped teachers incorporate practices that promoted student-to-student interaction in classrooms where she pushes in as an ENL teacher. To support teachers in upper grade classrooms comprising large numbers of ELs, Nancy met with the teachers in groups to review situations from classroom observations of how teachers were helping their ELs access academic language from grade level content.

## Evidence of Teacher Learning and Student Learning

### *Evidence of Teacher Learning*

As noted in TLMS Domains I and IV, student learning is closely tied to teacher learning, and teacher leaders have an important role to play in designing the kind of professional development that will lead to student learning. On completion of the first professional learning series for all faculty, we collected feedback from teachers to gather data on their learning several weeks after they had returned to their classrooms to try out new strategies. We asked for examples of practices they were using before they were exposed to the core teaching practices, as well as practices they had learned during the professional learning series and had tried in their classrooms later. We also gathered information about the kinds of additional support they felt they needed to be effective teachers of ELs.

We learned that teachers were trying out research-based practices that included (1) being mindful of the vocabulary demands for ELs (e.g., teaching common vocabulary and not just content-specific academic vocabulary), (2) strategically using ELs' home language to enrich content learning (e.g., giving assignments in Spanish and teaching Spanish/English cognates when introducing new vocabulary), (3) differentiating informal assessments based on language proficiency (e.g., providing ELs opportunities to communicate what they know nonverbally), (4) strategically grouping ELs with English-proficient students, (5) adding visual supports to instruction (e.g., adding photos to word problems), and (6) differentiating activities based on ELs' language proficiency (e.g., giving ELs at lower levels of English language proficiency sentence frames to scaffold academic writing).

We also solicited questions and concerns teachers had about effectively meeting the needs of ELs. The most common challenge was to differentiate instruction for ELs at lower levels of English proficiency using grade level curriculum. Similar challenges have become the focus of our long-term planning for professional development and classroom support.

Teachers attending the second professional learning series, focused on preparing children for the NYSESLAT, completed a survey of their knowledge of important aspects of the state language proficiency expectations, and learnt how to prepare ELs using the existing curriculum. All teachers responded that they were better informed about how to prepare students for the NYSESLAT, and all but one had a new understanding of the expectations for language proficiency outlined in the speaking and writing rubrics. Teachers found that the most useful part of the professional learning series was using the NYSESLAT rubrics to score their own students. They explained that this helped them to understand what ELs should be able to do at the different proficiency levels, and it better informed their instructional decisions. However, given the complexity of the rubrics and the ToMs, many requested further support in applying the ToMs, assessing ELs' learning, and adapting their instruction to address them.

### *Evidence of Student Learning*

ELs' academic achievement and improved language proficiency is our ultimate goal in the collaborative work we have described in this chapter.

Results of our evaluations of teacher learning offer evidence of teachers having learned to apply new practices in their instruction to support their ELs, but we want to know whether ELs themselves are benefiting from these changes in practice. Two kinds of evidence help us to assess ELs' learning: anecdotal, classroom-based evidence, and standardized assessments. Examples of anecdotal, classroom-based evidence include teachers' reflections on changes in ELs' performance and observations of student engagement in classrooms. This type of evidence is important but must be accompanied by formal assessments. Therefore, we also looked for changes in ELs' language proficiency levels based on the results of standardized assessments such as the NYSESLAT.

**Classroom-based evidence of ELs' learning in the pds.** In spring 2017, Yokaira and a preservice candidate used the Developmental Reading Assessment (DRA) (Beaver & Carter, n.d.) to assess the reading levels of ELs in Yokaira's class. The DRA is a standardized reading test used to determine a student's instructional level in reading. Based on their review of the results of students' DRAs, Yokaira and the preservice candidate noticed that ELs were successfully using a range of strategies to decode and figure out unknown words. However, students were unable to retell accurately what they read. They did not include all the details from the beginning, middle, and end of the story, and had difficulty identifying a favorite part of the story and making self-to-text connections to explain why they liked it. Working collaboratively to solve the problem (TLMS Domain I), Yokaira restructured her small group instruction by assigning groups to the preservice candidate, thereby doubling the opportunities her ELs had to receive targeted instruction in retelling and describing a favorite part of a story with a teacher. After a few weeks, Yokaira noticed that students who previously struggled to retell the story were doing much better at including details in their retellings, identifying a favorite part, and explaining connections between the story and their experiences. Yokaira observed that the teacher candidate not only prepared the ELs to reach high reading levels on the DRA assessment, but she also helped them improve their English vocabulary and their speaking and listening skills.

One of the challenges identified by the upper grade teachers was to keep ELs at the beginning levels of proficiency engaged in class lessons where the language demands were well above their proficiency level. In response, Nancy piloted an observation instrument to document beginning ELs' behaviors during a lesson. One to two beginning ELs were selected as the focus of each observation, and their behaviors were documented in 1- to-2-minute intervals over the course of a lesson. The results suggested that students at the beginning levels of English proficiency appeared more engaged when there were frequent opportunities for interacting with more proficient English speakers. In these interactions, they generally relied on their more proficient partners to initiate the conversation due to the academic language demands. The instrument was revised and will be used to document ELs' engagement in lessons at the beginning of the next school year. If next year's findings support the previous trend, we will explore different mechanisms to ensure that teachers provide ELs with structured opportunities for peer interaction to develop their oral language skills.

**Standardized measures of English language proficiency.** The fifth domain of the TLMS focuses on the use of assessments and data for school and district improvement. To meet the expectations in this domain, teacher leaders must be able to build their colleagues' capacity to identify and use assessment tools that are aligned to state and local standards to improve student learning. In order to assess changes in the language proficiency levels of our ELs, Maria analyzed NYSESLAT data over a two-year period (2016 and 2017). The NYSESLAT results for each language modality (i.e., speaking, listening comprehension, reading, and writing) were averaged by grade level and compared. Table 1 shows the results.

In 2017, average scores in listening comprehension improved by grade 3, though in grade 5 there was a small decline. Average scores in speaking improved in grades 1, 2, 4, and 5, and there was a slight decline in grade 3. Average scores in reading improved at all grade levels; and average scores in writing varied across grade levels, increasing in grades K, 1, 2, and 5, but decreasing in grades 3 and 4. We also noted that the decrease in the number of fifth graders taking the NYSESLAT in 2017 was a result of a large percentage of students passing the test in fourth grade in 2016. These data helped us to set new goals. In the coming year, we will focus on preparing teachers to develop additional academic questioning practices around read-alouds and expose students to a wider variety of writing genres that promote the kinds of academic listening comprehension and writing skills that meet state standards and are measured by the NYSESLAT.

**Long-term effects.** To evaluate the long-term effects of our efforts on ELs' language proficiency development, we are collecting data on passing rates at each grade level over a period of several years to determine how the school NYSESLAT trends compare to districtwide trends. For example, in the school district approximately 50% of ELs who enter school in kindergarten pass the NYSESLAT within four years (Kiefer & Parker, 2016). We will monitor the progress of our ELs to see whether our efforts are leading to ELs development of academic English proficiency at similar or better rates, and make adjustments to our work with teachers based on this information.

Table 1: 2016 and 2017 NYSESLAT Averages by Grade and Modality.

| | Listening | | Speaking | | Reading | | Writing | |
|---|---|---|---|---|---|---|---|---|
| | 2016 | 2017 | 2016 | 2017 | 2016 | 2017 | 2016 | 2017 |
| Kindergarten | 13.935 $N=31$ | 13.666 $N=36$ | 15.322 $N=31$ | 14.58 $N=36$ | 14.645 $N=31$ | 15.8 $N=36$ | 8.709 $N=31$ | 8.75 $N=36$ |
| First | 13.050 $N=40$ | 12.05 $N=20$ | 15.150 $N=40$ | 17.7 $N=20$ | 10.975 $N=40$ | 11.5 $N=20$ | 3.525 $N=40$ | 3.55 $N=20$ |
| Second | 16.083 $N=24$ | 15.7 $N=40$ | 16.125 $N=24$ | 17.075 $N=40$ | 15.083 $N=24$ | 16.675 $N=40$ | 3.791 $N=24$ | 5.25 $N=40$ |
| Third | 12.931 $N=29$ | 13.964 $N=28$ | 16.482 $N=29$ | 16.428 $N=28$ | 13.724 $N=29$ | 14.107 $N=28$ | 4.413 $N=29$ | 4.142 $N=28$ |
| Fourth | 16.323 $N=34$ | 16.857 $N=28$ | 15.852 $N=34$ | 17.75 $N=28$ | 18.264 $N=34$ | 18.642 $N=28$ | 5.970 $N=34$ | 5.785 $N=28$ |
| Fifth | 14.086 $N=23$ | 13.777 $N=18$ | 13.652 $N=23$ | 15.333 $N=18$ | 13.826 $N=23$ | 14.555 $N=18$ | 4.956 $N=23$ | 5.333 $N=18$ |

## CONCLUSION

In a study of how teachers define leadership, Cosenza (2015) discovered that teachers felt empowered as leaders when sharing best practices that influenced others' teaching and viewed teacher leadership as an opportunity to collaborate with colleagues. For all four authors, the PDS offers a space for defining best practices and exploring their impact on learners. Our PDS work to improve learning for ELs has greatly enriched our individual and collective understandings of teaching and learning. As a natural part of collaborative planning and implementation, teacher leadership skills were revealed and supported, and in the process everyone benefited: the teachers at PS 291, the preservice candidates at Lehman, and most importantly, our ELs.

## References

Beaver, J., & Carter, M. (n.d.) Developmental reading assessment (2nd ed.). Pearson Publishing.

Cave, A., & Brown, C. W. (2010). When learning is at stake: Exploration of the role of teacher training and professional development schools on elementary students' math achievement. *National Forum of Teacher Education Journal, 20,* 1–21.

Cosenza, M. N. (2015). Defining teacher leadership: Affirming the teacher leader model standards. *Issues in Teacher Education, 24,* 79–99.

deJong, E. J., & Harper, C. A. (2005). Preparing mainstream teachers for English-language learners: Is being a good teacher good enough? *Teacher Education Quarterly,* 101–124.

Dubetz, N. E., & Collett. J. (2016). Identifying core teaching practices that ensure academic success for English learners. Paper presented at the Annual Meeting of the American Association of Educational Research, Baltimore, MD, April 8–12, 2016.

Harrison, C., & Killion, J. (2007). Ten roles for teacher leaders. *Educational Leadership, 65,* 74–77.

Holmes Group. (1986). *Tomorrow's teachers: A report of the Holmes Group.* East Lansing, MI: Author.

Holmes Group. (1990). *Tomorrow's schools: A report of the Holmes Group.* East Lansing, MI: Author.

Houston, W. R., Hollis, L. Y., Clay, D., Ligons, C. M., & Roff, L. (1999). Effects of collaboration on urban teacher education programs and professional development schools. In D. M. Byrd & D. J. McIntyre (Eds.), Research on professional development schools: Teacher education yearbook VII (pp. 6–28). Thousand Oaks, CA: Corwin Press.

Kieffer, M. J., & Parker, C. E. (2016). Patterns of English learner student reclassification in New York City public schools (REL 2017–200). Washington, DC: U.S. Department of Education, Institute of Education Sciences, National Center for Education Evaluation and Regional Assistance, Regional Educational Laboratory Northeast & Islands. Retrieved from http:// ies.ed.gov/ncee/edlabs

Klinger, J., Ahwee, S., van Garderen, D., & Hernandez, C. (2004). Closing the gap: Enhancing student outcomes in an urban professional development school. *Teacher Education and Special Education, 27,* 292–230.

Lawrence, A., & Dubetz, N. (2001). An urban collaboration: Improving student learning through a professional development network. *Action in Teacher Education, 22,* 1–14.

Marchant, G. J. (2002). Professional development schools and indicators of student achievement. *The Teacher Educator, 38,* 112–125.

McDonald, M., Kazemi, E., & Kavanagh, S. (2013). Core practices and pedagogies of teacher education: A call for a common language and collective activity. *Journal of Teacher Education, 64,* 378–386.

National Center for Educational Statistics. (2017, March). English Language Learners in Public Schools. Retrieved from https://nces.ed.gov/programs/coe/indicator_cgf.asp

New York City Department of Education. (2016, November). English Language Learner Demographic Report for the 2015–2016 School Year. Retrieved from http://schools.nyc.gov/NR/rdonlyres/0183D51C-377B-4ED7-BCBE-607AE4669D54/0/201415ELLDemographicReport.pdf

Teacher Leadership Exploratory Consortium. (2012). Teacher Leader Model Standards. Retrieved from http://www.teacherleaderstandards.org/index.php

Teitel, L. (2001). *How professional development schools make a difference: A review of the research.* Washington, DC: National Council for Accreditation of Teacher Education.

United States Department of Education. (2012). National evaluation of Title III implementation: Report on state and local implementation. Retrieved from http://www2.ed.gov/rschstat/eval/title-iii/state-local-implementation-report.pdf

Chapter 4

# De-Tracking Ninth Grade Algebra: A Teacher Leadership Success Story

*Rhonda Baynes Jeffries*

### Abstract

This chapter explores the alignment of teacher leadership and student learning in a professional development school (PDS) by reporting on a successful teacher-initiated PDS project at a southeastern United States high school. De-tracking efforts using teacher collaboration and efficacy in ninth grade Algebra I College Prep courses were examined for effectiveness to improve the achievement in mathematics of students who enter high school without pre-algebra skills. The chapter critiques the lack of democracy inherent in educational tracking as a default system of student grouping because it perpetuates inequities, particularly for students most likely to experience challenges with academic achievement.

*Keywords:* Mathematics; de-tracking; self-fulfilling prophecy; teacher leadership; teacher collaboration; teacher efficacy; mastery learning

In education, a fundamental expectation of professional development is that schools will improve through focused reform efforts. Schools improve when administrators create inclusive environments where instructional and student personnel find opportunities to thrive and achieve their professional and academic goals. Often opportunities of this type are crafted through a professional development school (PDS) collaboration where key personnel in schools and universities use research-based theory to inform practices that facilitate academic excellence. The PDS model, grounded in democratic principles, is an effective means of combatting academic and social inequities that manifest in myriad ways in school environments (Zenkov, Corrigan, & Beebe, 2013). Democracy-driven professional development is possible when there is "a shared commitment to innovative and reflective practice by all participants" as noted by the National Association for Professional Development Schools (2017, para 4). Changing teacher perceptions and expectations of students who are most in need of support is a critical aspect of ongoing professional development. Supportive leadership and cooperative professional development can produce a culture of teacher belief that is reflected in teachers' ability to positively impact student achievement (Goddard, Goddard, Kim, & Miller, 2015).

One of the hallmarks of the PDS model is the use of collaborative instruction based on the principles of the National Network for Educational Renewal's (NNER) Agenda for Education in a Democracy. This agenda, in particular, highlights teacher leadership as an essential element of effective PDSs as well as the importance of collaboration among teachers to foster a democratic learning environment (Ronfeldt, Farmer, McQueen, & Grissom, 2015). Collaboration among teachers is sustainable in a democratic environment, but with multiple competing agendas, democratic collaboration may suffer (Datnow & Stringfield, 2000). Exploring the elements of outcome-driven PDS partnerships may reveal clear guidelines for the creation and maintenance of focused, relevant, and effective reform.

The initiative under investigation explores the alignment of teacher leadership and student learning in a PDS. In particular, it critiques the lack of democracy inherent in educational tracking as a default system of student grouping because it perpetuates inequities, particularly for students most likely to experience challenges with academic achievement. Broadly, the research explores one school's ability to prioritize PDS initiatives while negotiating Common Core State Standards, district and building administration shifts, and end-of-course testing expectations, among other demands on multiple resources. The chapter reports data from a de-tracking pilot project and two years of full implementation at a southeastern United States high school. Based on a redesigned mastery learning model in ninth grade Algebra I College Prep (CP), the PDS initiative was examined for its effectiveness to improve achievement for students who enter high school without pre-algebra skills in the face of no state-approved course that teaches pre-algebra skills at the high school level. Specific efficacy aspects examined include instructional leadership, teacher buy-in, and most importantly, student learning outcomes resulting from the PDS initiative. The primary question addressed was, how does heterogeneous grouping of ninth grade Algebra 1 CP mathematics students impact instructional leadership, teacher buy-in, and student learning outcomes?

## Theoretical Framework/Literature Review

The theoretical frameworks used to understand this PDS initiative are instructional leadership theories grounded in teacher collaboration, efficacy, and self-fulfilling prophecy. Instructional leadership theories grounded in teacher collaboration and efficacy suggest that teachers emerge as leaders once productive collaboration has occurred, and productivity among instructional personnel is a direct by-product of self-assessed efficacy. This framework is used in conjunction with self-fulfilling prophecy theory, also known as the Pygmalion Effect, which emphasizes the influence of teachers' expectations on student performance. Self-fulfilling prophecy theory helps explain how leadership beliefs, teachers' ability to design effective curriculum, and high teacher efficacy impact student performance positively.

Instructional leadership grounded in teacher collaboration is recognized as a natural outgrowth of school–university partnerships where enhanced student achievement thrives on the high interdependence of both agencies (Darling-Hammond, Bullmaster, & Cobb, 1995). Beyond interagency partnerships, the collaborations that occur among instructional personnel are the essence of outcome-producing reform. Hunzicker's (2013) research highlighted the interrelated nature of teacher effectiveness using inquiry-based learning, which increased teachers' willingness to embrace leadership roles. Primarily, teacher leaders "aim to increase student learning and achievement by directly supporting teachers toward effective instructional practices through various forms of positive influence, such as modeling, providing information, coaching, offering feedback, and analyzing data together." (Hunzicker, 2017, p. 13). Angelle and Teague (2014) found that teachers respond more positively to teacher-generated reform than administrator-led change. This supports the idea that teacherpreneurs, hybrid classroom instructors, and other organic leaders hold much promise for positively impacting teacher quality and student learning outcomes (Berry, 2015; Huang, 2016; Hunzicker, 2013).

Instructional leadership and efficacy research demonstrate that teachers are more likely to adopt an educational reform effort if the initiative supports their ability to see evidence of their own effectiveness. Teacher efficacy, and more specifically teachers' self-assessment of their ability to promote student achievement, is positively correlated with the use of instructional strategies that support the diverse learning needs of students who are heterogeneously grouped into classes (Dixon, Yssel, McConnel, & Hardin, 2014). Furthermore, effective teachers have a tremendous influence on their colleagues' willingness to embrace reform that expressly resides in the professional development realm. Teacher leaders in PDSs have become the persuasive force behind school reform intended to directly impact student achievement (Gonzales & Lambert, 2001). While administrative leadership has significant impact on school culture and the successful integration of PDS reform, teacher leaders have powerful influence on teacher buy in (defined as collaboration and efficacy) regarding the implementation of reform that changes teachers' instructional strategies and student expectations, which directly benefit student achievement.

Rosenthal and Jacobsen's (1968a, 1968b) seminal work on the professional development of teachers originally described the self-fulfilling prophecy as high teacher expectations positively influencing student learning outcomes, and low teacher expectations negatively influencing student learning outcomes. Considering the impact of teacher bias on student learning outcomes, this theory was undergirded by research that rejected the deficit models, which previously attempted to explain the poor performance of students of color and students from low-income families. Nearly 50 years after, recommendations from this work have yet to be fully integrated into schools and classrooms. Nevertheless, educators continue to lament the student learning outcomes for demographically diverse students. While some theorists have argued the limitations of self-fulfilling prophecy theory (Brophy, 1983; Jussim, 1989; Wineburg, 1987), they present no preferred treatment of the problem. Furthermore, continued research on the positive outcomes produced from the effective application of self-fulfilling prophecy theory suggests that students who are racial/ethnic and economic minorities respond best when they are taught by teachers who exhibit tenets of the theory (Madon, Willard, Guyll, & Scherr, 2011). In other words, teachers who contradictorily have high expectations of students who typically exhibit low academic performance are particularly well suited to disrupt the pervasive pattern of underachievement. The sooner academically disadvantaged students encounter a teacher whose practice is grounded in democratic instructional practices the better. For example, Sorhagen's (2013) study suggested that low teacher expectations beginning in elementary school continue to negatively affect marginalized students' high school performance. These studies suggest that successfully implemented PDS initiatives provide meaningful pathways for teachers to sustain their belief in and use of equity pedagogies.

## Background

The participant school where the research was conducted is a PDS site, which collaborated with a partnering university that required the utilization of the NNER's Agenda for Education in a Democracy. However, the overall agenda for sustaining PDS work between the high school and the university had been overshadowed in recent years by district and state mandates that did not necessarily support emphasis on inquiry-based teaching and learning or the promotion of research for dissemination. This chapter reflects on the explicit efforts of a school-based teacherpreneur, identified in this chapter by the pseudonym, Heather Rogers, and a university professor, the author, to specifically design and implement a PDS initiative, which transformed the mathematics department at a high school and is now scheduled for replication at other high schools in the district.

The participant school enrolled approximately 1,600 students with a racial composition of 48% black, 46% white, 3% Latino, 1% Asian, and 2% others during the pilot year 2011–2012. At the participant school, a disproportionate number of students eligible for free and reduced lunch (49%) were recommended for Foundations of Algebra, the developmental course for high school students with little to no exposure to pre-algebra skills, in contrast to the total percentage of free/reduced lunch students (28%). Likewise, a disproportionate number of students of color (77%) were recommended for Foundations of Algebra in contrast to the total percentage of students of color (54%). The school's reliance on tracking as the method for classifying students according to their report card grades in middle school, state standardized test scores, and teacher recommendations created significant barriers for students who wanted to change their academic station. Based on historical mathematics performance at the high school, it was evident that tracking did not support the democratic principles of the PDS model.

This overrepresentation of economically and racially disadvantaged students prompted the design of an informal pilot project with 49 students who were tracked into Foundations of Algebra. Despite being registered across two sections of Foundations of Algebra with Heather Rogers, students were told by Heather that they were in CP algebra sections, and she assigned the students CP level work. Students in the pilot project passed the course at a rate of 90%, which was significant considering that 99% of this group were low-income students of color. Heather's pilot project suggested that a majority of this student group was capable of performing at a higher level of mathematics when offered appropriate instructional strategies.

During academic years 2011–2012 through 2014–2015, a PDS collaboration grew from the pilot project to full implementation, with data collection guiding the development and subsequent utilization of a teacher collaboration model (Figure 1).

Project implementation included research and redesign in response to instructional personnel changes. The specific teachers involved in the project are described in detail in the following section.

## Research Methods

This single case study employed qualitative research methods and descriptive statistics to explore the PDS initiative. Data collection included interviews of teacher participants, review of student outcome data, and review of archival documents. The purposefully selected sample included 8 Algebra 1 CP classroom teachers, 49 students during the pilot project year, no students during the administrative support and model project research year, and an average of 380 students during the two full implementation years.

From pilot project through year two of full implementation, total school instructional personnel at the high school averaged 94 teachers per year. The specific teacher participants included six females and two males: six were white and two were black. Their years of teaching experience ranged from a 36-year veteran to a first-year novice teacher. Heather, a black female, had 22 years of teaching experience during the pilot project year.

Case study research designed around a bounded phenomenon – the achievement of students enrolled in Algebra 1 CP – was utilized to explore multiple points of evidence for credibility and trustworthiness

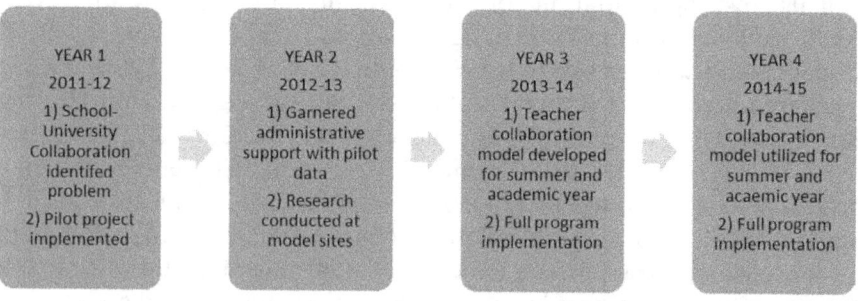

Figure 1. Project Implementation Timeline.

(Yin, 2009). Interviews with the teacher leader and the participant teachers, e-mail correspondence and parent communications, and student grades and end-of-course tests were the primary data sources. Multiple interviews with the teacher leader were conducted to gauge the tone, response to, and effectiveness of the PDS initiative. Foundations of Algebra student placements were evaluated with the guidance department chair to determine the effectiveness of the registration process. Triangulation of data-generated themes and member checks, and peer debriefings provided credibility and trustworthiness of the data set.

## Findings

### *Instructional Leadership*

Instructional leadership often originates from a single individual who is compelled to conceive an initiative; however, collaboration across school and university personnel helps to give an initiative life. While the pilot project data supported replication of the project with a wider audience, many aspects of full implementation remained unresolved. The teacher leader, in consultation with the author, explored the feasibility of the project with the school principal and Algebra 1 CP teachers to establish support. She then solicited the assistance of the guidance department because of their essential role with the intricate scheduling that needed to occur for implementation. The high school operates on a modified block schedule, and blocks are 90-minute frames that can be divided into two 45-minute periods as needed. Algebra 1 CP teachers spent the summer before year one, full implementation collaborating with the guidance department to develop a structure that provided 45 minutes of preteaching the Foundations of Algebra-recommended students in a required elective course entitled Math Seminar. These same students moved directly from the Math Seminar course to the Algebra 1 CP course for an additional 45 minutes of instruction in an integrated section of students who entered ninth grade on track for Algebra 1 CP. Four teams of two Algebra 1 CP teachers partnered in order for one team member to conduct the Math Seminar section for the subgroup of Foundations of Algebra students from both teachers' Algebra 1 CP classes (Figure 2).

All Algebra 1 CP teachers agreed to synchronize the curriculum, lesson plans, and assessments, which were designed during the summer planning sessions. They agreed to meet on a weekly basis during the school year to make adjustments as needed. The Algebra 1 CP teachers

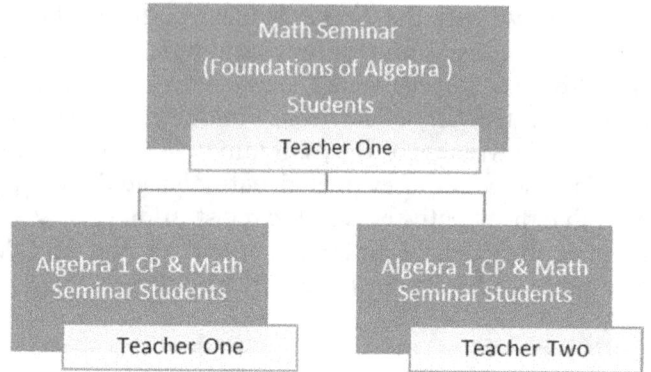

Figure 2. Algebra 1 CP Math Team Format.

and the university partner collaborated on the information that should be distributed to every Algebra 1 CP parent to create transparency and garner family support. Learning objectives and goals were clearly outlined. A flyer distributed to parents at the beginning of the academic year read in part as follows:

> The course will provide students with the necessary skills of algebra that will be needed for success in future courses and increase the ability to use those skills to solve realistic problems they may encounter in their lives. Our learning objectives will be called Learning Objective Goals (LOG). Thirteen LOGs are covered in the course.

Mastery learning is based on the philosophy that all children can become achievers when taught at a level of their own proficiency and encouraged to progress at a rate of their ability to master clearly defined units of learning. Mastery learning proposes that all students can learn when provided with the appropriate classroom learning conditions. Also explained in the flyer, the mastery learning design included the following plan:

- Students will take a series of mini quizzes before a unit test is given.
- Teachers will assess each quiz to check for student misconceptions of content.
- Teachers will target student misconceptions and reteach objectives as appropriate.
- After all unit objectives are taught, students will take the unit test.

- If the student does not score 77% or higher on the unit test, he or she must retake it.
- Students must attend tutoring before retaking a unit test. This can be done during lunch, after school, or before school.
- Unit tests must be retaken until unit objectives are mastered. Students will have the opportunity to improve test grades, but they cannot replace the grade. Therefore, it is of great importance that students come prepared the first time.

Early reactions to the project were predominantly positive. For example, district administration responded to the de-tracking initiative with the following e-mail correspondence to Heather: "The plan that you all have is working. Parents really loved the message that you communicated at the beginning of the year at orientation. Keep up the good work!" However, while most parents expressed support of the initiative, early responses were not completely positive. One concerned mother wrote:

> My son...has come home daily stating that...quite a few students are unfamiliar with a lot of the information that... was supposed to have been taught last year. Because of this issue, the teacher has had to spend the first couple of days teaching...instead of simply reviewing. My concern is that the teacher will end up spending most of her time teaching information that should have been learned in eighth grade.

The team of teachers addressed parent concerns when they arose and supported the goals and objectives that needed to be met for continued and expanded improvement in student learning outcomes. To accomplish this, teacher buy-in was critical.

### *Teacher Buy-in*

Teachers who were a part of the de-tracking initiative respected its research-based approach and were eager to demonstrate that they could raise test scores and improve students' learning outcomes through their commitment to de-tracking. Teachers' initial responses, based on their buy-in to the project, were cautiously optimistic, as seen in the following teacher comment:

> I have mixed emotions because I do believe that many of the kids have stepped up and are doing fine in CP instead

of Foundations. I don't think that would be the case if it weren't for the extra time to work and get more help during seminar [preview sessions] so I think the seminar is working well for most of the kids in it.

Another teacher commented, "I thought it was a good idea in theory, but I wasn't sure it would work in practice. It has exceeded my initial expectations, so far." This suggested that while teachers were willing to follow a strong teacher leader, they embraced the initiative because it was research-based and student learning was outcome-driven.

The team was also strengthened by the support they received from the school's administrative team. In one parent communication, the assistant principal concluded, "There is a district pacing guide that will be followed, so [all ninth grade content] will be covered." Due to this type of administrative support, a veteran teacher who was initially ambivalent about the project stood by Heather's leadership and embraced the project goals. In one communication to a concerned parent, this teacher wrote, "We are working on [helping your son to feel comfortable with the new course structure], and it does take time." While the veteran teacher fulfilled the primary expectations to respond to the concerned parent and support the school administrator and teacher leader, an early career teacher acknowledged the social justice implications of the initiative that aligned with her personal teaching philosophy:

> Tracking is something that always concerned me even when I was in high school. Some students will never have the opportunity to take a calculus course solely based on the track that they were given. The new system gives everyone an equal opportunity to succeed mathematically, and I love that.

As the project gained traction, a colleague from another department noted its success and recognized that enhanced student learning outcomes were a direct result of the PDS work: "One of your students told me she only missed ONE problem on the first part of the test! You are working wonders with her!" The teacher leadership, collaboration, and efficacy displayed in the de-tracking initiative were critical elements of its creation and preservation, but the essential indicator of effectiveness was student learning outcomes. Academic gains and increased learning opportunities were the ultimate goals of the initiative, and it is in this arena that the data are robust.

## Student Learning Outcomes

The challenge to show growth within the school and among the district was motivation for each Algebra 1 CP team, and student learning outcomes for these previously low performing mathematics students were positive. For full implementation year one, 2013–2014, the Math Seminar students performed well in Algebra 1 CP, with 159 students placed in CP and 119 (75%) passing at the end of the semester. The remaining 40 students (25%) were rescheduled to a Foundations of Algebra section in order to prevent failure and gain credit. Foundations of Algebra counts as 1/2 high school math credit. However, students on this track typically do not complete Algebra 2, the baseline mathematics readiness course for college attendance. The de-tracking initiative increased the number of students on track for college readiness with CP mathematics by 53%. Project recognition was noted from the district mathematics coordinator in the following e-mail: "Parents are impressed with the consistency in protocol, procedures, fairness/equity, and impact. Thank you so much for all that you have done to support freshman algebra learning to maximize individual potential [for] secondary mathematics."

The district administration's recognition was in direct response to data that demonstrated how declining Algebra 1 CP student learning outcomes were improved with the mastery learning curriculum implemented through the de-tracking initiative. Algebra 1 CP end-of-course test passing rates showed gains from the traditional tracking system during the academic year 2010–2011, to the second year of full implementation in 2014–2015. During the academic year ending 2011, the pass rate was 87.2%, which was strong but still below the top high schools in the district. During the academic year ending 2012, the pilot project year, the pass rate dropped to 83.2%, which was below the district's top high school. One possible reason for the dip may have been the fact that student enrollment in the participant high school was redistributed prior to the academic year 2011–2012, and the school's demographics had changed significantly. During the academic year 2012–2013, perhaps due to the process of gaining administration endorsement and preparatory research for the de-tracking initiative, scores fell to their lowest at 81.2%. During the academic year 2013–2014, the first year of full implementation, scores rose to 86.6%. During the academic year 2014–2015, the second year of full implementation, scores were the highest in school history and surpassed all other high schools in the district at 90.1% (see Table 1).

The Algebra 1 CP end-of-course tests with data disaggregation for Math Seminar students and all ninth grade Algebra 1 CP students

Table 1: Algebra I CP End-of-Course Passing Rates.

| Academic Year | End-of-Course Test Passing Rates (%) | Project Implementation |
| --- | --- | --- |
| 2010–2011 | 87.2 | Traditional tracking system |
| 2011–2012 | 83.2 | Project pilot |
| 2012–2013 | 81.2 | Project planning and preparation |
| 2013–2014 | 86.6 | Full implementation: First year |
| 2014–2015 | 90.1 | Full implementation: Second year |

demonstrates the capacity of the de-tracking initiative to increase academic achievement. The project assisted with remediation and provided equity to the Math Seminar students who passed after two years of full implementation at a rate of 89.4%. These data also show that the initiative did not compromise the academic goals of the full, ninth grade Algebra 1 CP student group who passed at a rate of 92.7%.

Based on the associated race/ethnicity and socioeconomic status demographics of the Math Seminar students identified in the pilot project, de-tracking improved academic opportunities and learning outcomes for students of low-income category and for students of color. These data demonstrate advantages of a research-based, collaborative PDS project and debunk the common perceptions that perpetuate tracking. This study provides evidence that supports collaborative professional development grounded in social justice and framed by leadership theories including teacher collaboration and teacher efficacy, and self-fulfilling prophecy theory to support teacher development. As a result of the project's demonstrated success in improving the mathematics achievement of students who enter high school without pre-algebra skills, the de-tracking program is now scheduled for replication at other high schools in the district.

## Discussion

The findings of this study suggest that a leadership framework based on teacher collaboration and teacher efficacy, coupled with self-fulfilling prophecy theory, effectively informed the design of a PDS initiative that impacted student learning outcomes. The data revealed a sequential pattern of instructional leadership generated by the initiative that led to teacher buy-in. Teachers embraced the de-tracking initiative in response to a school–university partnership that provided research-based strategies and sound teacher leadership. Teacher buy-in subsequently led to enhanced student learning outcomes. As teachers began to see the effects of the initiative on their self-efficacy, the self-fulfilling prophecy of expectation increased teacher buy-in and bolstered student learning outcomes. These findings suggest that CP mathematics can be successfully accessed by greater numbers of students when offered with appropriate instructional supports, including effective leadership and a school culture that supports and promotes democratic ideals.

PDS initiatives grounded in democratic instructional practice hold much promise in improving teacher efficacy and the resulting academic performances of students most in need of success. While administrative leadership is necessary for instructional advancement, teacher leaders who prioritize student learning by supporting their colleagues' skill sets are at the greatest advantage for producing effective outcomes through professional development. Unlike external consultants who lack intimate knowledge regarding the culture of instructional and student personnel, teacher leaders understand the intricate requirements of both populations. This knowledge enables teacher leaders to design PDS efforts that specifically address the academic needs of students, the professional needs of teachers, and the structural needs of the school as an organization (Danielson, 2006; Leana, 2011; Nappi, 2014).

Essentially, developing mathematical knowledge for teaching is unlikely to flourish in schools where equity pedagogy is not the fundamental impetus for instruction. Pilot project research and full implementation of this initiative found that end-of-course testing continued to improve and significantly alter the academic and life opportunities for marginalized students. Faulkner, Stiff, Marshall, Nietfeld, and Crossland (2014) noted the significance of student race and teacher orientation as predictors of Algebra 1 placement where students of color are disproportionately recommended for lower level classes despite academic performance. This research indicates that PDS initiatives based on the NNER agenda may increase opportunities for teachers to cultivate proficiency with equity pedagogies. District and building level administrators must certainly consider their roles in creating a culture where high expectations of teachers are supported by policies and procedures that enable instructional efficacy. Modeling democracy at the school, district, and university levels will positively modify the practices that perpetuate high identification of culturally marginalized mathematics students in foundation level classes.

## Conclusion

The plethora of research exploring impactful PDS initiatives tends to focus on partnerships that ultimately support a social justice agenda. However, most have failed to provide specific curriculum plans and instructional techniques that might be incorporated into the goals and objectives of the classroom (Zenkov et al., 2013). Campbell and Lee (2017) noted that democracy is a critical element for effective mathematics classrooms, and professional development models often fall short of creating the specific skills needed to help marginalized students. The ability of teachers to collectively build pedagogical skills around mathematical knowledge is crucial to structuring successful lessons that change student learning outcomes.

Pantić and Florian (2015) confirmed that these collaborative practices include teacher leaders who garner administrative endorsement, facilitate the professional growth of their colleagues, engender the support of parents and families, and most importantly, create excitement for learning among a group of students who have never before experienced true academic success. Low-income and racial minority students are overwhelmingly represented in the lowest track for mathematics instruction, and these practices detrimentally affect academic as well as life outcomes (Sullivan, 2015). More attention must be given to assisting this population of students to achieve mathematics excellence. PDS projects such as the de-tracking initiative described in this chapter develop clear, operational strategies for sustained teacher collaboration that can produce tangible improvements in student learning outcomes. Accordingly, the project provides an example of teacher leadership through a teacher-initiated PDS project that in turn developed many teachers' abilities to practice equity pedagogies that produced student success.

## References

Angelle, P., & Teague, G. M. (2014). Teacher leadership and collective efficacy: Teacher perceptions in three US school districts. *Journal of Educational Administration, 52*(6), 738–753.

Berry, B. (2015). Teacherpreneurs: Cultivating and scaling up a bold brand of teacher leadership. *The New Education, 11*(2), 146–160.

Brophy, J. (1983). Research on the self-fulfilling prophecy and teacher expectations. *Journal of Educational Psychology, 75*(5), 631–661.

Campbell, M. P., & Lee, H. S. (2017). Examining secondary mathematics teachers' opportunities to develop mathematically in professional learning communities. *School Science and Mathematics,* 117, 115–126. doi:10.1111/ssm.12209

Danielson, C. (2006). *Teacher leadership that strengthens professional practice.* Alexandria, VA: ASCD.

Darling-Hammond, L., Bullmaster, M. L., & Cobb, V. L. (1995). Rethinking teacher leadership through professional development schools. *The Elementary School Journal, 96*(1), 87–106.

Datnow, A., & Stringfield, S. (2000). Working together for reliable school reform. *Journal of Education for Students Placed at Risk (JESPAR), 5*(1–2), 183–204.

Dixon, F. A., Yssel, N., McConnell, J. M., & Hardin, T. (2014). Differentiated instruction, professional development, and teacher efficacy. *Journal for the Education of the Gifted, 37*(2), 111–127.

Faulkner, V. N., Stiff, L. V., Marshall, P. L., Nietfeld, J., & Crossland, C. L. (2014). Race and teacher evaluations as predictors of algebra placement. *Journal for Research in Mathematics Education, 45*(3), 288–311.

Goddard, R., Goddard, Y., Kim, E. S., & Miller, R. (2015). A theoretical and empirical analysis of the roles of instructional leadership, teacher collaboration, and collective efficacy beliefs in support of student learning. *American Journal of Education, 121*(4), 501–530.

Gonzales, S., & Lambert, L. (2001). Teacher leadership in professional development schools: Emerging conceptions, identities, and practices. *Journal of School Leadership, 11*(1), 6–24.

Huang, T. (2016). Linking the private and public: Teacher leadership and teacher education in the reflexive modernity. *European Journal of Teacher Education, 39*(2), 222–237.

Hunzicker, J. (2013). Attitude has a lot to do with it: Dispositions of emerging teacher leadership. *Teacher Development, 17*(4), 538–561.

Hunzicker, J. (2017). Using Danielson's framework to develop teacher leaders. *Kappa Delta Pi Record, 53*(1), 12–17.

Jussim, L. (1989). Teacher expectations: Self-fulfilling prophecies, perceptual biases, and accuracy. *Journal of Personality and Social Psychology, 57*(3), 469–480.

Leana, C. (2011). The missing link in school reform. Stanford Social Innovation Review. Retrieved from http://www.ssireview.org /articles/entry/the_missing_link_in_ school_reform/

Madon, S., Willard, J., Guyll, M., & Scherr, K. C. (2011). Self-fulfilling prophecies: Mechanisms, power, and links to social problems. *Social and Personality Psychology Compass, 5*(8), 578–590.

Nappi, J. S. (2014). The teacher leader: Improving schools by building social capital through shared leadership. *Principal's Research Review, 9*(6), 1–6.

National Association for Professional Development Schools. (2017). *Nine essentials*. Retrieved from http://napds.org/nine-essentials/

Pantić, N., & Florian, L. (2015). Developing teachers as agents of inclusion and social justice. *Education Inquiry, 6*(3), 333–351. doi:http://dx.doi.org/10.3402/edui.v6.27311.

Ronfeldt, M., Farmer, S., McQueen, K., & Grissom, J. A. (2015). Teacher collaboration in instructional teams and student achievement. *American Educational Research Journal, 52*(3), 475–514.

Rosenthal, R., & Jacobson, L. (1968a). *Pygmalion in the classroom: Teacher expectation and pupils' intellectual development*. Austin, TX: Holt, Rinehart & Winston.

Rosenthal, R., & Jacobson, L. (1968b). Teacher expectations for the disadvantaged. *Scientific American, 218*(4), 19–23.

Sorhagen, N. S. (2013). Early teacher expectations disproportionately affect poor children's high school performance. *Journal of Educational Psychology, 105*(2), 465–477.

Sullivan, P. (2015). Maximising opportunities in mathematics for all students: Addressing within-school and within-class differences. In A. Bishop, H. Tan, & T. Barkatsas (Eds.), *Diversity in mathematics education: Towards inclusive practices* (pp. 239–254). New York, NY: Springer.

Wineburg, S. (1987). The self-fulfillment of the self-fulfilling prophecy. *Educational Researcher, 16*(9), 28–37.

Yin, R. K. (2009). *Case study research: Design and methods* (4th ed.). Thousand Oaks, CA: Sage.

Zenkov, K., Corrigan, D., & Beebe, R. S. (2013). Professional development schools and social justice education. In K. Zenkov, D. Corrigan, R. S. Beebe, & C. R. Sell (Eds.), *Professional development schools and social justice: Schools and universities partnering to make a difference* (pp. 3–10). Lanham, MD: Rowman & Littlefield.

Chapter 5

# Moving from Collaborative Teacher Inquiry to Leadership: Four Stories from Project Teacher Leadership

*Clare Kruft and Diane Wood*

**Abstract**

Project Teacher Leadership is a PDS initiative, which has formed university–school teams to foster collaboration, inquiry, and leadership. University professors, intern teachers, and veteran K-12 teachers engaged in collaborative conversations about authentic experiences in their work to uncover troubling problems of practice and develop strategies for addressing them. In doing so, participants began to develop increased professional agency and leadership. The project drew strength from examining problems through varied perspectives and systematic inquiry, and the inquiry process motivated participants to advocate for changed practices better suited to ensure all students' learning.

*Keywords:* Collaboration; inquiry; professional development school; teacher leadership; advocacy; student learning; professional agency

Teachers touch students' lives and learning every day, yet they are rarely consulted – and sometimes even intentionally excluded – from official policy deliberations. Meanwhile, new policies take shape, spawning new mandates and regulations, which profoundly impact teaching and learning in classrooms across the country. No matter how well intentioned, many of these policies are poorly implemented, often because they lack the "reality checks" teachers could easily provide. Compounding the chaos are the short attention spans of politicians and administrators who, pressed for "results," often underestimate both the time and the comprehensive team effort that sustainable school change requires (Cochran-Smith & Lytle, 2009; Elmore, 2004; Fullan & Quinn, 2015). Unfortunately, these problems have become wearying not only to the general public but to teachers themselves, particularly because the latter find themselves scrambling to master and implement endless parades of reform ideas that eventually get interrupted, abandoned, or replaced. Sadly, the long history of school reform, punctuated with more failures than successes, has exacted heavy costs in terms of labor, treasure, and morale. Worse still, despite all these efforts, as well intentioned as they are, we have yet to capture the elusive holy grail: equitable, accessible, engaging, and productive learning for *all* students.

We, the authors of this chapter, are convinced that teachers working as collaborative inquirers, can help move schools and districts out of this cyclical morass and that professional development schools (PDS) may be the best possible context to figure out how to do so. As City et al. (2009) have emphasized, this is precisely the kind of inquiry originally envisioned and recommended as key work for professional development schools by the Holmes Group (1995). Moreover, there is wide agreement that, without teachers' active participation, insight, and know-how, reform efforts are bound to fail (Bond, 2015; Cochran-Smith & Lytle, 2009; Fullan & Quinn, 2015; Lieberman & Wood, 2003). Teacher leaders, in fact, have already proven themselves to be effective school reformers in some places (Boone, 2015). In the context of the project we describe in this chapter, we define teacher leaders, much as Wenner and Campbell (2017, p. 140) have, as full-time teachers who extend their sense of responsibility beyond their classrooms. To that definition, however, we add that teacher leaders collaborate with colleagues to name and address problems of practice that negatively affect students' learning and well-being. We are not necessarily referring to a formal, institutional role, such as team leader, instructional coach, or subject matter specialist. Like Taylor, Goeke, Klein, Onore, and Geist (2011), we view teachers as leaders when they exercise agency and influence to advocate for and lead positive school change for the sake of more productive and equitable student learning.

Our conceptualization of teacher leadership draws particularly on Heifetz and Linsky's (2002) "adaptive leadership," Cochran-Smith and Lytle's (2009) "inquiry stance," Hargreaves and Fullan's (2012) conception of building "professional capital" toward the improvement of teaching, and the Teacher Leadership Exploratory Consortium's (2012) Domain 7, "Advocating for Student Learning and the Profession." (p. 47). Heifetz and Linsky claim that contemporary organizations, roiled by unpredictable and multidimensional changes, should extricate from the hierarchical, chain-of-command structures in order to foster distributive leadership, multiple perspectives, continual questioning, and innovation. Cochran-Smith and Lytle describe and defend an inquiring professional "stance" for teachers that is likely to uncover the needed change and sustain the kind of shared questioning, decision-making, consideration of multiple perspectives, and ongoing innovation, which will better serve students. Hargreaves and Fullan argue convincingly for an investment in teacher professionalism and teacher-centered professional development as the most promising routes for schools to promote and sustain responsive and effective teaching in light of shifting student demographics, cultural conditions, and social needs. Domain 7 of the Teacher Leader Model Standards clearly indicates the consortium's position that teachers ought to influence education policies and practices. Hence, we envision teacher leaders who lead through advocacy, shared leadership, systematic questioning, collaboration, innovation, and moral purpose.

Katzenmeyer and Moller (2009) have argued that it is long past time for those truly interested in improving public education to "awaken the sleeping giant," that is, to tap into the considerable expertise and leadership potential of the teaching force. We also believe that teachers ought to become genuine leaders in their own profession by collaboratively confronting and addressing shared concerns about students' learning, development, and well-being and then advocating for more promising practices. In an effort to support teachers who want to undertake this kind of work, we launched a joint school system and university initiative called Project Teacher Leadership in fall 2016. Our intention was to create teams of university and school educators to collaboratively inquire into authentic problems of practice, build local knowledge, make participants' growing expertise public, and develop teacher leadership in the process.

The project brought together hybrid teams of veteran teachers, interns, college instructors, and – in one case – students. Clearly, there are many stories to narrate about each team. For purposes of this chapter, which describes the project only midway into its first iteration (two semesters of a three-semester process), we look especially closely at the leadership development in veteran teachers. The chapter traces the project's conceptualization; its rationale and implementation; four examples of collaborative teams working on problems of practice; what we, as project designers and implementers, have learned so far; and, finally, our recommendations, questions, and challenges regarding continuing this work.

## Why *Teacher* Leadership? Why Collaborative Inquiry? Why Professional Development Schools?

At the start of every year, effective teachers learn quickly a dizzying array of idiosyncratic quirks and unique backgrounds of their students. They learn what it will take to lure each student into meaningful, sustained learning; and they recognize how much context, personalities, relationships, and cultural/socioeconomic conditions matter to learning. Because effective teachers grasp complexities regarding individual students, learning environments, and nested contexts (i.e., the institutional contexts of classroom, school, and district; the political contexts of local expectations and district, state, and national policies; the cultural contexts of place, professional and peer relationships, families, and so forth) and learn to navigate these complexities, they are particularly well equipped to be leaders in making schools work better for students. Three principles have guided our thinking in this regard. Effective teachers are as follows:

1. A major factor in students' development, learning, and well-being (Darling-Hammond, 2007; Delpit, 2006; Durlak, Domitrovich, Weissberg, & Gullotta, 2015; Hargreaves & Fullan, 2012).
2. A crucial resource for school change (Boone, 2015; Cochran-Smith & Lytle, 2009; Hargreaves & Fullan, 2012; Katzenmeyer & Moller, 2009; Schlechty, 2016).
3. A chief asset for building professional capital and elevating the teaching profession (Hargreaves & Fullan, 2012; Whitford & Wood, 2010).

Despite the profound impact teachers can possibly have, their work is often humbling, rife with the potential and potency of reality. Classrooms act as crucibles where promising theories, "best practices," and heroic efforts clash with hard realities, ultimately yielding more questions and dilemmas than answers: What is going on here? Why are teachers always complaining in the faculty room about kids like Jamie? How can our grade level team keep Rosa engaged? What can we do to get kids like Hussein working harder? Why are kids from the same demographic group always getting suspended? Why are some students bullying each other?

Questions such as these become catalysts for ongoing inquiry – critical reading, reflection, dialog, observation, listening, and assessment. Systematic, collaborative inquiry builds local knowledge, or "knowledge *of* practice," (Cochran-Smith & Lytle, 2009) a kind of knowledge necessary for teaching but different from "knowledge *for* practice," which is the knowledge emanating from sources outside of schools, usually universities, and different from "knowledge *in* practice," which is the knowledge teachers construct from classroom experience. "Knowledge *of* practice" is deliberately constructed knowledge, vetted by disciplined collegial conversations, reflection, study, and observations. Once teachers recognize the value of "knowledge *of* practice," they also realize that they are the only ones positioned to build it, but that they must do it collaboratively. As they internalize the importance and worth of building knowledge collaboratively, they develop individually and as a group a sense of professional authority about what they know and what they want for students. Moreover, they begin to feel authorized by their professional relationships to advocate for better ways to serve students (Wood & Lieberman, 2000). Ultimately, this combination of conscious and collaborative advocacy and knowledge-making can become a pathway to authentic teacher leadership (Cochran-Smith & Stern, 2015).

PDSs that are genuinely interested in two-way learning between school practitioners and university professors and supervisors provide particularly promising settings for this type of inquiry. Within this kind of PDS, teachers, empowered as knowledge contributors as well as recipients, have much to offer the university in terms of "knowledge *of* practice" (Cochran-Smith & Lytle, 2009) and teacher preparation. The interns placed in these schools have opportunities to witness teachers actively pursuing challenges of practice and building knowledge for the sake of student learning. One intern from our project put it this way, "This project was a great way to make interns involved in the school. I got insight as an intern at how teachers can change and improve their school environments" (January 28, 2017).

Motivated by this notion of schools as "centers of inquiry" (Robert Schaefer called for this vision of schools in 1967 – fifty years ago!), we recognized that authentic teacher leadership, borne of collaborative inquiry, requires intellectual space, time, and resources so that teachers internalize the idea that the knowledge they need to be successful does not always have to come from outside the profession. Teachers, working together, have the power to build valuable knowledge from within. We also know that teacher leadership initiatives frequently encounter institutional and cultural barriers. They can be profoundly countercultural, flying in the face of school and university bureaucracies, which position teachers as audiences for professional development, as technicians and implementers, and as hosts for intern placements. Despite pockets of teacher inquiry that occur in some settings, the practice is not widespread. In too many schools, teachers hide questions, uncertainty, and doubt under a cloak of the so-called expertise or wait in hope for a professional development experience to provide answers. This situation is particularly regrettable because teachers' uncertainties, doubts, and questions are the very grounds for serious inquiry into problems of practice and for building the kind of knowledge that can help all children learn.

## The Project

Project Teacher Leadership was designed by Baltimore County Public Schools (BCPS) and Towson University (TU), specifically to promote teacher leadership through experiences in collaborative inquiry. We envisioned a process that recalls Goodlad's notion of "simultaneous renewal," (Goodlad, 1998) that is, teachers and interns conceiving of their schools as living laboratories for study and innovation and then sharing that knowledge with others. The charge to teams was to name, confront, and explore an authentic and troubling question about schools and/or classrooms. Participants received a clear mandate to develop their own questioning, thinking, and deliberations oriented from and toward education practices. We shared with the participants our hope that the experience of collaborative inquiry would lend participating teachers a sense of agency so that together they could reach new understandings and develop new ideas and strategies to (1) improve BCPS K-12 student learning, (2) advance the professional expertise of TU interns, (3) provide professional development for BCPS veteran teachers and TU faculty, (4) strengthen the TU/BCPS partnership and enhance their PDS, and (5) develop in themselves and others leadership capacity. All of this placed veteran teachers, in particular, at the center of inquiry; they, after all, had the deepest experiences regarding these troubling questions.

### The Context

TU celebrated its 150th anniversary in 2016 as a higher education institution devoted largely to teacher preparation. Approximately 550 Towson education majors graduate, ready to teach, each year. Interns from early childhood, elementary, secondary, special education, and many other specialties (from physical education to nursing interns) are placed within the university's 180 PDS placements in BCPS, Baltimore City, other nearby counties, and some private schools. TU's campus is located within Baltimore County, and BCPS is the 27th largest school system in the country. Over 111,000 students attend one of the 189 schools within the BCPS. These individual schools vary in demographic population characteristics, but the county overall has 41% black, 10% Hispanic, and 43% white students enrolled, with about 8% English language learners (ELLs) and 49% of all eligible for free and reduced lunch, with the aggregate BCPS diversity growing each year. Forty-five of TU's PDS sites are located within the BCPS system, and this Project Teacher Leadership concept was introduced to all 45 sites. Teams from four sites, representing varied demographics and age levels of student populations, decided to participate in the initial pilot year of Project Teacher Leadership. The final four teams – a high school, a middle school, and two elementary schools – attended a weekend workshop and created action plans for their school partnerships.

## *The Process*

The first step to enable this work was to secure funding by TU and BCPS leaders (with each institution contributing matching grant funding of $5,000 toward final awards to be given as $1,500–$3,000 mini-grants for truly promising action plans). The second step for interested TU and BCPS educators was to hear more about opportunities offered through Project Teacher Leadership. Thus, the planning team, including representatives from TU and BCPS, advertised the new initiative with the liaisons from TU. They, in turn, explained the initiative to their school partners. News spread to principals, site coordinators, and other university contacts. As it addressed both partners simultaneously, the dissemination plan communicated mutual respect as it generated curiosity.

Project Teacher Leadership laid out a series of work phases, ensuring an ongoing process that would allow for current teams to deepen implementation plans, and prepare participating teachers to orient future teams as a new cycle began. These phases of each Project Teacher Leadership cycle are explained below.

**Phase one: information meeting.** Interested representatives from four schools attended the after-school information session conducted at the university. After hearing the rationale and the process for developing teacher leadership and local knowledge through collaborative inquiry, interested participants formed five-to-eight person, cross-institutional teams. These teams comprised of mentor and/or veteran K-12 teachers, university professors, university teaching interns placed at PDS sites, and students (if appropriate for secondary teams). Next, these teams submitted a brief application, which asked for the topic to be addressed, a paragraph explaining the rationale, and a list of participants and their roles.

**Phase two: weekend workshop.** We launched the Project Teacher Leadership Workshop on a Friday evening in January from 5:00 to 8:00 p.m. After a hot buffet and greetings from the TU dean of the College of Education and the BCPS Coordinator of Teacher Development, the evening kicked off with a keynote speech by a TU professor on the importance of teacher inquiry and advocacy. Inspired by the keynote, teams plunged into a work session to articulate and discuss problems of practice. Through these intense discussions, the participants recognized and questioned implicit assumptions, saw more clearly what they needed to know and understand, and began to develop inquiry questions. One participant wrote about this process on her evaluation: "I appreciated the open and free time to discuss issues/solutions" (January 28, 2017). She captured the importance of creating sustained time for teachers to wrestle with problems of practice –the kind of reflective time that Katzenmeyer and Moller (2009) recommend for elevating the teaching profession and developing leadership.

The second day (Saturday) of the workshop began with an overview of the day's goal: to help teams move toward developing fully fleshed-out inquiry projects, including their working theories of action and implementation steps toward addressing identified problems in their schools. Each component of the workshop that Saturday was designed to move teams from abstract questioning into concrete action plans. As participants tacked back and forth between the abstract and the concrete, they continued to deepen their grasp of the problems and what they needed to better understand. As a result, inquiry questions evolved, became more tightly focused, and felt more satisfying to participants. As one teacher put it, "This was an amazingly frustrating experience – sitting with a diverse group of educators to develop our question took almost our whole time...which is time well spent! I appreciated the perspectives and rich discussions" (January 28, 2017).

We designed the day intentionally to provide not only maximum work time for team discussions, but also for school–university, cross-sectional teams to collaborate. In addition, we arranged for sessions with cross-team critique and with "critical friends" (professionals from outside of the school community) to comment on the drafts as they emerged. A highlight of the critical feedback segment occurred when school teams participated in a "gallery walk." Each team visually represented their inquiry project on large chart paper and hung it on the wall or projected information from computers onto whiteboards. One or two members of each team stayed behind to field questions and explain while the rest of the team rotated in timed sequences through others' projects. This part of the day served several crucial purposes in that it developed capacities for giving and receiving critical feedback, setting strong purposes, aligning equally strong implementation plans, and arguing convincingly for needed changes in school practices. All of these served participants well when they returned to their respective schools to advocate for their projects and promote further participation by colleagues and administrators. Many participants commented that this portion of the gallery walk was the most useful for clarifying their problem statements, rationales, and inquiry questions. One teacher wrote on her evaluation, "The gallery walk was extremely helpful because it allowed us to verbalize our thinking to a new 'set of eyes'. It initiated discussion and allowed us to adapt our rationale, which we had been going back and forth on how to word appropriately" (January 28, 2017).

The collaboration between the TU and BCPS participants, which began with the planning committee and then expanded once the project got underway, offered cross-institutional peer response and critique. Participants commented positively about the intergroup feedback and two-way learning they experienced. One university professor wrote on her evaluation, "The planning committee members walked around and gave valuable feedback, asked questions, and shared resources. I also feel that the gallery walk was beneficial as we were given good suggestions from other school teams" (January 28, 2017).

Particularly impressive to the planning team was the way teachers, interns, and professors were "stepping up" to wrestle with school and classroom problems. Despite not being paid for their efforts, participants unanimously reported that the time devoted to intense question and learning justified the time invested. We witnessed veteran teachers, fueled by their desire to make a difference, taking up leadership roles to see through their projects, and university professors not simply offering expertise but also learning from teachers' perspectives and knowledge. The very fact that teachers were asking hard questions about their concerns and problems intrinsically motivated everyone in the room to work together to make students' school experiences richer and more satisfying. One teacher wrote:

Thank you for giving us the opportunity and support to make our school better. The questions that you posed made us delve deeper into the root causes and identify solutions. This weekend and all the activities/agenda was [sic] useful and conducive to growth. (January 28, 2017).

Another participating teacher commented on the practical benefits of this phase. He summarized, "I left both meeting days with a sense of accomplishment. We actually created a realistic plan which can be implemented and create positive change" (January 28, 2017).

**Phase three: funding and implementation.** The next phase of the Project Teacher Leadership cycle involved funding the implementation activities of each team's project. The cross-institutional planning team reviewed action plan drafts; subsequently, revision suggestions were sent to all of the teams. Each team had a planning team advisor to turn to for questions, advice, or school visits. Upon successful completion of revisions, team plans were reviewed by the planning committee again, and teams were awarded grant funding to pursue their respective inquiry projects. The planning team allocated funds from both the school system and university budgets, following the regulations of each institution carefully.

As project action plans were approved by the cross-institutional planning team, PDS teams received approval to make expenditures to support their funding requests (see Appendix A). Funding requests could be made in the categories of stipends for 10-month teachers for after-school or summer work, professional conference registrations, books and other supplies/materials, consultant fees, and food costs. Across all of the four plans, each of these categories was present in one or more of the plans.

The final critical step in this cycle was for the teams to explain how they planned to rally their entire PDS, including both TU and BCPS players, to participate in – or at least approve of – their inquiry projects. Teachers especially needed to exercise leadership as advocates for their projects with colleagues and administrators. Team acceptance of funds included other specific requirements, which also involved leadership; an end-of-year progress report, a fall report the subsequent year, and sharing of experiences and insights by team representatives at the informational meeting during the next year's Project Teacher Leadership cycle. Furthermore, some team representatives accepted the planning team's invitation to "go public" by presenting at the Maryland PDS Statewide Conference.

**Phase four: reflections to improve next year's process** The final stage was to reflect on ways to enhance the Project Teacher Leadership cycle not only for another round of invitations to the 45 TU/BCPS PDS sites, but also for the possibility of extending the partnership invitation to TU's PDS sites in another school system. We realize that those working in school–university partnerships, who learn about this project through conferences or publications, such as this chapter, would ultimately need to make adjustments to fit their own contexts and purposes. We want, therefore, to share this final phase of planned revisions to our approach hoping that they will be instructive for those who decide to undertake this work.

Crucial to our design process was the ongoing expectation for the project planning team to meet for reflection as they accomplished each phase of the project cycle. In doing so, our Project Teacher Leadership planning team realized that we needed to make the following changes to improve our outcomes for next year's teams. First, teachers and professors may be wonderful in the classroom, but that does not mean they know how to take leadership in creating effective action plans for their entire school faculties. While we did provide a chart to help teams construct their action plans, we realize now that a better approach would be for members of the planning team to provide tips and coaching for various parts of the plan as teams work through them. For future teams, we plan to move through different "stations," representing different segments of the action plan and staffed by members of the planning team, in order to obtain clarification and have questions answered. Our stations would target the following:

1. Constructing needs assessments that will help teams or school faculties tease out important root causes of the inquiry target, in order to plan for the highest-leverage actions that will move the PDS site forward.
2. Mapping backward to determine how to move from intended outcomes back to underlying meaningful professional learning opportunities, especially moving from one-time events to job-embedded, differentiated support for school and/or university faculty.
3. Understanding requirements from the school system and the university in creating and submitting the necessary budgets to be funded from the grants provided.

Second, the teachers with whom we worked needed to understand qualitative inquiry and action research as processes they can design and implement in their respective sites. While many teachers may have taken a research course some time along the way, participants in this project needed guidance in articulating strong and researchable questions, designing data collection plans, and creating data analysis protocols in order to assess progress.

Third, teacher–professor–intern collaboration was critical throughout all phases of the weekend workshop. Many participants wrote in their evaluations that the most powerful part of this collaborative feedback and questioning process involved the "gallery walk" time. Many participants, however, appreciated the suggestion one team member made that the rotation give way to mini-presentations (six-minute limit), presenting highlights of each team's work in progress so that all participants could benefit from hearing questions, concerns, and suggestions raised by others. We plan to try this new approach in next year's cycle.

Finally, all team applicants were accepted this year. Although we anticipate more interest next year, we have decided to invite all applying teams to the weekend workshop to give them the opportunity to learn together and to participate in powerful collaborative inquiry processes. Unfortunately, we will also need to make it clear that we can only fund four or five of the top team submissions because of limited funding.

## Examples from the Field and New Learning

The team inquiry projects ranged from reimagining and rebuilding school climate around restorative practices to differentiating instruction around gender and learning style differences. University partners offered academic resources and ongoing support as teams finalized their action plans and began to pursue their questions. Such support included, among other things, expertise on brain research and advice on action research. One intern reflected, "As a Towson intern, this experience has been monumental! I admire the collaboration and passion that was clear in all members" (January 28, 2017).

As the teams worked together, interns offered fresh, untainted-by-experience questions and enthusiasm, which sometimes shocked their team members into reexamining assumptions. One intern, for instance, asked her team members to clarify what they meant by repeatedly calling their high school "high-powered" in terms of academics. Ultimately, she pressed, "It's not high powered for a lot of kids; some aren't doing well at all." She pointed out that some groups of youths were not flourishing academically, usually poorer kids from the surrounding neighborhood including pockets of recent immigrants. The rest of the team conceded and began to question how any high school, no matter its reputation or test scores, could be deemed "high powered" if there were groups of students lacking a sense of belonging and feeling marginalized and disengaged.

As one of the veterans, an English teacher, said, "We have got to think about how we work with all of each kid – not just his or her brain!"

As the project continues to unfold, teachers are learning how to create effective plans, negotiate these plans in the face of school realities, and marshal support. We started with the idea of developing leadership, but found that we had landed on a particularly powerful way of going about it. Our theory of action has further evolved: through collaborative inquiry, teachers can construct useful local knowledge that no one else can produce, and building this knowledge develops in teachers both the desire and the wherewithal to lead. Moreover, interns who participate in collaborative inquiry develop from the start an expansive conception of the role of teachers, which includes the practices of inquiry and leadership. The four evolving inquiry projects are indicative of the important issues that teachers, interns, and university professors can address collaboratively. Some highlights of each are provided as follows:

*Elementary School (Primary)*

This Pre-K through grade 3 elementary school has a 70% free and reduced lunch population and close to 20% of its population are ELLs. They focused on the inquiry question: what are some curricular models that permit high-quality differentiation for a flex-grouping of high achieving children? Both university- and school-based participants were convinced of the mutual benefits of their collaboration. The team's university professor played a crucial role by being both a "critical friend" and by contributing academic expertise. The university professor's participation also served her own professional interests by fulfilling the university's service expectation, contributing to her own professional development, and allowing her an opportunity to explore possibilities for ongoing research. Practitioners on the team benefitted from two after-school workshops, provided by the professor (one targeted especially for the team and another for the entire faculty). Subsequent to these workshops, the team decided to deepen their work by creating teacher-centered professional development plans for the summer, using a large part of their funding to pay interested teachers for participating. The goal was to harness teachers' collaborative power to redesign instructional approaches for differentiation and enrichment. In the spirit of Taylor et al. (2011), we view teachers like these as leaders when they exercise agency and influence to advocate for and then lead implementation of positive school change.

Indeed, the team presented their plan to the school principal, and she was so convinced of the quality of this project that she reallocated summer professional development funds from her Title I budget to double the funding from the grant and allow math differentiation projects to be produced for half of the students at the school, instead of just for one grade level. With this increased funding, team members recruited other faculty members who had been intrigued by the previously mentioned workshops. Then university interns, veteran teachers, and university instructors worked alongside one another multiple days during the summer to construct the enrichment projects math students would be offered throughout the following school year. Ongoing data will be collected as these enrichment projects are implemented.

### *Elementary School (Intermediate)*

This elementary school population with a 30% mobility rate comprised of 38% African-American, 29% Asian, 16% white, 11% Hispanic, and 6% mixed race students. This team focused on the inquiry question: what strategies can we implement in order to motivate boys to be actively engaged in reading? One of this team's preservice interns was especially influential in helping the team move forward. She suggested a book line with a multiple "solve-your-own-adventure" format that the entire team agreed might be especially enticing for young boys. The professor on the team agreed, as did the teachers, and so they launched a new initiative, a boys' book club, and decided that buying books from the line would be a smart investment. The team conducted a survey immediately following the Project Teacher Leadership weekend workshop that allowed them to "hear" the direct voices of the boys about whom they were concerned. This led to the realization that the key factor holding the boys back was not a lack of reading skills but a pervasive attitude – quite simply, they hated reading! Consequently, the team identified engaging texts for these boys and gave them choices in buying texts, created a fun reading club, and helped the boys discover the joys of reading. The work of this team exemplifies Wenner and Campbell's (2017) description of teachers advocating for students beyond those in their own classrooms.

### *Middle School*

This middle school with a 23% mobility rate comprised of 61% white, 18% Hispanic, 11% African-American, and 10% other races of students.

The team focused on the inquiry question: how can we change the school culture via a restorative practices approach? In this case, it was the cross-team discussions and the exchange of expertise that made all the difference. As the middle school team learned from their peers in other institutions, they made increasingly informed, solid decisions about their project plans. They decided to differentiate professional development, based on the willingness of faculty members to try new restorative and community-building practices. Influenced by the suggestions of one university professor, they decided to weave in a framework for how people adapt to change at different rates. This became the underlying premise for constructing a differentiated professional development initiative to educate staff about restorative practices and support them in their implementation. They planned to provide more information and support for more hesitant educators to explore and try out the new practices, provide coaching for those eager to adopt them, and promote early adopters already experiencing success. For the latter, they encouraged teachers to take on the role of group leaders charged with helping colleagues by providing demonstration lessons and authentic stories of successes with students. By the end of the first year, the lead teacher reported substantial progress in moving most of the schools' educators toward greater understanding and implementation of restorative practices. The dogged efforts of the Project Leadership school team exemplify Domain VII's emphasis on advocacy and professional service (Teacher Leadership Exploratory Consortium, 2012).

## *High School*

This high school with fewer than 5% mobility and 5% free and reduced lunch rate comprised of 55% white, 20% African-American, 18% Asian, and 7% other races. This team focused on the inquiry question: how can we foster the community that we envision at our school? Unique to this team is the participation of three students particularly invested in the problem behind the question, why do too many students lack a sense of belonging in the school? The question, which sprang from the disconnectedness between the school's vision and students' perceptions regarding community, was intentionally open-ended because the team did not want to assume causes. Ideas were bandied about, based on preliminary data collected by the students in informal peer groups. These ideas included suspected mainstream biases toward students from "different" demographic backgrounds and a sense that there was too much emphasis on academic competition and achievement. Ultimately, the question proved prophetic. Subsequent to the workshop in January, an uprising at the school with clear racial overtones made headlines. The team's inquiry question, clearly on target, provided positive momentum as team members were especially well positioned to help the school stay ahead of the issue. Thus, these teachers, seeing themselves as change agents in the midst of an organizational crisis, demonstrated the kind of adaptive leadership Heifetz and Linsky (2002) describe and urged the school into a deeper exploration of schoolwide equity and climate issues. A series of dialog circles ensued that spring.

## Lessons Learned and Future Directions

Having launched Project Teacher Leadership for the first time in the fall of 2016, at the time of this writing, we are finishing the first year of a two-year process. As described earlier, our plan is to introduce subsequent opportunities for new teams for at least another year. Despite the early stage of this initiative, we see evidence that our original theory of action has merit. As we have explained, we based the initiative on the idea that engaging practitioners in collaborative inquiry would promote collaboration and leadership. We summarize our lessons learned below.

### "Outing" of Problems of Practice Generates Questions, Encourages Inquiry, and Builds Collaboration

Members of all four teams openly discussed the problems teachers were experiencing in their respective schools. These discussions generated questions, which team members, even those outside the school site, found intriguing. All members found an entry point. Teachers sought to correct the problems; interns wanted to witness and become problem-solving teachers; professors looked to experience the realities of practice through teachers' eyes. Everyone found reasons to work together, to learn from one another, and to find ways to approach the problems and make a difference for students. One professor involved with an elementary school said in a private conversation that she found it "inspiring" to work so closely with practitioners.

## Adopting a "Stance of Inquiry" Shows Promise for Elevating Teacher Professionalism and Building Professional Capital

Participants in the project demonstrated professional agency in multiple ways. First and foremost, they moved their problems of practice to questions for study. In the case of the high school, the team faced unfolding events that threatened to place their inquiry project on the back burner. Rather than let that happen, the team took the initiative to approach the principal and explain how she could capitalize on their project, building on it to heal a community under siege. Through this experience, both the teachers involved and the principal recognized the value of building professional capital throughout the school and then drawing from that capital when needed; that is, tapping into the expertise, knowledge, decision-making, and leadership of teachers when problems arise. The middle school recognized that their principal had mandated participation by all in the concept of restorative practices, but in sharing their own observations of colleagues concluded that the real leverage point for change was a needs-based model of differentiation for the faculty. The team was able to build on and draw from the professional capital of teachers to create this differentiated plan.

## Collaborative Inquiry Develops Local Knowledge, Needed Innovation, and Teacher Leadership

So far, we see clear signs that the teams are taking their questions seriously and searching for greater understanding and better answers. This pursuit has led to innovative ideas. For instance, one of the elementary schools initiated the boys' book club, while the other took a whole new approach to differentiating instruction for particularly capable students as well as designing scaffolded enrichment opportunities for struggling learners. These innovative ideas, coupled with the support of the overall project, became so compelling that participants stepped up to leadership roles seemingly without hesitation, meeting with administrators and school leadership teams to garner support, promoting plans through formal and informal structures, engaging the expertise of university professors to help study their ongoing progress and results, and becoming advocates and coaches with other colleagues to share their lessons learned as mentors for new teams and other teachers interested in hearing more about their work at professional conferences.

### And Yet a Caveat...

Although we are encouraged by each of these lessons, we are not naïve to issues of power and control, which can derail our efforts. Again, this project entails countercultural work and necessarily involves navigating bureaucratic and often top-down professional cultures that exist both in schools and, to a somewhat lesser extent, in colleges of education. There are those in power in both institutions who easily dismiss or strongly resist the ultimate worth of teachers asking hard questions, building local knowledge, or exercising leadership. Some principals resist initiatives that do not emanate from their offices. We, however, have concluded that it is essential to this project for participating teachers to feel genuine authorship and ownership for their inquiry projects.

There are other challenges to initiatives like Project Teacher Leadership. For instance, educators in K-12 schools are surrounded by calls to reform. Increasingly, the same is true of colleges of education. Perhaps as a defensive posture, in both settings, educators can be quick to seek and adopt ideas and strategies from outsiders claiming research-based authority. This can result in overdependence on outside knowledge, dismissal of lived experience, suppression of doubts, and concealment of mistakes. Although we hope that, in the case of universities, these tendencies will be resisted, there are accumulating signs, particularly embedded in accountability requirements, indicating unfortunate trends are encroaching. In the case of K-12 schools, the train has definitely left the station. Additionally, both in K-12 and university settings, ongoing candid and authentic conversations about the struggles of teaching are all too rare.

We are still determining the best structures to empower teams to work through these potential challenges. We have considered, for instance, asking principals to attend orientation sessions when teams apply. During those sessions, we hope to provide evidence and models for teacher leadership, encourage conversations about shared visions and decision-making, the value of knowledge-of-practice, and the benefits of building professional capital. We are also encouraging a stance of inquiry and dialogic processes for faculty in both university and school settings. Our hope is to work toward institutionalizing these principles in PDS sites over time so that more and more educators can engage in collaborative inquiry and exercise professional leadership. We draw hope from the fact that, so far, all of the teams are finding ways to embed this work in their respective cultures.

## Concluding Thoughts

The Project Teacher Leadership process has helped teachers see the power of collaborative inquiry as they implement change processes to address problems of practice and to document their progress. From the beginning, we wanted to facilitate the building of "knowledge *of* practice." (Cochran-Smith & Lytle, 2009) Although we recognize that outside expertise can be quite valuable, the purpose of this project was to foster the kind of collaboration, inquiry, and leadership to build expertise from within, and this is exactly what we saw happening. Honest conversations about teaching struggles spurred questions, drew team members together, sparked professional agency and leadership in veteran teachers, and modeled these processes for interns. The project has solidified determination to discover better approaches, and has motivated participants to play leadership roles in order to move their inquiry projects forward by rallying support. In doing so, they have modeled the power of teacher leadership in their local settings for both administrators and colleagues. Indeed, teacher leadership has created a backbone for school improvement efforts in a capacity-building, systemic, and sustainable way.

## References

Bond, N. (Ed.). (2015). *The power of teacher leaders: Their roles, influence, and impact*. New York, NY: Routledge.

Boone, S. C. (2015). Teacher leaders as school reformers. In N. Bond (Ed.), *The power of teacher leaders: Their roles, influence, and impact* (pp. 105–119). New York, NY: Routledge.

City, E. A., Elmore, R. F., Fiarman, S. E., & Teitel, L. (2009). *Instructional rounds in education: A network approach to improving teaching and learning*. Cambridge, MA: Harvard University Press.

Cochran-Smith, M., & Lytle, S. (2009). *Inquiry as stance: Practitioner Research for the next generation*. New York, NY: Teachers College Press.

Cochran-Smith, M., & Stern, R. (2015). The role of inquiry in teacher leadership. In N. Bond (Ed.), *The power of teacher leaders: Their roles, influence, and impact* (pp. 196–209). New York, NY: Routledge.

Darling-Hammond, L. (2007). *Preparing teachers for a changing world: What teachers should learn and be able to do*. San Francisco, CA: Jossey Bass.

Delpit, L. (2006). *Other people's children: Cultural conflict in the classroom*. New York, NY: The New Press.

Durlak, J. A., Domitrovich, C. E., Weissberg, R. P., & Gullotta, T. P. (2015). *Handbook of social and emotional learning: Research and Practice*. New York, NY: The Guilford Press.

Elmore, R. (2004). *School change from the inside out: Policy, practice, and performance*. Cambridge, MA: Harvard University Press.

Fullan, M., & Quinn, J. (2015). *Coherence: The right drivers in action for schools, districts, and systems*. Thousand Oaks, CA: Corwin Press.

Goodlad, J. I. (1998). *Educational renewal: Better teachers, better schools*. San Francisco, CA: Jossey-Bass.

Hargreaves, A., & Fullan, M. (2012). *Professional capital: Transforming teaching in every school*. New York, NY: Teachers College Press.

Heifetz, R. A., & Linsky, M. (2002). *Leadership on the line: Staying alive through the dangers of leading*. Cambridge, MA: Harvard Business Review Press.

Holmes Group. (1995). *Tomorrow's schools of education: A report of the Holmes Group*. East Lansing, MI: Holmes Group, Inc.

Katzenmeyer, M. H., & Moller, G. V. (2009). *Awakening the sleeping giant: Helping teachers develop as leaders*. Thousand Oaks, CA: Corwin Press.

Lieberman, A., & Wood, D. R. (2003). *Inside the National Writing Project: Connecting network learning and classroom teaching*. New York: Teachers College Press.

Schaefer, R. (1967). *Schools as centers of inquiry*. New York, NY: Harper & Row.

Schlechty, P. *Leading for learning: How to transform schools into learning organizations*. Hoboken, NJ: Jossey-Bass Publishers.

Taylor, M., Goeke, J., Klein, E., Onore, C., & Geist, K. (2011). Changing leadership: Teachers lead the way for schools that learn. *Teaching and Teacher Education, 27*(5), 920–929.

Teacher Leadership Exploratory Consortium. (2012). *Teacher Leader Model Standards*. Retrieved from http://www.teacherleaderstandards.org

Wenner, J. A., & Campbell, T. (2017). The theoretical and empirical basis of teacher leadership: A review of the literature. *Review of Educational Research. 87*(1), 134–171.

Whitford, B. L., & Wood, D. R. (2010). *Teachers learning in community: Realities and possibilities*. Albany, NY: SUNY Press.

Wood, D. R., & Lieberman, A. (2000). Teachers as authors: The National Writing Project's approach to professional development. *International Journal of Leadership in Education. 3*(3), 255–273.

## Appendix A: Project Teacher Leadership Completed Action Plan

*Problem Statement*: Instructional activities in mathematics are differentiated to enhance learning for all children; however, according to the 2016 PARCC results, only 38.2% of third grade students met or exceeded grade level expectations.

*Rationale*: Our school has two SPP goals in math that directly relate to this topic. One goal is to focus on enrichment for all students, and another is to differentiate learning tasks based on formative assessments.

Although all teachers on the third grade team believe they are differentiating mathematics instruction, only 38.2% of third grade students met or exceeded grade level expectation on the 2016 PARCC Assessment. Teachers feel that students' critical thinking skills are not being addressed effectively. Teachers are seeking strategies and resources for enhancing and extending critical thinking skills.

| Inquiry Questions | Key Actions/ Events/Dates | Key People | *Budget (See Back of Page) | Anticipated Outcomes and Evidence of Change |
|---|---|---|---|---|
| What curriculum instructional knowledge and needs exist among the NES faculty? | • Needs Assessment – Teacher Knowledge & Comfort Level in differentiation strategies – By 2/28 (2-stages – general differentiation strategies now in use; specific needs; definition/understanding of critical thinking) | • Dr. McCormick, • Dr. Schroth, • J. Pilarski, • M. Gorecki | • NONE | • Direction/topics for PD; to establish a cadre of in-house specialists |
| What are some curricular models that permit high quality differentiation for a flex-grouping of high achieving children? | • Purchase book for school Faculty Library – *Parallel Curriculum* – SP17<br>• PD – *Tool Kit and Overview Pt. 1* – Grade 3 team – March 27 – 9–11 am.<br>• PD – Differentiation Tool Kit Pt. 2 – SP 17 (full faculty) – May 8 – 3:30–4:30 pm | • J. Pilarski • Dr. Schroth • Dr. McCormick | • 18–$40 per book × 2 = **$36–$80** | • Pre- and Post-Assessments of Professional Development<br>• Examples of differentiated units |
| What curriculum units do the NES faculty need to differentiate math instruction? | • SP & Sum of 2017 – Workshops to develop differentiated projects/strategies for math units in Grade 3 | • Grade 3 team; TL team | • $30.26/hr. per BCPS faculty members; 3 days @ 4 hours per day × 6 teachers = $2,178.72 *plus* | • Differentiated math units |

| | | | |
|---|---|---|---|
| What data points are needed to determine project progress? | • Develop pre-/post-assessments of math units starting with the unit developed in the spring (Grade 3 unit 6); results of this assessment may drive development of further units<br>　○ Assessment of student learning outcomes using current grade 3 pre- and post-Unit Assessments (pulling out complex problems from Unit Assessments); take all students, that is, Enrichment for All; also we third grade teachers will track which students complete the entire enrichment task to further validate results.<br>　○ Pre- and post-data, as well as the number of students completing the project in each class, will be collected in the quarterly | • Team | $195 for food (summer) + 1 after school for 3 hours for 6 teachers in spring = $544.68<br>• See above budget requests | • Adjusted instruction based on formative assessment through the differentiated choice enrichment activities |

*(Continued)*

| Inquiry Questions | Key Actions/Events/Dates | Key People | *Budget (See Below) | Anticipated Outcomes and Evidence of Change |
|---|---|---|---|---|
| | data summary spreadsheet to be reviewed and discussed during grade level meetings.<br>○ Assessment of changes in teacher practice/understanding based on participation in project. (Anecdotal journals or pre-post-survey; assessment tools TBD)<br>○ Possible IRB needed | • Third grade teachers | | |
| Are other personnel essential to the project? | • Invite L. Sizemore (BCPS Math Resource Teacher assigned to school) to consult on unit projects developed | • Dr. McCormick<br>• J. Ruppert | • Is he 10 mo. or 12 mo BCPS employee? This will determine need to compensate | • Informed alignment with BCPS Math Curricular Goals and Objectives |

*Budgetary Resources Categories:*
? Stipends for teachers for approved project work done outside of the duty day ($30.26 per hour for BCPS guidelines)
? Space rental (for meetings/professional development)
? Consultant fees (for presenters)
? Supplies (books and materials)
? Food (minimal allowance – needs pre-approval)
*Every group has $1,500. You need to justify anything in your budget above this, which may or may not be funded (up to a maximum of $3,000).*

Chapter 6

# Teacher Leader Reflections: Teacher Leadership and Student Learning

## Abstract

This chapter features three personal reflections written by practicing teacher leaders from Florida, Ohio, and Maryland. The first reflection describes a collegial partnership between a practicing special education teacher and an undergraduate intern which has been sustained for many years. The second recounts a teacher leader's serendipitous experience in cultivating new teacher leaders through collegiality, collaboration, and leading by example. The third describes how a college instructor's participation in Project Teacher Leadership provided new leadership opportunities and inspired educational and professional growth. The chapter concludes with five questions for discussion and reflection.

*Keywords:* Teacher preparation; internship; teacher leadership; school–university partnership; professional development school; special education; continuous improvement; collaboration; restorative practices; Project Teacher Leadership

## A Courageous, Collegial Partnership

*Keri Haley and Christopher Urquhart*

Upon hearing you are being placed in charge with a promising future educator who is in the culminating undergraduate teaching experience to learn the ropes of the daily events of being a teacher, you instantly feel privileged…until swept by fear with more essential questions than those that guide your instructional lessons. Will this be the right fit? Will he know more about the latest practices than I? Will I demonstrate the best modeling opportunities in such a short period of time? Will I leave an impression that lasts a lifetime?

Then you meet. He is dressed for success, clearly intending to make an impact and wondering what potential disaster he just stepped into. You, on the other hand, demonstrate within your first hours serving as mentor how not to read directions on the laminator, break it, and attempt to shield yourself from the wrath of the media specialist. At that moment you grasp your neglectfulness, unintentionally laying the groundwork for an impression you never envisioned while unknowingly cultivating a collegial partnership that blossomed on day one. That bond has since weathered educational forces that neither of us anticipated and remains in effect today as we carve our own paths toward becoming teacher leaders in special education. It is a collegial partnership like few others.

It is no secret that special education is a critical shortage area. With fewer individuals becoming special educators, the pool of candidates wishing to lead in special education is shortchanged as well. Teacher leaders are born as a by-product of quality leadership at the university level from faculty who recognize the value of connecting research to practice in a hands-on and purposeful way. Through collegial partnerships, future teacher leaders can be groomed, whether they aim to serve in leadership at the school/district level or choose to become a change agent in a different capacity. Our unique union merged a special education teacher finishing a doctorate (Keri) with an intern from the undergraduate program in the same university (Chris). Linked by a shared vision, we were both in position to become leaders in our own right. My intended path was to move beyond the school district and become a leader for change in higher education. Chris' intended path was to enact change as a leader within the school district.

Forging a collegial partnership beyond the mentor/mentee, the teacher/intern role was not our original purpose. In my position as Chris' mentor teacher, I gave him every opportunity to learn how to become a special education teacher in the classroom and beyond. Acting as the liaison between the school and university, I allowed him experiences other mentors may not have offered due to my comprehensive knowledge of the expectations of his undergraduate program. As a doctoral student under the tutelage of the professors who linked our university–school partnership, I knew how to complement Chris' coursework with experiences in the field. There was value in extending his learning opportunities, thereby placing his development as a proficient beginning teacher on the fast track. Chris was allowed to write Individualized Education Program (IEP) plans, assist in IEP meetings with parents, participate in data discussions with school and district administrators to defend the use of research-supported practices unfamiliar to those in the district, and gain an understanding of the operational aspects that support special education programs in schools with large populations of students in need; all opportunities his cohort members did not experience.

Also unlike his fellow undergraduates, Chris and I crafted a collegial partnership that withstood criticism. In the face of mounting pressure to maintain pace with the curricular calendars, we relied on our university–school partnership to hold true to what we knew related to teaching mathematics. We consciously decided to focus on the core skills that students needed and teach to mastery, all while refusing to succumb to pressure to stay on the pacing calendar. Chris taught math using the research-supported practices in which we were both versed; and I ran interference, deflecting criticism that we were not exposing students to all the content for the statewide assessment. As a young intern, Chris' decision to hold strong to such an approach spoke volumes. Ironically, our decision to do what was right for kids was hailed at the end of the school year when scores on the state assessment showed incredible gains made by those very same students who were taught, not just exposed. To this day, Chris uses the same instructional approach and supports his decision-making with evidence of better student outcomes.

A few years removed from our first year together, what makes our collegial partnership unique? Knowing our alliance was cultivated in a university environment allowed us the confidence to maintain instructional autonomy in our classroom, to support each other in being the voice and in doing what was right for kids, and to not be afraid of taking risks as long as they were grounded in research and supported by data. Had it not been for the university–school partnership that brought us together during Chris' intern year, we perhaps would not be blazing our own trails as future leaders in our field; I at the University of West Florida in Pensacola, Florida, seeking relationships with local school districts to connect research and practice, and Chris, now an experienced teacher in Hillsborough County, Florida, acting as an agent for change, demonstrating his ability to lead, and encouraging in-service teachers to focus on the best interests of students. Our collegial partnership has exceeded expectations as we have presented at numerous conferences and continue to rely on each other routinely, leading change in the field of special education. It is truly a collegial partnership in the best sense of the word, and for that we are thankful.

## From One To Many

*Nancy Cryder Jones*

I am old school. There are so many things that need to be taught in today's classrooms, and I wanted to teach it all. Because I have always been one to organize and take charge, I had many jobs within my job. For 36 years, I enjoyed trying my best each day to make learning a wonderful experience for my first grade students at Zane Trace Elementary School in Chillicothe, Ohio. I also enjoyed sharing information with my colleagues in hopes of preparing them for the tasks that lay ahead. In my old school style, I have a story about teacher leadership that started with one and ignited many.

In my later years of teaching, as my colleagues were getting younger and younger, I found it important to teach my grade level peers to be self-reliant leaders. Having a class full of six-year-olds was difficult enough; I wanted to share my experiences to help my colleagues make this hectic job easier. I worked with wonderful people, and together we learned all of the new trends that were presented to us through professional development. With each new trend, I shared my ideas and hopefully instilled in the younger teachers ways to make their jobs manageable without disturbing the quality of instruction. I was the one who always kept our grade level staff on task, but I tried to show the younger teachers how to be proactive and assertive in acquiring and distributing information to other teachers in the school – to keep them on task. After all, I was getting close to retirement!

One year, I was selected by my superintendent to serve on our district's Continuous Improvement Plan (CIP) Committee. The CIP Committee met in our district office and there, we learned of the new laws, rules, requirements, objectives, standards, etc. in which educators and schools were to become compliant. The committee worked together to establish a plan for our district to cover all aspects of continuous improvement. We had many sessions and discussions about how our district would approach the CIP.

Being the person that I am, after the committee meetings, I would always write a summary of what the committee did at each meeting and share it with my fellow Zane Trace teachers via e-mail. Consequently, our school staff was well informed of the CIP, upcoming changes, and additions to the curriculum and to the district. Sometimes, even the principal learned something new through my e-mails! At the time, I didn't perceive myself as a leader; I was only trying to keep my friends and co-workers informed because I felt this was an important thing to do. They needed to know what was in the plans since it affected them, and we educated one another with discussions about the best ways to incorporate CIP ideas. Plus, I received teachers' input on controversial topics that I could share with the committee at the next meeting.

As a result of the Zane Trace staff knowing what was in store for them, our first grade level team came up with a plan of our own to implement the CIP. We each took a section of the curriculum and created a web establishing standards to be taught, a timeline, and possible learning activities. We developed an extensive method of teaching our first grade curriculum. Later that year, our entire grade level staff attended a county-wide professional development meeting at the Ross County Educational Service Center. It became apparent at this meeting that we almost knew more than the presenters. Our staff shared much of the stage that day, showing our grade level plan and advising others how to establish their own plans to ensure their districts' CIPs.

The point of all of this is that it began with teacher leadership. The information was given to my fellow teachers and from there, we worked as a team to cultivate and produce a plan that became our guide to teaching for the next few years, and at the same time reinforced our district's CIP. For the younger teachers, the experience was a lesson too, on how to take charge of an idea, get organized, and go with it. It showed them that being informed gave them an advantage over districts that hadn't shared the CIP information with teachers. The Zane Trace teachers became very popular at that county meeting as other teachers asked to see our course of action.

My fellow teachers and I gained self-assurance that day. Our determination in developing and incorporating a grade level plan to accompany the CIP brought us self-respect as well as the respect of our peers. Once confidence is gained, it becomes easier to be a teacher leader. Leadership in the workplace (especially in a school) can provide an arena for generating ideas that are pertinent to making our jobs easier in the long run. As a result of getting organized and participating, all of our first grade staff became leaders. It takes one person to get the ball rolling, and once everyone is on board, there's no limit to what can be done!

## Learning and Leading Through Collaboration

### Jamie Silverman

Had you told me just eight years ago as I was sitting (or rather standing) at home with four children under the age of three that I would soon be a full-time lecturer in the Department of Secondary and Middle School Education (SMED) at Towson University in Towson, Maryland – and leading interns whose seats I myself had occupied many years prior in Towson's Secondary Education Professional Development School (PDS) in Baltimore County – I don't know if I would have believed you. Recently, a special partnership between Baltimore County Public Schools and Towson University called Project Teacher Leadership provided me with a new leadership opportunity that has inspired my continued journey of educational and professional growth.

In the fall of 2016, I had the pleasure of leading a semester-long seminar for SMED part-time interns at Holabird Middle School in Dundalk, Maryland. I had never been to Holabird, located in a postindustrial and struggling East Baltimore neighborhood, but I quickly learned that this was a school where the teachers and administrators cared deeply not only for the academic growth of their students, but for students' social-emotional growth as well. One of Holabird's goals for the year was to introduce and implement restorative practices in the school community. Restorative practices aim to engage students, teachers, and other adults in doing things together (rather than adults always doing things for students), to build rapport, and to create a more positive school climate. Unfortunately, implementation did not unfold as expected that fall.

Yet there was a need for restorative practice at Holabird. The students who attend this middle school come from various feeder elementary schools, and when they meet in the halls of Holabird in sixth grade there are noticeable rifts between them. Holabird is unique in that it serves grades four through eight. Students attend Norwood Elementary School, a pre-kindergarten through third grade site, and then in fourth grade transition quite smoothly to Holabird – literally across the street. However, in sixth grade many students begin to meet new students who arrive at Holabird from other feeder schools in the county. It is at this point when

Holabird teachers note the beginning of many tensions. For the first time, students who attended Norwood and Holabird begin to form new friendships, and some students feel threatened by the new faces.

Fast forward to February 2017. Project Teacher Leadership provided an impactful opportunity for teachers in its PDSs to identify a problem and create an action plan to resolve it. Little did I know that when I agreed to be the Towson representative for Holabird, the project would provide new leadership opportunities and inspire my own educational and professional growth.

My team consisted of three Holabird teachers and one of my former SMED interns who was currently student teaching at Holabird. We met for a day and a half to create an action plan to effectively implement restorative practices at Holabird. First, we determined that it was important to learn much about restorative practices in order to become school experts. Then, we planned several professional development teacher trainings to facilitate the social-emotional growth of Holabird's community. As a result of our efforts, I have observed a different energy in our group; the teachers, the intern, and I are excited about the ideas we bring and continue to build our action plan because we feel empowered by our leadership roles. I am proud of the meaningful inquiry we have started, and I am most proud of my former intern who has invested his energy into the project by creating surveys to determine teacher attitudes toward and knowledge of restorative practices as an essential starting point to our action plan.

Becoming an active participant in Project Teacher Leadership has sparked my desire to develop new professional and educational goals. I have already reached out to faculty members who implement restorative practices at other schools in Baltimore County so that I can learn more about their approaches and the impact on their students and school communities. In addition, because I want to learn as much as possible about restorative practices, I have decided to pursue a graduate certificate from the International Institute for Restorative Practices so that I can teach my Towson colleagues more about this important movement in social justice. I also plan to present Holabird's Project Teacher Leadership journey at the 2018 National Association for Professional Development Schools Conference. Moreover, in addition to adding a significant restorative practices piece to an adolescent development course that I teach, I plan to charge my new interns with designing and implementing a restorative practices service project at Holabird this fall, and present it at the Maryland Professional Development Schools Conference next spring. I have always been one to jump at opportunity and to lead when given the chance. Now, my interns also will become leaders by taking on restorative practices leadership roles early in their teaching careers.

## Questions for Further Reflection

*Jana Hunzicker*

1. Keri and Christopher describe how they first became acquainted and have partnered professionally ever since. Is an ongoing, collegial partnership between a school district representative and a university representative a true partnership? Why or why not? To what extent should such partnerships be encouraged and recognized?
2. Nancy demonstrated teacher leadership by taking action to address grade level, school, and district needs that she considered important. What internal and external factors and conditions do you believe support the expansion of teacher leadership from one teacher to many teachers? Which factor or condition may be most influential in expanding teacher leadership from one to many?
3. Through Project Teacher Leadership, Jamie developed an ambitious list of professional goals related to her teaching, research, service, and leadership responsibilities as well as to two different leadership projects for her interns. As a full-time university lecturer, is Jamie a teacher leader? Why or why not? How might Jamie's experience help to broaden – or narrow – current notions of teacher leadership?
4. In all three reflections, students were better served when teacher leaders employed sound instructional practices amidst pressure to maintain the status quo, engaged in work that extended beyond their assigned teaching duties, and collaborated to identify and address specific student needs. If teacher leaders are absent – or dormant – in today's schools, does it mean that students will be underserved? Why or why not?
5. In all three reflections, collegial partnerships and/or teacher leadership developed unintentionally, even with PDS relationships and/or school–university partnerships in place. Considering the chapters and reflections in this section, is it possible that unintentional partnerships and teacher leadership efforts are more authentically student-centered than those that are intentionally planned? How can intentional school–university partnerships and teacher leadership efforts be designed to offer greater authenticity in regard to student-centeredness?

Chapter 7

# Teacher Leadership and Student Learning

*Bernard J. Badiali*

### Abstract

This chapter synthesizes Chapters 3–6, traces contemporary educational policy, and explores its impact on teaching and learning in today's schools before exploring professional development schools (PDS) as communities where teaching, learning, and leadership can thrive. Drawing from classic literature on educational leadership, the chapter weaves together implications for teacher leadership and student learning with recent and current standards for teacher leadership and for PDSs. It asserts that, rather than standards, Goodlad, Mantle-Bromley, and Goodlad's (2004) Agenda for Education in a Democracy may impart greater meaning to teacher leaders' contributions to the PDS movement.

*Keywords:* Teacher leadership; professional development school; organizational leadership; student learning; educational policy

"Within every school there is a *sleeping giant* of teacher leadership that can be a strong catalyst for making changes to improve student learning." (Katzenmeyer & Moller, 2009, p. 2).

It has been my privilege to reflect on and now respond to Chapters 4–6 connecting professional development schools (PDSs) and teacher leadership with student learning. All four chapters address very well, in their own way, calls for empirical evidence that PDS and teacher leadership have an impact on student learning. These chapters contribute to our knowledge about the nature of teacher leadership in its many forms and of the power that lies within a PDS community to encourage and support actions and activities that ultimately mean better, more humane, educational experiences for students, teachers, and college faculty alike. These accounts of teacher leadership also highlight the power that stories have to explore and explain complicated interactions by situating them in context.

Our charge for writing these "synthesis chapters" was to pull together research findings, best practices, and innovative concepts across the four contributed chapters and offer generalizations, insights, and implications for future practice related to that section's focus area. To those ends, this chapter briefly discusses the idea of student learning writ large and how it is fostered by teacher leadership within PDS communities. It also discusses how and why the PDS is an ideal environment for teacher leadership by contrasting schools as organizations and schools as communities using Chapters 3–6 as illustrations. The chapter concludes with reflections on teacher leadership and student learning in PDSs.

## Student Learning: Beyond Test Scores

Surely by now most teacher educators recognize that the concept of student learning is far too complex to be reduced to scores on any standardized battery. In fact, the most important things students learn in schools may not be test sensitive at all (Badiali & Peters, 2013). When talking about P-12 achievement, what was true in the past continues to be true today; the best predictor of high test scores is parental income and zip code (Berliner & Glass, 2014). Chapters 4–6 take a broader view of student learning. They address directly and indirectly student learning in primary and secondary schools, but they also address how postsecondary students and professional educators continue to learn. In fact, is it not the goal of PDSs to place everyone in the role of learner? Should we not think of ourselves as students? In a PDS, we are all students of teaching and learning regardless of title. Surely that is what assuming an inquiry stance toward teaching demands (Cochran-Smith & Lytle, 1993).

With regard to conceptual understanding of student learning, the story of contemporary educational policy in this area is a dismal one. Largely driven by fear generated by reports such as A Nation at Risk in 1983 and also by hyperbolic reactions to National Assessment of Educational Progress results, policy in the age we live in seems to have turned away from the original purpose of public schooling in America and toward narratives of accountability and economic utility (Berliner, 2011; Ravitch, 2013). The Elementary and Secondary Education Act, a policy originally intended to level the playing field for poor children, was changed during the Bush administration to No Child Left Behind (NCLB), a policy directed at holding teachers and schools accountable for student scores on standardized tests. This shift in emphasis from supporting children to punishing teachers and schools has had dire consequences.

Proponents of NCLB would take exception to that claim. They would argue that NCLB was intended to provide more equitable access to a quality curriculum for all children. Driven by good evidence that minority children are being short changed in some schools and by some teachers, the original intention behind NCLB was to create greater educational equality as well as to increase America's economic competitiveness. Unfortunately, its implementation twisted. According to Bullough and Rosenberg (2018), this was a time when a punishing psychology dominated federal policy. Under NCLB any school that received federal funding (virtually every public school) was required to test children in reading and math in grades three through eight every year and at least once in high school. School students had to increase their test scores in order for a school to achieve Adequate Yearly Progress or face possible loss of revenue or even closure. For accountability purposes, the concept of student achievement was mainly reduced to mean student scores on standardized tests. NCLB's unrealistic goals and overreliance and misuse of testing data eventually led to its repeal. It took a divided congress until 2015 to replace NCLB with the Every Student Can Succeed Act, but not before the law created a sense of crisis, lending credibility to claims that American public education is failing (Ravitch, 2013).

One unfortunate legacy of NCLB was narrowing the curriculum to focus on math and reading. Time in the school day for social studies, arts, and even science was reduced in order to focus on test readiness. A second legacy of NCLB is that test scores continue to be synonymous with student achievement in the minds of many educators and policymakers. My first thought regarding this perspective comes from Sergiovanni and Starratt's (2007) wry observation that people would rather have an exact answer to the wrong questions than an approximate answer to the right questions. This simplistic view of student achievement misrepresents the complexity and diversity of social and cultural factors that influence learning (Bullough & Rosenberg, 2018). Moreover, an overreliance on test scores as substitutes or synonyms for student achievement is an impoverished representation of what students actually learn in school.

It would be a disservice to the efforts of teacher leaders to believe that there could be a one-to-one correspondence between their actions and test score results alone. Among other problems, teacher leaders understand that overreliance on test scores as *the* measure of achievement is no incentive for teachers to perform well; it is simply a reason to narrow the curriculum to ensure that students get good test scores. Sergiovanni and Starratt (2007) would call teachers (and administrators) who base their actions on policy compliance ahead of their own good judgment, bureaucrats, not professionals. Bureaucrats, they argue, see themselves as subordinate to their work system. Professionals, by contrast, see themselves as superordinate to their work system.

In Chapter 5, Kruft and Wood assert basically the same argument. They view teachers as leaders when they exercise agency and influence to advocate for positive school change for the sake of more productive and equitable student learning. They conceptualize student learning capaciously when they describe teacher leadership initiatives that result in student learning, which goes well beyond test scores. Consider the excellent questions developed by teacher leaders who responded to what students needed in their school contexts. At the elementary level, what are some curricular models that permit high-quality differentiation for a flex-grouping of high achieving children? This question attends to the variety of student learning needs. It addresses the need to carefully and collaboratively design lessons that will reach all students. We can look forward to learning more about the fruits of their labor, that is, what outcomes these co-designed lessons brought about. In their chapter, teacher leaders also asked, what strategies can we implement in order to motivate boys to be actively engaged in reading? While this issue is not unique to their PDS, the fact that teachers made it a priority based on local data gave the inquiry more legitimacy, urgency, and imperative. At the middle school level, Kruft and Wood describe an inquiry initiative that connects to the very purpose of schooling itself: How can we change the school culture via a restorative practices approach? Restorative practices are aimed at establishing social skills vital to a thriving democracy. As educators across the nation recognize the importance of fostering positive, healthy school climates and helping students learn from their mistakes, they are partnering with parents, students, district officials, community organizations, and policymakers to move away from harmful and counterproductive zero-tolerance discipline policies and toward proven restorative approaches to addressing conflict in schools (Schott Foundation, n.d.). Likewise at the high school level, teachers have taken on this essential question: How can we foster the community that we envision at our school? Implicit in these good questions are outcomes of student achievement that matter.

In Chapter 3, Dubetz, Fella, LaChapell, and Rivera provide another sound illustration of teacher learning that impacts student learning based on needs in their context. As the number of English language learners (ELLs) continues to increase in schools, the need has never been greater to help them succeed. Through collaborative efforts enabled by their PDS, these authors developed a program based on core practices for teaching ELLs. Because of their actions, children's learning is enhanced, yet much of what they learn cannot be documented by a standardized test. What becomes clear while reading their story is that test performance is not given high priority in their thinking or planning. As in most PDSs, their collaboration does not emphasize test performance when preparing the next generation of teachers. Their goals include using cultural and linguistic resources to promote comprehension and increase oral language development across a spectrum of content areas. It is stories like theirs that give nuance and richness to the concept of student achievement.

## PDSs as Communities

The PDS is an ideal environment for teacher leadership, in part because it flattens the organizational hierarchy, which means everyone has the opportunity, if not the responsibility, to learn as well as to lead. PDSs are communities of learning – for everyone – as indicated specifically in two of the National Association for Professional Development Schools (NAPDS) Nine Essentials (2008):

- Essential 3: Ongoing and reciprocal professional development for all participants guided by need.
- Essential 4: A shared commitment to innovative and reflective practice by all participants.

There are significant differences between communities and organizations though. As long as we continue to think of schools as organizations and not as true communities, opportunities for teacher leadership will be few. For generations, schools have tried to reconcile the incongruity of the desire for teacher leadership with the obstacles of organizational constraints. Institutional barriers to teacher leadership are well documented (Kowalski, 1995). These obstacles are basically attributable to the organizational bureaucracy that has persisted for generations.

According to Sergiovanni (1994), we have been taught to think of schools as formal organizations. The paradigm is difficult to change. The problem is that formal organizations seek legitimacy by appearing to be rational. They often mirror business and industry by developing management structures, reporting lines and procedures that purport to result in a means-ends chain intended to accomplish objectives. Schools are organized by departments and grade levels often with formal job descriptions for leaders. School administrators attempt to convince everyone that they are in control by using rules and regulations and by monitoring teachers' instruction. The school as organization is a logical response to state and federal mandates as well as a defense from public criticism. But over time, organizations tend to take on a life of their own and get separated from the people who inhabit them. Policies and regulations become more important than the people they are supposed to serve. As a paradigm, the school as organization remains strong in public education and probably stronger in private education, especially when the motive is profit and not service.

But organizations are not communities. Anyone who has taught in schools knows that the organizational paradigm breaks down when educators endeavor to meet the learning needs of the children in their care. Simply changing the language we used to describe schools without changing the culture does not work. In Chapter 4, Jeffries explains how PDS work between the high school and the university has been overshadowed by district and state mandates that did not necessarily support emphasis on inquiry-based teaching and learning. Jeffries troubles the organizational practice of tracking students. She questions the ethics of a practice that puts marginalized students at a disadvantage. Jeffries' study exemplifies what happens when an organizational breakdown occurs. Her chapter illustrates that in a PDS it is teacher leaders who find ways to cope with the demands of the formal organization while attending to the needs of children. An important message in Chapter 4 is that teacher leaders tend to accomplish their goals by forming relationships and alliances that make better, more equitable, student achievement possible. The findings of her research support her assertions about the power of teacher leadership.

A healthy PDS is a community even though it is situated between two formal organizations. It is the figurative space between. PDSs hold together not because of contracts, memorandums of understanding, or reporting lines, but because the people who work in them have commitments to a shared sense of purpose. PDSs rely on relationships and commitments to the fundamental notion that teaching the young to the best of our ability is one of the most important responsibilities in society.

Partners in a PDS are bound together by common values, sentiments, and beliefs strong enough to set aside self-interest for the welfare of the whole. Glickman (1993) has called this a "covenant" where individuals have a common vision and a cause beyond oneself.

This is not to say that tensions do not exist within a PDS, they do. In fact, disagreements about how best to fulfill our commitments may be a constant in communities that value innovation and inquiry. There may be disagreements about how best to achieve our purpose, but fewer disagreements about what our purpose actually is. Different points of view, given the nature of where the partners come from, can raise respectful tensions about how best to prepare, support, and enhance learning at every level.

PDSs are communities bound together by commitments and common purpose, not by contracts. Unlike formal organizations that rely on external control, a PDS community relies more on norms, shared values, purposes, collegiality, and natural interdependencies. Perhaps one of its most foundational attributes is that the PDS relies on teacher leadership. Therefore, when a mentor teacher decides with her intern to modify the curriculum to better meet the needs of students as described in Chapter 6, the two may do so despite organizational constraints and pressures. The PDS gives them courage to do so. It may also provide a kind of cover. As Haley and Urquhart explain in Chapter 6, the PDS gave them space to "… craft a collegial partnership that withstood criticism. In the face of mounting pressure to maintain pace with the curricular calendars, we relied on our university–school partnership to hold true to what we knew related to teaching mathematics." (p. 101). Jones' and Silverman's descriptions of grade level and team-based collaborations on behalf of students further illustrate the kinds of teacher-to-teacher relationships that are foundational to PDS communities.

In my visits to PDS sites across the country, I have witnessed consistently high levels of enthusiasm from the educators who work in them. To be blunt, mentors, college professors, clinical supervisors, and especially teacher leaders are on fire with regard to their commitment to the work. The freedom of working within a community, relatively unfettered from organizational obstacles is exhilarating. Even when tasks are difficult and problems abound, their commitment to a common vision and a moral purpose results in going well beyond the expectations of their job.

There may be no better source that makes the distinction between organizations and communities than Tom Sergiovanni's *Building Community in Schools*. Sergiovanni (1999) differentiates authentic communities from counterfeit communities:

> Authentic community requires us to do more than pepper our language with the word "community," label ourselves as a community in our mission statement, and organize teachers into teams [think PLCs] and schools into families. It requires us to think community, believe in community and practice community – to change the basic metaphor for the school itself to community. We are into authentic community when community becomes embodied in the school's policy structure itself, when community values are at the center of our thinking. (p. xiii)

Sergiovanni asks us to question and to change our current metaphor of schooling making very clear distinctions between organizations and communities.

## An Agenda for Teacher Leadership

In *Educating Teachers for Leadership and Change*, the Association of Teacher Educators (ATE) Teacher Education Yearbook III, Ken Sirotnik (1995) offers an elegant definition of leadership for educators: "Leadership is the exercise of significant and responsible influence." (p. 236). This definition contains three key words: exercise, significant, and responsible. He explains that *exercise* means deliberate, decision-oriented, action-taking behavior. It is not passive or laissez-faire. By *significant*, Sirotnik means actions of substance and importance, not trivial, bureaucratic, or ritualistic. Most importantly, by *responsible* he argues that leadership for educators has strong moral connotations. Responsible, he asserts, derives from the tacit agreements entered into by all educators that by virtue of their occupation they devote themselves to profoundly influencing the lives of children and youth. He concludes his extended definition by saying that, above all, teacher leaders must attend to the moral and ethical dimension of their profession.

There is an inspiring literature on teacher leadership that began decades ago (Hilty, 2011). Teacher leadership is implicit in most of the literature on PDSs. The two constructs are natural allies. Both ideas have evolved steadily in such a way that it is difficult to write knowledgably about one without integrating the other. Throughout the literature on both PDSs and teacher leadership there are calls for more evidence as to their effectiveness. The chapters in this section respond to those calls by connecting teacher leadership with student achievement.

In Chapter 3, Dubetz and colleagues illustrate the power of teacher leadership and collaborative effort among classroom teachers, teacher candidates, and college faculty. In Chapter 4, Jeffries gives us a classic research study that provides evidence of the effects teacher leadership can have on school practices such as tracking. In Chapter 5, Kruft and Wood provide a wonderful structure for enabling teacher leadership in a PDS through Project Teacher Leadership, including a roadmap for us to replicate their efforts. In Chapter 6, we have authentic accounts of the influence of teacher leadership on student learning in a variety of PDS settings. All of the authors address the demand for research on the impact PDSs on student learning and school change.

Setting standards is a sign of the times. The Teacher Leadership Exploratory Consortium, a diverse group of 10 national organizations (including the National Education Association), 8 institutions of higher education, 10 practitioners, and 11 state education agencies, examined research, conducted surveys, debated, and shared experiences to produce a set of standards to stimulate discussion among stakeholders of the teaching profession about what constitutes the knowledge, skills, and competencies that teachers need to assume teacher leadership roles in their schools, districts, and the profession.

The Teacher Leader Model Standards consist of seven domains that describe the various attributes of teacher leadership:

- Domain I: Fostering a collaborative culture to support educator development and student learning
- Domain II: Accessing and using research to improve practice and student learning
- Domain III: Promoting professional learning for continuous improvement
- Domain IV: Facilitating improvements in instruction and student learning
- Domain V: Promoting the use of assessments and data for school and district improvement
- Domain VI: Improving outreach and collaboration with families and community
- Domain VII: Advocating for student learning and the profession. (National Education Association, 2002–2017, para 3)

It becomes evident when we read the teacher leadership standards that the descriptions in Chapters 3–6 align well.

Perhaps the time has come for the PDS community to revisit its own set of standards or perhaps standards are not the appropriate vehicle to communicate the differences between PDSs and traditional schools. In 2001, the National Council for the Accreditation of Teacher Education (NCATE) published Standards for Professional Development Schools, but these standards are no longer found in the new accrediting body, the Council for the Accreditation of Educator Preparation. It is difficult to determine what effect, if any, resulted when these standards were employed. The NCATE standards were:

Standard 1: Learning Community
Standard 2: Accountability and Quality Assurance
Standard 3: Collaboration
Standard 4: Diversity and Equity
Standard 5: Structures, Resources, and Roles

In 2008, the NAPDS published the Nine PDS Essentials. They were written to help partnerships identify whether they were PDSs or not. But the Nine Essentials were created to define what a PDS is; they are not standards for accreditation, nor are they standards for determining a national agenda for PDSs.

Alternative to standards, and more in keeping with the idea of community, John Goodlad et al. (2004) chose to call guiding principles for PDSs an "agenda." The Agenda for Education in a Democracy embraces teacher leadership as indispensable to PDSs. The agenda is not prescriptive in the same way standards are prescriptive. Goodlad was too wise to prescribe actions and behaviors without considering context. Instead he and his associates argue for a set of principles that could be interpreted by educators according to their own settings. Many of these principles are in place in partner schools and PDSs today. Those who aspire to teacher leadership within a PDS should become conscious of the Agenda as it will give more meaning and direction to their efforts. Certainly, the chapters in this section exemplify aspects of the Agenda, but the Agenda could be the conceptual framework that imparts more meaning to their contributions to the PDS movement.

## References

Badiali, B. J., & Peters, B. (2013, February). The influence of PDS interns on student academic performance on standardized tests. Paper presented at the National Association for Professional Development Schools (NAPDS) Annual Conference, New Orleans, LA.

Berliner, D. C. (2011). Rational responses to high stakes testing: The case of curriculum narrowing and the harm that follows. *Cambridge Journal of Education, 41*(3), 287–302.

Berliner, D. C., & Glass, G. V. (2014). *50 Myths and lies that threaten America's public schools: The real crisis in education.* New York, NY: Teachers College Press.

Bullough & Rosenberg (2018). Schooling, democracy and the quest for wisdom: Partnerships and the moral dimensions of teaching. New Brunswick, NJ: Rutgers University Press.

Cochran-Smith, M. J., & Lytle, S. (1993). *Inside/outside teacher research and knowledge.* New York, NY: Teachers College Press.

Glickman, C. (1993). *Renewing America's schools: A guide for school-based action.* Hoboken, NJ: Jossey-Bass.

Glickman, C. (2003). *Holding sacred ground: Essays on leadership, courage, and endurance in our schools.* San Francisco, CA: Jossey-Bass.

Goodlad, J. I., Mantle-Bromley, C., & Goodlad, S. J. (2004). *Education for everyone: Agenda for education in a democracy.* San Francisco, CA: Josey Bass.

Hilty, E. B. (Ed.) (2011). *Teacher leadership: The new foundations of teacher education.* New York, NY: Peter Lang.

Katzenmeyer, M., & Moller, G. (2009). *Awakening the sleeping giant: Helping teachers develop as leaders* (3rd ed.). Thousand Oaks, CA: Corwin.

Kowalski, T. J. (1995). Preparing teachers to be leaders: Barriers in the workplace. *Educational Leadership Faculty Publications.* Paper 47. Retrieved from http://ecommons.udayton.edu/eda_fac_pub/47

National Association for Professional Development Schools. (2008). *What it means to be a professional development school.* Retrieved from http://napds.org/9%20Essentials/statement.pdf

National Council for Accreditation of Teacher Education. (2001). *Standards for professional development schools.* Retrieved from http://www.ncate.org/ProfessionalDevelopmentSchools/tabid/497/Default.aspx

National Education Association. (2002–2017). *Teacher Leader Model Standards.* Retrieved from http://www.nea.org/home/43946.htm

O'Hair, M. J., & Odell, S. J. (Eds.) (1995). *Educating teachers for leadership and change: Teacher education Yearbook III.* Thousand Oaks, CA: Corwin Press.

Ravitch, D. (2013). *Reign of error: The hoax of the privatization movement and the danger to America's public schools.* New York, NY: Alfred A. Knopf.

Schott Foundation. (n.d.). *Restorative practices: A guide for educators.* Retrieved from http://schottfoundation.org/restorative-practices

Sergiovanni, T. J. (1994). *Building community in schools.* San Francisco, CA: Jossey-Bass.

Sergiovanni, T. J. (1999). *The lifeworld of leadership: Creating culture, community, and personal meaning in our schools.* San Francisco, CA: Jossey-Bass.

Sergiovanni, T. J., & Starratt, R. J. (2007). *Supervision: A redefinition*. New York, NY: McGraw-Hill.

Sirotnik, K. A. (1995). Curriculum: Reflections and implications. In M. J. O-Hair & S. J. Odell (Eds.), *Educating teachers for leadership and change: Teacher education yearbook III* (pp. 235–242). Los Angeles, CA: Sage Publications.

# Section II

# Definitions, Structures, and Cultures that Promote Teacher Leadership

Chapter 8

# Teacher Leader Identities and Influences as Defined by Liaisons-in-Residence

*Jennifer L. Snow, Sarah Anderson, Carolyn Cort, Sherry Dismuke and A. J. Zenkert*

**Abstract**

Recognizing the importance of developing professional identities and valuing the work of school-based teacher educators, this chapter outlines a specific context in which teacher leaders self-identified and worked across contexts to support teacher development within their schools. This chapter's primary focus includes the perceptions and experiences of teacher leaders in school–university partnerships connected to one university in one identified role: liaison-in-residence. Three themes resulted from analysis of transcripts, journals, and memos: teacher leader identity developed within democratic leadership; teacher leader positionality stirs tensions in professional identity; and service and equity as key guideposts for leading and learning.

*Keywords:* Teacher leadership; leadership development; site-based clinical supervision; phenomenological case study; democratic leadership; servant leadership; reciprocal learning

> It has been interesting. The positive aspects are getting to know the teachers in my building better and having a chance to help them develop as mentors. The negatives are that sometimes I get caught in the middle between a mentor and

a candidate when they really need to be talking to each other. (*Liaison-in-Residence Journal*, March/April, 2017 p. 1).

As Wenner and Campbell (2016) have identified, "an often-underreported outcome of teacher leadership is the effect it has on those taking up these roles." (p. 29). Even more specifically, Gordon, Jacobs, Croteau, and Solis (2017) have identified a need for future research from "informal teacher leaders themselves." (p. 35). Hence, this chapter primarily focuses on the perceptions and experiences of teacher leaders in partnerships connected to one university in one identified role. In this chapter, researchers outline an experience in which liaison-in-residence is conceived by classroom-based teachers in school–university partnerships. The liaison-in-residence concept emerged organically from the work of these teachers highlighting democratic leadership (Woods, 2004). In short, liaisons-in-residence are classroom teachers in school–university partnerships who serve as clinical supervisors for teacher candidates in their building. The liaison-in-residence also supports mentor teachers in their work and shares responsibility for teacher candidate development and evaluation with a university-based liaison. In this partnership, all liaisons-in-residence had served as mentors to teacher candidates with university-based liaison support. As liaisons-in-residence, they were now interested in furthering their work with teacher candidates while remaining full-time classroom teachers.

Recognizing the importance of developing professional identities and valuing the work of school-based teacher educators, this chapter outlines a specific space in which teacher leaders self-identify and work in nested contexts to support teacher development. They work within their own classrooms as mentor teachers of teacher candidates who are assigned another liaison for evaluation purposes. They also work in other classrooms in their buildings, supervising teacher candidates and supporting peers as mentor teachers. Finally, they work outside of their buildings in larger university contexts where candidates, liaisons, and mentors from across partnerships come together for workshops, seminars, and professional development opportunities. The work of these liaisons-in-residence highlights "teachers' intentional use of their professional space." (Oolbekkink-Marchand, Hadar, Smith, Helleve, & Ulvik, 2017) Considering the agency and purposeful action inherent in becoming a liaison-in-residence, we, as clinical supervision partners, gathered perceptions of the teacher leaders themselves to better investigate this space where they serve as teacher leaders with positional authority. The "third space terrain" (Martin, Snow, & Torrez, 2011) in this study pushes the continuum of formal to informal teacher leadership where more fluidity and boundary crossing occurs in terms of leadership structure. This chapter provides data and interpretations for the following research questions:

1. How have participants come to envision their role as a liaison-in-residence?
2. What effect does being a liaison-in-residence have on professional work? As a teacher? As a teacher leader? As a mentor teacher? As a colleague in a professional context?
3. How does the liaison-in-residence role influence the learning of students?
4. How do liaisons-in-residence describe their influence on equitable opportunities for others (e.g., colleagues, teacher candidates, students, or traditionally marginalized groups), if at all?

This chapter will first identify a theoretical framework within which to consider partnership contexts and teacher leadership. Both constructs have allowed for the liaison-in-residence role to emerge in this study. A description of the phenomenological research design follows. Following which, initial findings connected to the professional identities that these liaisons-in-residence take up and experience in their new leadership roles are shared, and the study significance is outlined.

## Theoretical Framework for Partnerships, Teacher Leadership, and Identity

### School–University Partnerships

Building from work theorizing school–university partnership contexts (Bullough, Draper, Smith, & Birrell, 2004; Darling-Hammond, 2006; Snow-Gerono, 2009; Teitel, 2003) and developing agency for teachers through inquiry (Dana, Silva, & Snow-Gerono, 2002) this research study examines a context focused on simultaneous renewal and professional growth (Darling-Hammond, 1994). For decades, school and university partners have been working together for professional year field experiences in this context. University-based partners work weekly in schools to support teacher candidates and mentor teachers.

An emphasis on clinically based teacher preparation is geared toward teaching professional practice (Grossman et al., 2009). Teaching and learning to teach are complex phenomena in which aspects of teaching practice may be considered through representations, approximations, and a deconstruction of practice (Grossman et al., 2009). An understanding of teaching professional practice through this framework provided a focus on the complex interactions undertaken by educators. Working with the belief that merging the teaching and learning of practice in school contexts pushes "third space terrain," our school–university partnerships have grown and developed over time to involve school-based teacher educators more fully in this practice-centered teacher education. This involvement means that school-based teacher educators are not only mentor teachers but also key participants in the development and evaluation of teacher candidates, serving the dual purpose of renewal for veteran teachers, university-based teacher educators, and teacher candidates. It is important to recognize the school–university partnership context as a significant terrain or space necessitating purposeful navigation when teacher educators take on hybrid roles for professional learning (Martin, Snow, & Torrez, 2011).

### Teacher Leadership as Democratic Leadership

Within our school–university partnership context, focused on hybrid roles and reciprocal learning, we identified a guiding structure for leadership development of clinical educators. One of the most common theoretical frameworks for teacher leadership is distributed leadership (Wenner & Campbell, 2016; Woods, 2004). In this sense leadership is shared, or distributed, among multiple partners. This is appropriate in nested systems of schools; however, naming shared leadership often reiterates traditional power hierarchies and leadership structures (Anderson, 2011). In this study, liaisons-in-residence reportedly did not serve in these roles to become leaders as much as to serve their students and teacher candidates in new and more purposeful ways. This motivation and the organic emergence of a liaison-in-residence role aligned their identity development more with democratic leadership (Woods, 2004) than simply a sharing of leadership responsibilities. A moral alignment within teacher leadership literature may identify these participants as informal teacher leaders (Gordon et al., 2017).

These participants align with several descriptions in the literature of both formal and informal teacher leadership roles (Lai & Cheung, 2015; Lee Bae, Hayes, O'Connor, Seitz, & Distefano, 2016; Mujis & Harris, 2006; Wenner & Campbell, 2016) while at the same time embodying described characteristics of teacher leaders, such as student-centered, collaborative, and in pursuit of professional growth (Hunzicker, 2013; Jacobs, Gordon, & Solis, 2016). Recognizing the "moral understandings of leadership concerned with struggles over contradictions and conflicts in values, beliefs and the interests of all," (Anderson, 2011, p. 329) this chapter works from the engagement of power differentials and human agency in a moral endeavor. This refined lens allows for a deeper look into a leadership structure and the experiences of people involved with/in hierarchical systems and structures.

Identifying multiple sites for teacher development in school–university partnerships, our leadership perspective builds on activity theory (Engestrom, 1999, 2000) where "the focus of action circulates to one person, then another according to the social and environmental context and the flow of actions." (Woods, 2004, p. 6). Identifying an even deeper connection with constructing identity and enacting agency around ethical roles and responsibilities pushed distributed leadership into a framework for democratic or constructivist leadership. Therefore, the research highlighted in this chapter has adopted a democratic leadership theory (Woods, 2004) to better understand agent experiences.

## *Framing a Professional Leadership Identity*

Teachers are important players in the development of future teachers due to their daily involvement in the complex work of teaching (Mangin & Stoelinga, 2008). Likewise, past scholarship has identified key benefits noted by teacher leaders, including feelings of confidence, empowerment, or value (Beachum & Dentith, 2004; Hunzicker, 2012). At the same time, teacher leadership as something "added to" the already rigorous work of daily classroom teaching can be stressful and contribute to vulnerability and negative relationships with colleagues (Brooks, Scribner, & Eferakorho, 2004). By reviewing teacher leadership through a democratic leadership theory, this chapter highlights a space for possibilities within the benefits and challenges. Teacher leadership, when working from within a classroom, can certainly be seen as something "added" to an already full role as a teacher. However, teacher leadership from within a classroom may also be viewed through a lens of opportunity and a continuum of more positive and more challenging experiences. Situating the space of teacher leadership in this way allowed for nuanced understandings of hybrid teacher leadership experiences and contexts.

An underexplored construct in teacher leadership includes how professional identities evolve or are constructed with new leadership structures. In this study, we viewed the development of teacher identity as a sociocultural process (Lasky, 2005) involving individual teacher agency and the influence of social contexts. Considering "the interplay among teacher identity, structure and agency," (Pillen et al., 2013) the research study shared here worked to examine the experiences of individual teachers within a certain structure for clinical supervision and as a support for teacher leadership identity construction.

Oolbekkink-Marchand et al. (2017) explored teacher agency enacted across teacher leader careers, highlighting that "teacher beliefs appeared to be a factor of considerable importance." (p. 45). Likewise, democratic theories of leadership can be described as "organic governance" connecting "structure, agency and the person." (Woods, 2004, p. 11). In this study, all liaisons-in-residence opted to become site supervisors while maintaining full classroom teaching duties even as this responsibility also meant passing a rigorous proficiency assessment connected to a framework for teaching (Danielson, 2013). Having a shared structure for discussing teacher development – how all teachers in the state are evaluated and how teacher candidates are evaluated – made for a boundary crossing of development for self and other, allowing structure, agency, and individuals to integrate in experiences contributing to identity development.

## Research Design

### Phenomenological Case Study

This phenomenological case study (Merriam, 1998) aimed to determine what the essence of the experience (Moustakas, 1994) of being a liaison-in-residence was for participants. Liaison-in-residence was defined by classroom teachers who actively sought the opportunity to serve as clinical supervisors (known as "liaison" in this partnership) for teacher candidates. They also worked as contacts for mentor teachers in their buildings, facilitators for cross-context teacher candidate workshops, and passed the required state proficiency assessment for teacher evaluation. The university fulfills contracts for the liaisons-in-residence following the same protocol as for all adjunct supervisors.

This case study focused primarily on interviewing and journaling to elicit narratives of experience from the participants themselves. Findings were grounded in the exact words of the participants to characterize the experiences of liaisons-in-residence considering multiple professional responsibilities of participants. Participants included five liaisons-in-residence, all teaching in elementary or middle school classrooms. Their four university-based partner liaisons also served as contributing authors to this chapter and participated in focus group interviews and individual journaling. This case study was bound within the role of the liaison-in-residence in a specific university-partnership context.

## *Data Sources*

Data sources to gather liaison-in-residence perceptions included individual surveys and journal prompts examining why and how participants believed they came to participate in this role; how they constructed their professional responsibilities in the dual roles of classroom teacher and university liaison; and what they considered their key motivations and challenges in this structure. Additionally, all participants engaged in two focus group discussions around similar topics. This design provided individual and collective notions on the essence of experiences in this situated context. Participants were asked to journal weekly from February through April, describing their experiences and feelings about the study research questions (i.e., they were provided with prompts about equity, collegial relationships, influences, and construction of their professional identities). The researchers and co-authors kept journals identifying observations of liaisons-in-residence working in their multiple contexts.

## *Data Analysis*

All interviews and researcher or participant journals were transcribed and considered verbatim to code for initial themes. Inductive coding was conducted (Patton, 1990), and researchers memoed and engaged in dialog through data debriefing discussions to develop an initial theory of teacher leader professional identity and the essence of the experience as a liaison-in-residence. Memos and key findings were shared with the liaisons-in-residence for member checking. Triangulation of individual and focus group transcripts with researcher journals and field notes (Creswell, 1998; Patton, 1990) substantiate claims about how this role influences teacher identity and student and teacher learning.

## Teacher Leadership as Servant Learning

In line with Gordon, Jacobs, Croteau, and Solis's (2017) study on informal teacher leadership, liaisons-in-residence in this study all evidenced dedication to professional learning – for themselves and others – while at the same time focusing on student learning. All liaisons-in-residence had the desire to take on new responsibilities in service to education, in particular the profession of teaching. They found themselves often pulled among their interests in serving all roles and responsibilities not just well, but in "truly excellent" ways. As they took on new roles as site supervisors within their buildings, they found themselves identifying the need to meet their student learning (as a teacher), serve their own teacher candidate learning (as mentor teachers), and serve their teacher colleagues and building administrators (as teacher leader). Each of these identities intertwined and overlapped throughout their work. They therefore identified the need for support in sustaining an emergent leadership role to maintain their overall professional identity. Highlighting the notions of professional growth and struggle on a continuum of teacher leadership experiences allowed for an organic leadership structure where collective voice informed teacher development across the professional life span.

Participants did not deny the possibility of the liaison-in-residence growing into a stronger teacher leadership role in their buildings. However, the complexity of the negotiation of roles in identity construction caused some difficulty in fully embracing the liaison-in-residence role at all times. Three themes resulted from analysis of transcripts, journals, and memos in this study: teacher leader identity development within democratic leadership; teacher leader positionality stirs tensions in professional identity; and service and equity as key guideposts for leading and learning. Reviewing all data sources and resulting themes with a focus on the development of participant identity and contextual influences on leadership in a democratic framework allowed for nuances in the description of the experiences and themes that follow.

### *Teacher Leader Identity Development within Democratic Leadership*

As identified previously, these liaisons-in-residence emerged as teacher leaders in a conscious manner by choosing this work (teacher candidate support and development) over other more traditional school leadership roles (e.g., building level principals or department chairperson). Their emphasis on the work necessary for being a liaison-in-residence stemmed from a commitment to personal, professional growth while at the same time bettering opportunities for their students and teacher candidates. A key facet of their identity development was their emphasis on doing work within the building that typically came from someone external to the building (e.g., the university).

**Access Matters: Being "Coach in the Copy Room".** Being involved in this "bottom up" structure aligned with democratic leadership and met these teachers developing identities as servants to new teachers and their students at the same time. The key was being able to serve while being "embedded" in the building. One liaison-in-residence shared that the impetus for her growth was being "embedded in the building" and "it was just borne from discussions on improvement and how to better serve students and candidates and mentor teachers." (FG#1, 1/2017, p. 1). Similarly, another participant described being a liaison-in-residence as "a resource in the building." (FG#1, 1/2017, p. 2). The idea that the liaison-in-residence was purposefully positioned as a teacher educator within the building allowed for the facilitation of candidate support in new ways.

For example, the notion of "coach in the copy room" became a frame for embedded service for teacher development. Liaisons-in-residence as teacher leaders were being leveraged due to accessibility in buildings. When one participant was describing an encounter with a teacher candidate who was feeling bad about a lesson she had just taught, she said, "It's like, let that piece go… move forward…It's like the coach in the copy room. Focus on what are you doing this afternoon. It's that conversation at the copier." (FG#2, 4/2016, p. 2). The ability to have an immediate response or subtle coaching moment was empowering and important for all participants. Focus on different roles in the same building context allowed for nuances of practice and responsibility so that layers of need could support teacher development at multiple levels and in different spaces within the building.

Another liaison-in-residence agreed saying, "The in-person as opposed to email or text conversation is so important" (FG#2, 4/2017, p. 2) when identifying their presence within the building as being sometimes more powerful than the university-based liaison who may only be scheduled to stop in the building once weekly. University-based liaisons agreed it was incredibly helpful to have classroom teachers serving officially in these liaison roles so that immediate needs were met.

Interestingly, an unanticipated outcome of this new presence was serving as a mentor or coach not only for other mentor teachers but for all teachers in the building.

> I find that in our building, too. People will come and say, 'hey!' They see me around the building and just, yeah, people come to me and ask me about things. … because we're

> more visible in the building. We're in people's classrooms.... If I didn't have this position, I probably would never see the 4th–6th grade teachers. Even though we have a tiny building, and they are just around the corner. But, yeah, I'm out of my classroom, I'm forming relationships with other teachers because of it. That's a huge component of teacher leadership that this liaison-in-residence role takes on. (FG#2, 4/2017, p. 3)

These liaisons-in-residence may not have seen themselves as "active" in all parts of their school buildings before taking on this new role; however, they acknowledged their colleagues did identify them as classroom leaders. One participant shared:

> No one in my building was surprised that I was taking this on. I'm already on our leadership team. As far as I know, most people are fine with my position, and some teachers come to me for advice even if they aren't mentors. (Liaison-in-Residence Journal, March/April, p. 1)

It is important to note this apparent comfort with being viewed as a leader in the building when working within the tensions of being strained by felt challenges or resistance to new roles.

**Access Matters: Self-Development while Serving Others.** Overall, the liaisons-in-residence demonstrated a value for professional growth – their own, their colleagues', their teacher candidates', and their students'. One participant shared, "I have always had a difficult time speaking in front of peers and colleagues. This has helped me climb out from underneath my shell and find a voice in a way that feels comfortable." (Liaison-in-Residence Journal, March/April, p. 1). Other participants agreed: "I'm a better teacher all around. It makes me question myself as a teacher and as a person. How am I behaving professionally? Inside the classroom. Outside the classroom." (FG#2, 4/2017, p. 4). And, being a better teacher sometimes spanned to being better when communicating outside the teaching context.

> I feel like I'm getting better at having crucial conversations with people. That has never been my strong suit. … being able to sit down and have a difficult conversation. And, I feel like that's translating over into my life in general. (FG#2, 4/2017, p. 9)

Considerations of how liaisons-in-residence grew from their work as teacher leaders as well as how they reframed their professional identities also came up in focus groups and individual journal reflections.

> I like the school-wide identity I have now. I got good feedback as a classroom teacher but now I'm in a lot of classrooms. And, it's a different sense. I'm not just a teacher in my room. I'm a teacher in the building. (FG#2, 4/2017, p. 4)

Space for reflection on identity development also demonstrated how one participant internalized her new role with what she could learn from her university-based partner liaison. "I'm taking my professional development personally… teaching adults is a different way to instruct… I use that model as a professional development tool… so it helps spread the skill/the craft of teaching." (FG#1, 1/2017, p. 3).

In their newer work with adults and identifying teacher learning spaces, they also recognized the additional time this took. Again, they valued the opportunity, sought out the professional growth, and recognized that it was potentially taking away from some other work they may need to do.

> I found that I was at school a lot earlier preparing for PLCs for the candidates to further support them in lesson components, general classroom administration, safety training, Code of Ethics and various other needs that resulted in discussion from mentor meetings. I also found that I love the process of working with new teachers and look forward to interaction with the candidates, but I work really hard to provide thorough and detailed feedback which consumes my time as well as my after school hours. (Liaison-in-Residence Journal, March/April, pp. 1–2)

Another example of a pull on professional identity included the prioritizing of different roles based on immediate needs. One liaison-in-residence shared:

> I needed to be a first grade teacher today. Because we moved this little guy, this person from one room into the next, and I just needed to be there with him today. It's sort of a fine line with me sometimes, feeling like I'm just competent and on top of the world, and then I'm just the worst at everything because I'm not doing anything well. (FG#2, 4/2017, p. 8)

One of the highlights in finding a way through these tensions is identified by the liaisons-in-residence as the importance of partnership. One participant used the example of empowering the teacher candidates to work in their classrooms if the liaison-in-residence needed to be in another room. Also, partnering with a university-based liaison who is there when someone has "to be a first grade teacher today." She said:

> I think it works well as a partnership. Otherwise we'd be out of our room way too much... and then it would be a problem. Because now you have a student candidate running your class... who may not be at that developmental level to deliver instruction with fidelity. So I think it's good that we're partnered and we don't shoulder the entire liaison responsibility. (FG#2, 4/2017, p. 6)

Honoring the pulls on multiple roles as a teacher leader consistently returned to an appreciation for the multiple partners the school–university partnership could provide:

> There is energy in my classroom too... [teacher candidates] bring a different energy than I do. So I feel like we can bounce off each other. If you really get along and do well, it's fun!... you can problem-solve right then and there and the kids love to see the interaction ... between two adults professionally. (FG#2, 4/2017, pp. 6–7)

All participants identified overwhelming benefits to themselves personally and professionally along with felt benefits to colleagues and their classroom students. However, it could not be overlooked that there were realities of stress and discomfort to being in a classroom role and a leadership role at the same time.

### Teacher Leadership Positionality Stirs Tensions in Professional Identity

When asked to describe their feelings about serving as a liaison-in-residence, the participants identified feelings of "great honor and respect." One participant said:

> I feel honored by the trust the university has placed in me. Seeing me as someone, yes, we want you in the building and

we trust you with our candidates. And we trust your judgment about placements and we trust you when you go in and do an observation ... That gives me a lot of validation. (FG#2, 4/2017, pp. 3–4)

Although this validation is important, it has also provided the space where liaisons-in-residence are being called upon to serve in other leadership roles or decision-making in their buildings.

**Tensions in Knowing What You Know.** As liaisons-in-residence appreciated the value they – and others – found in their new roles, they also found discomfort in the spotlight. One of the liaisons-in-residence tried to explain this discomfort in the following way:

> I just never saw myself in admin positions. And, knowing the information that you get when you go in there... is sometimes heavy. And, that's hard to take. Sometimes, you just end up... I'm not going to go out and blab it or anything, but you're also trying to process in your own head. (FG#2, 4/2017, p. 5)

Another participant followed up with, "And, I don't want that information. I don't want to know that a colleague down the row is not doing well... that's hard...." (FG#2, 4/2017, p. 5). Another participant concurred: "Most difficult is getting an insight into colleagues that is not necessarily complimentary." (FG#1, 1/2017, p. 5). It would appear some of the discomfort was in having information about colleagues one did not really want to have. There was also discomfort, though, in how colleagues in the building might respond to these new structures.

Liaisons felt explicit tensions with forming perceptions about colleagues, at the same time they recognized tension from the perceptions of their peers. "My partner teacher seems a little annoyed sometimes with my [university] responsibilities and even commented in front of candidates that she doesn't like that I have this position." (Liaison-in-Residence Journal, March/April, p. 1). This participant continued to share, "One teacher actually called me a brownnose." (Liaison-in-Residence Journal, March/April, p. 2). Another study participant said:

> Sometimes, I'll be in with the principal, and I'll come out of the office, and my partner teacher will say, oh, what was that about? And, I'll hesitate for a minute, and she'll say 'oh, was it a liaison thing?' because she knows I'm kind of privy and I'm not going to tell her... (FG#2, 4/2017, p. 5)

The tensions in positionality involve information sharing along with responsibility for leading teacher development and learning. These tensions occurred alongside the "coach in the copy room" instances for liaisons-in-residence and their colleagues.

**Tensions in prioritizing roles.** Another tension included sometimes desiring their own space in the classroom: "Um, sometimes I really like having my kids to myself. Right now my candidate is … out of my room for math. And, I really look forward to math and doing my own thing." (FG#2, April 2017, p. 6). When pushed to identify more specific tensions they might feel in their roles as teacher leaders, participants could unanimously agree to a key practical tension. They all played a large and critical role in placing the teacher candidates in their buildings by matching them appropriately with mentor teachers. They identified that they, personally, needed a strong candidate as they would often be observing other teacher candidates in the building and may not be in their own classroom. Therefore, a key practical tension was "getting the best candidate." One liaison-in-residence shared:

> People get bent about that…. But one thing I used to find so pleasing was seeing a candidate who was struggling and being that teacher that got to see them and say okay we got it figured out! And, we won't get that candidate who is going to need intensive work because then we can't do our job… but I'm asking everyone else to take one. (FG#2, 4/2017, p. 7)

Another liaison-in-residence thought her candidate might not get enough attention: "like she's good. She's fine. But she could have had more support from me, pulling back and modeling again." (FG#2, 4/2017, p. 7).

Having long discussions with a partner university-based liaison guided one liaison-in-residence. She shared that they wondered together, "Am I the best classroom teacher as well as the best intern teacher to my candidate, at the same time being the best liaison…starting to feel a really strong pull…and something had to give." (FG#2, 4/2017, p. 8). Another participant worried about her students having "too much new and not enough constant. They see me coming and going. …." (FG#2, April 2017, p. 9). Taking their multiple roles seriously and working to find balance among them is likely one of the trajectories from being a teacher leader. With deeper systemic change and organic structures, the balance and give and take may become more established and sustainable.

### Service and Equity as Key Guideposts for Leading and Learning

In terms of describing candidate learning, one liaison-in-residence shared that her candidate may learn more than she intends. This liaison-in-residence served as the Response to Intervention Lead for her entire building. She explained:

> My candidate sees…and they're not easy issues. A lot of them I've had to be confrontational. That's not a good word, but I've had to be confrontational…Things aren't happening. It's equity, right? Things aren't happening that should be happening. So, the whole time she's shadowing me and she's with me. It's hard. It's extremely confidential information…"You need to know how I dealt with it in the hallway," I said. "I realize this feels weird, and I'm not gossiping, but I need you to know I took care of this,"…hopefully having that professional conversation. But it's like, is this too much for them to know? (FG#2, 4/2017, p. 3)

Becoming a model for difficult discussions and advocating for students or other teachers was a by-product of these liaisons-in-residence working closely with teacher candidates while at the same time serving their other professional roles. Liaisons-in-residence did not want to protect candidates from information about teacher practice not following equitable processes. One participant shared:

> I was really shocked when I first started observing. You guys [university-based liaisons] see this all the time. But, I was, I mean you see practices occurring in your building…Because they [teacher candidates] are mimicking, especially the initial interns. And, that created a lot of angst for me. Because I mean, we have a model here. How do I work with that? (FG#1, 1/2017, p. 4)

Liaisons-in-residence also recognized a potential need for better scaffolding in these situations. It is difficult to pull candidates – or colleagues – into other situations involving practicing teachers. However, helping candidates to see equitable practices through their work with students makes those opportunities more meaningful. All liaisons-in-residence identified having extra support in the classroom with their teacher candidates as a way to better meet diverse student learning needs.

> I'm at a Title I school, and this year we were blessed with kids that are just learning the alphabet and kids that are learning novels. And… figure it out. But it's so much easier: formative assessments and who is going to work with who and… I love the co-teaching and the co-planning. (FG#2, 4/2017, p. 7)

Serving as a liaison-in-residence boiled down to benefits for students: "It is more beneficial for my students when they have access to two teachers in the classroom. Student needs are met more frequently and supported through the efforts of both student teacher and mentor teacher in the classroom." (Liaison-in-Residence Journal, February, p. 1). Another participant identified, "It has also made me think about my students' learning styles and try a variety of strategies to focus on each style in a lesson, reaching more students at one time." (Liaison-in-Residence Journal, February, p. 1).

In addition to working in classrooms together, a participant shared that the professional growth comes from working through crucial conversations:

> I'm not as judgmental of others as I typically can be. … it's an appreciation for the hard conversations. Even today I had to have a calibrating conversation with an intern. I've only observed her twice. They are really intense issues. How do you say this? How do you form it so she can grow? (FG#2, April 2017, p. 7)

Initial findings indicate a persistence of liaisons-in-residence to serve teacher candidates and the students in their buildings at the same time. All study participants took on the liaison-in-residence role as a part of their own professional growth and commitment. Participants identified specific challenges (like working with colleagues in new ways) and benefits (like shared conversations about professional practice with new teachers as being reciprocally renewing). Serving as liaison-in-residence has pulled classroom teachers from some of their primary responsibilities. However, it has also pushed them into professional space where their agency may influence deeper equity in educational systems and student learning.

## Concluding Remarks for Hybrid Teacher Leadership

Classroom teachers serving as liaisons-in-residence in this study clearly demonstrated that allowing voice in building key aspects of school–university partnership structures cultivates teacher leadership, whether intended or not. If teacher educators and school–university partners identify the tensions along a continuum of benefits and challenges in teacher leadership work within professional spaces, they may be able to create democratic leadership structures where multiple voices carry deliberative weight in decision-making. Likewise, a deeper examination of the identities of teacher leaders in hybrid spaces like school–university partnerships could further enlighten how teacher leader identities emerge and may be cultivated and supported in education systems.

Investigating this hybrid structure could create a more fluid space for professional agency around the moral imperative of teacher education for creating equitable opportunities for all learners and teachers. There may also be more of a democratic than distributed model of leadership in these instances. Each person has roles and responsibilities, yet each person also has pulls on individual time. Consequently, shared roles with different structures may be a response to supporting teacher leadership over time. Therefore, school–university partnerships provide an important context, or space, for cultivating teacher leadership in collaboration.

Acknowledging key benefits of teacher leadership (Beachum & Dentith, 2004; Hunzicker, 2012) and at the same time, honoring emotions of stress or discomfort (Brooks, Scribner, & Eferakorho, 2004) brings forth possibilities for sustaining a teacher leadership continuum where individual actors may be at different spaces on any given day or time, making the construct more of a hybrid teacher leadership structure. If the structures are in place to support moves along the benefit–challenge continuum, the desire of classroom teachers to emerge as leaders and remain in their classrooms may be a possible future and theorized hybridity. Additionally, such a support structure may be able to emphasize equity in terms of access, opportunity, and advocacy for students if identified as the fulcrum of the continuum.

In a democratic structure focused on equity, teacher education and institutional policymakers need to also consider how to emphasize equity in sharing voice and honoring time and commitment. Different compensation or workload structures may have to be considered to better support teacher leadership from within partnership systems. University faculty and school administrators might work together more purposefully such that "organic structures" (Woods, 2004) for leadership might emerge for hybrid teacher leadership; identifying multiple spaces for teachers to enact professional agency, build confidence in themselves and in others, and develop equity-based instructional practices to engage the tensions of tight and loose structure, such that teacher development and professional identity may continue to evolve over the professional life span. More significantly, deeper research needs to be conducted on various sites as spaces for teacher leadership and the enactment of roles and responsibilities within these spaces.

# References

Anderson, M. (2011). The struggle for collective leadership: Thinking and practice in a multi-campus school setting. *Educational Management, Administration & Leadership, 40*(3), 328–342.

Beachum, F., & Dentith, A. M. (2004). Teacher leaders creating cultures of school renewal and transformation. *Educational Forum, 68*(3), 276–286.

Brooks, J. S., Scribner, J. P., & Eferakorho, J. (2004). Teacher leadership in the context of whole school reform. *Journal of School Leadership, 14*(3), 242–265.

Bullough, R. V., Draper, R. J., Smith, L., & Birrell, J. R. (2004). Moving beyond collusion: Clinical faculty and university/public school partnership. *Teaching and Teacher Education, 20*, 505–521.

Creswell, J. W. (1998). *Qualitative inquiry and research design: Choosing among five traditions.* Thousand Oaks, CA: Sage Publications.

Dana, N. F., Silva, D. Y., & Snow-Gerono, J. L. (2002). Building a culture of inquiry in a professional development school. *Teacher Education & Practice 15*(4), 71–89.

Danielson, C. (2013). *Enhancing Professional Practice: A Framework for Teaching* (2nd ed.). Alexandria, VA: ASCD.

Darling-Hammond, L. (2006). *Powerful teacher education: Lessons from exemplary programs.* San Francisco, CA: Jossey Bass.

Darling-Hammond, L. (1994). *Professional Development Schools: Schools for developing a profession.* New York, NY: Teachers College Press.

Gordon, S. P., Jacobs, J., Croteau, S. M., & Solis, R. (2017, April). Informal teacher leaders' activities, characteristics, relationships, and impact. Paper presented at the Annual American Educational Research Association, San Antonio, Texas.

Grossman, P., Compton, C., Igra, D., Ronfeldt, M., Shahan, E., & Williamson, P. (2009). Teaching practice: A cross-professional perspective. Teachers College Record, 111(9), pp. 2055–2100.

Hunzicker, J. (2012). Professional development and job-embedded collaboration: How teachers learn to exercise leadership. *Professional Development in Education, 38*(2), 267–289.

Hunzicker, J. (2013). Attitude has a lot to do with it: Dispositions of emerging teacher leadership. *Teacher Development, 17*(4), 538–561.

Jacobs, J., Gordon, S. P., & Solis, R. (2016). Critical issues in teacher leadership: A national look at teachers' perceptions. *Journal of School Leadership, 26*(3), 374–406.

Lai, E., & Cheung, D. (2015). Enacting teacher leadership: The role of teachers in bringing about change. *Educational Management Administration & Leadership, 43*(5), 673–692.

Lee Bae, C. C., Hayes, K. N., O'Connor, D. M., Seitz, J. C., & Distefano, R. (2016). The diverse faces of teacher leadership: A typology and survey tool. *Journal of School Leadership, 26*(6), 900–937.

Mangin, M. M., & Stoelinga, S. R. (2008). Teacher leadership: What it I and why it matters. In M. M. Mangine & S. R. Stoelinga (Eds.) *Effective teacher leaderships: Using research to inform and reform* (pp. 1–9). New York, NY: Teachers College Press.

Martin, S., Snow, J. L. & Torrez, C. (2011). Navigating the terrain of third space: Tensions with/in relationships in school-university partnerships. *Journal of Teacher Education, 62*(3) 299–311.

Merriam, S. B. (1998) *Qualitative research and case study applications in education*. San Francisco: Jossey-Bass.

Moustakas, C. (1994). *Phenomenological research methods*. Thousand Oaks, CA: Sage Publications.

Muiis, D., & Harris, A., (2006). Teacher led school improvement: Teacher leadership in the UK. *Teaching and Teacher Education, 22*, 961–972.

Oolbekkink-Marchand, H. W., Hadar, L. L., Smith, K., Helleve, I., & Ulvik, M. (2017). Teachers' perceived professional space and their agency. *Teaching and Teacher Education, 62*, 37–46.

Patton, M. Q. (1990). *Qualitative evaluation and research methods*. Newbury Park, CA: Sage Publications.

Pillen, M., Beijaard, D., & denBrok, P. (2013). Tensions in beginning teachers' professional identity development, accompanying feelings and coping strategies. *European Journal of Teacher Education, 36*(3), 240–260.

Snow-Gerono, J. L. (2009). Voices less silenced: What do veteran teachers value in school–university partnerships and initial teacher preparation? *The Teacher Educator, 44*(4), 248–267.

Teitel, L. (2003). *The professional development schools handbook: Starting sustaining, and assessing partnerships that improve student learning*. Thousand Oaks, CA: Corwin Press.

Wenner, J. A., & Campbell, T. (2016). The theoretical and empirical basis of teacher leadership: A review of the literature. *Review of Educational Research*. (pp. 1–38) Retrieved from http://rer.aera.net

Woods, P. A. (2004). Democratic leadership: Drawing distinctions with distributed leadership. *International Journal of Leadership in Education, 7*(1), 3–26.

Chapter 9

# Lab School Teacher Leaders as Learners and Change Agents

*Margaret Hudson and Jayne Hellenberg*

**Abstract**

Partnerships between public schools and institutions of higher education provide teachers with opportunities for leadership. Teachers at the University of Wyoming (UW) Lab School belong to a community of learners and leaders partnering with the UW's Education College. In this school–university partnership, a strong culture endures in which teachers are viewed as leaders supporting the preparation of future educators and embracing active involvement in the school community. Professional development practices are implemented through the partnership to enhance teacher leadership skills. This chapter explores how professional learning communities, school learning walks, and co-teaching strategies support lab school teacher leaders as learners and change agents.

*Keywords:* Co-teaching; professional development; professional learning communities; school learning walks; school–university partnerships; teacher leadership

Policymakers, educators, and researchers agree that teacher quality is a key factor that contributes to student learning and school improvement.

According to Goodlad (1984), the development of quality teachers relies on quality schools where clinic-like learning occurs. A school–university partnership provides the setting for preparing high-quality teachers as well as enhancing professional development and teacher leadership opportunities for experienced teachers.

Teacher leadership has a significant impact on sustainable schoolwide reform (Vernon-Dotson & Floyd, 2012). Corrigan (2000) asserted that no single institution or professional can assume full responsibility for schools in which all children flourish and grow. Fullan, Hill, and Crevola (2006) added that school administrators are not solely responsible for educational leadership and coordination; teacher leaders play an important role. In addition, Elmore (2000) argued that a redefinition of leadership toward distributed views is necessary. Distributed leadership involves concerted action among those with different areas of expertise. According to Vernon-Dotson and Floyd (2012), in order for school improvement plans to be made effective, all school personnel must be involved in improving the entire school.

> Through distributed leadership models like school-based leadership teams, school leaders can promote all teachers as leaders by empowering their participation in school reform efforts, inspiring them to become competent in their practice, encouraging their collaboration, and creating partnerships both within and beyond the walls of the school for the benefit of all students. (p. 48). Within the collaborative setting of a school–university partnership, teacher leaders are part of a learning organization in which partners share the common goals of preparing quality teachers while improving the teaching and learning system to ensure that the needs of all members of the learning community are met.

This chapter describes professional development practices that enhance teacher leadership abilities and increase effectiveness in meeting the learning needs of students, preservice teachers, and school–university faculty. The partnership between the University of Wyoming (UW) Lab School and the UW's College of Education will be used to highlight examples of teacher leaders as learners and change agents in a school–university partnership. Professional development practices that build knowledge and skills in teacher leaders, along with lessons learned while implementing these practices, will be discussed.

## A School–University Partnership Setting

The UW Lab School is a public school of choice in Albany County School District #1. Located in the College of Education building on the UW campus, the school is unique to Wyoming public education for reasons that it strives to model learner-centered education for approximately 270 kindergarten through eighth grade students while partnering with a teacher education institution to serve as an educational learning site for hundreds of UW College of Education students each year. The student population is relatively diverse when compared to other Wyoming schools with approximately 20% nonwhite ethnicity. Although families must complete applications and enrollment is through a lottery, around 20% of the students receive free lunch, or lunch at reduced rates. The average number of students who qualify for special education services and are served through individual education plans is at or above state and national averages. Currently, the school employs eight elementary classroom teachers (K-4), six middle school teachers (5–8), two special education teachers, a math specialist, a reading specialist, and 1.5 Spanish teachers, along with special teachers for art, physical education, and music.

For over a hundred years, the UW Lab School has served a critical role in supporting the work of the College of Education's teacher education program. The school–university partnership is a complex system that purposely incorporates interaction of teacher leaders with college faculty and preservice educators to improve student learning while preparing future teachers for the profession. The mission of the UW Lab School is to create a positive learning community that will recognize, foster, and assess continuous improvement toward high levels of academic and social achievement for all students, preservice teachers, faculty, and staff. In addition to hosting 12–20 preservice educators for semester- or year-long residencies and internships, the school has over a thousand visits each year from university students completing observations, interviews, and other practicum requirements. Along with these clinic-like experiences, the school setting provides research opportunities for graduate students, school faculty, and university faculty.

The school's partnership with the College of Education and extensive utilization as a setting for field experiences has resulted in a culture in which all teachers are viewed as leaders who support the preparation of future educators and embrace their active involvement in the school community. This culture furthers teacher leadership roles through a shared commitment to innovative and reflective practice, collaboration, and ongoing professional development. Models, structures, and practices that enhance teacher leadership skills and honor the work of teachers beyond the classroom have been created and continue to evolve in response to developing needs.

## Ensuring Opportunities for Teacher Leader Development

Learning Forward, formerly the National Staff Development Council, has identified seven standards for professional learning. According to Learning Forward (2011), "The primary purpose of professional learning is to improve educator practice and student results." (p. 6). While all seven professional learning standards must work in conjunction to change educator knowledge, skills, and dispositions, Standard 1 regarding learning communities speaks directly to the learning of teacher leaders. This standard recommends professional development programming that involves organizing teachers into adult learning communities to "apply a cycle of continuous improvement to engage in inquiry, action research, data analysis, planning, implementation, reflection, and evaluation." (p. 24). Standard 2, regarding leadership, suggests that effective professional learning and collaboration requires shared leadership to guide continuous instructional improvement (Learning Forward, 2011). The right kind of continuous, structured professional development and collaboration improves the quality of teaching and makes a significant, immediate impact on student learning and professional morale (DuFour, DuFour, Eaker, & Many, 2006).

Developing teacher leaders as learners and change agents is about creating opportunities for actions that improve teaching and learning, tie school and community together through collaboration, and provide a local level of distributed leadership in the school and district (Crowther, Ferguson, & Hann, 2009). York-Barr and Duke (2004) asserted that developing teachers as leaders improves the culture and instruction in schools and enhances student learning.

> Teacher leadership is the ability of school professionals to forge a sense of community and share a commitment for increasing student achievement by engaging all faculty and staff and enhancing school climate with the overarching goal of building a capacity for change. (Vernon-Dotson & Floyd, 2012, p. 40). DuFour et al. (2006) confirmed that

teacher leaders need the opportunity to frequently participate in conversations focused on student learning, reflect on reform initiatives, advocate for high-quality education, and take leadership roles in professional development.

At the UW Lab School, teacher leaders initiate and participate in professional development experiences that lead to school and community improvement by increasing the learning opportunities for school and university faculty, preservice educators, and students. Lab school teacher leaders also play a significant role as change makers in the work of schools and in school improvement efforts. In addition to spontaneous, organic leadership efforts to enhance the school environment and student learning, teacher leaders take on semi-formal or formal leadership roles in professional development and in district, state, and national committees. These roles establish distributed leadership and a democratic environment while recognizing teacher expertise and the essential role of teachers as key players in educational reform. Professional practices that help develop lab school teachers as learners and change agents currently being studied, discussed, and implemented through the school–university partnership include professional learning communities (PLCs), school learning walks, and co-teaching strategies. These practices increase quality learning experiences that help to meet the needs of the entire learning community, and support teachers as change makers in their classrooms and beyond.

## *Professional Learning Communities*

After synthesizing over 800 meta-analyses on factors that impact student achievement, Hattie (2009) concluded that the best way to improve schools is to organize teachers into collaborative teams. The work of these teams will include clarifying student learning goals and indicators, gathering evidence of learning on an ongoing basis, and analyzing the results together to determine the effects of the instructional strategies. In other words, he advised schools to function as PLCs. Marzano (2003) agreed and described the PLC concept as one of the most powerful initiatives for school improvement. While the quality of individual teachers remains paramount in student learning, the PLC concept is the best strategy to create a system to ensure that good teaching happens in more classrooms more often. PLCs are characterized by a culture in which collaborative processes are deeply embedded into the daily life of the school. This culture supports regularly scheduled meetings of teachers and pre-service educators who share responsibility for assessing needs and developing solutions to improve all students' learning (DuFour et al., 2006).

Serving as a model for learner-centered education, the lab school does not utilize one core resource to address the curriculum standards. Instead, teachers are responsible for working in PLC teams to develop two-year rotating curriculum maps for the multi-age classrooms. This includes planning and implementing standards-based units using a variety of resources. Lab school teachers share leadership roles as they work on curriculum, instruction, and assessments with continual analysis to improve learning. Through the school–university partnership efforts, preservice teachers and college faculty become contributors to this work. After recent school and district level trainings, a more focused and continuous cycle of reviewing and updating curriculum maps is being implemented. By participating in structured conversations and sharing curriculum maps, the following outcomes are accomplished: (1) ensuring horizontal and vertical articulation of standards-based skills, strategies, and assessments, (2) outlining clear learning expectations for students, parents, preservice teachers, and college faculty, (3) allowing for the development of integrated learning experiences for multiple grades or the entire school, and (4) providing flexibility to change and adapting resources and units to best meet student learning needs.

As part of the school's continuous learning and progress in implementing PLCs, many teachers attended college- and state-sponsored assessment courses over the past several years. Teacher leaders then brought information back to the faculty to support best practices in assessment, grading, and reporting. Through staff-based training and PLC work, the school recently implemented a K-8 standards-referenced report card. Figure 1 provides an overview of the process that is now followed.

The report card identifies the performance level of the student with proficiency marks based on the achievement of standards-based priority learning goals taught during the grading period. It also includes an overview of the learning that has taken place and comments on individual students addressing areas of strength and areas where continued growth is needed. The math section of a seventh grade report card is shown in Figure 2.

*Lessons learned.* Effective implementation of PLCs continues to be an area of learning and growth for the school–university partnership. The partnership setting promotes collaborative work between school and college faculty and provides opportunities for disseminating successful educational approaches, which ultimately help bridge theory and practice in education courses. College faculty benefit from PLC work when teacher leaders serve as guest lecturers in college classrooms and share current

- Priority learning goals are identified from the standard and written in student-friendly language.
- Each priority learning goal is represented on a proficiency scale as a score of 3.0.
- Criteria are established up and down from this to inform the other proficiency scores.
- Students receive instruction and have multiple opportunities to build/demonstrate proficiency. Teachers document student performance recording proficiency marks on a variety of artifacts.
- Overall performance on the priority learning goal is determined by looking at the pattern of performance with strong consideration of the most recent artifacts.
- When determining criteria for a score of 4 on a priority learning goal, the next grade level standard is just one consideration. Another consideration is in addition to exhibiting Level 3 performance, there is evidence of in-depth inferences and applications beyond what was taught.
- The overall proficiency mark for each priority learning goal is averaged with other priority learning goals addressed during the learning period. This score is then used as the proficiency mark for the standard.
- The overall standard proficiency mark for each learning period reflects the priority learning goals taught and assessed. Level 3 (representing proficiency) is based on the end-of-year grade level standard.

Adapted from Heflebower et al. (2014).

Figure 1: Standards-Referenced Report Card Overview.

examples of research-based practices in curriculum, instruction, and assessment. Additionally, lab school teachers make a substantial contribution to the profession by conducting classroom research, leading and participating in study groups with colleagues and UW faculty, and sharing the results of innovative work through conference presentations or articles. For teachers to engage broadly in professional learning work, it is important to schedule collaborative time to develop ideas, implement projects, complete analysis and evaluation, and disseminate results. Financial resources are also needed to support presentations at state and national conferences. Building the leadership capacity of a diverse team creates a culture for distributed leadership and is key to sustaining successful PLCs.

## *School Learning Walks*

According to Fisher and Frey (2014), learning walks are organized classroom observations in which multiple classrooms are visited. The aim of a learning walk is to foster conversation about teaching and learning in order to develop a shared vision of high-quality instruction that impacts student learning. Learning walks are a transformative practice supporting school culture and fostering collaborative leadership. The process

| Academic Standard Proficiency Marks | | Academic Success Behaviors and Citizenship Marks | |
|---|---|---|---|
| 4 | Advanced | | |
| 3.5 | Approaching advanced | | |
| 3 | Proficient | (++) | All the time |
| 2.5 | Approaching proficient | (+) | Most of the time |
| 2 | Partially proficient | (−) | Some of the time |
| 1.5 | With help, partially proficient | (#) | Rarely/with assistance |
| 1 | Even with help, limited knowledge/skills for partial proficiency | | |
| 0 | No work or work not turned in | | |

| Academic Standard Proficiency Level | S1 | S2 |
|---|---|---|
| Ratios and proportional relationships – 7.R | NA | 3.5 |
| The number system – 7.NS | 3.5 | 4 |
| Expressions and equations – 7.EE | NA | 3.5 |
| Geometry – 7.G | 3 | 3.5 |
| Statistics and probability – 7.SP | NA | 3 |
| Mathematical practices – 7.MP | 3 | 3 |

| Academic Success Behaviors and Citizenship Marks | S1 | S2 |
|---|---|---|
| Perseverance and focus | ++ | ++ |
| Safety and responsibility with materials and environment | + | ++ |
| Kindness and respect for self and others | + | + |
| Homework | + | + |

**S1 Comments**

*Learning overview*: In 7th grade Math, students are working toward proficiency in six standard areas. The scores represent the student's knowledge as evidenced by their individual assessments. During the first semester students worked on: The Number System – to add, subtract, multiply, and divide rational numbers in real world and mathematical problems; and Geometry – involving area and perimeter of figures, and introducing scale drawings and similar figures. Students also demonstrated Mathematical Practice Standards, including the practices of collaboration, perseverance, precision, modeling, and explaining.

*Teacher comments*: Your student is a pleasure to have in our math class. He is usually very attentive, whether working with one partner or participating in a whole-class discussion. He continues to take his time and be thoughtful on assessments. Consequently, he shows proficient and above-proficient understanding of new concepts on chapter tests. Sometimes that involves learning from mistakes and doing better on retakes, which your child does. The point of the class is to learn, to be able to show proficiency, and to build a strong foundation for future mathematics. We are picking up the pace in the coming semester, and I expect him to do fine.

Figure 2: Seventh Grade Math Report Card.

facilitates reflection and discussion on what happens in classrooms, leads to development of new insights and understandings, builds connections and trust among staff, and identifies potential resources for providing support or furthering learning (Fisher & Frey, 2014).

Learning walks are being implemented at the UW Lab School as a tool to enhance learning for all members of the school–university partnership. One way in which learning walks are used is as a structured observation protocol with preservice educators. Early in their education program, preservice teachers complete a two-hour observation as part of their educational foundations course. In previous years, these observations provided a limited school experience, varied greatly, and often resulted in inaccurate assumptions and misconceptions. To address these issues, the learning walk model is being utilized to provide a structure for consistent, guided observation. An entire class of preservice teachers can be supported in developing a comprehensive understanding of a school as members of a learning walk team. Rather than a narrow experience focusing on an observation in a single classroom, the preservice teachers get a glimpse of many classrooms, identify commonalities across grade levels and content areas, and reflect on their observations individually and collectively. This allows them to connect the observations to their growing understanding about philosophies of learning.

Lab school teachers and college faculty also benefit from the learning walk model. Much like with preservice teachers, learning walks can serve as a learning tool for teachers and university faculty. Members of the school–university partnership are able to build understanding of school culture and consider how to support the inclusion of preservice teachers into this culture, share and discuss best practices, and foster a spirit of continual learning. Learning walks provide a format for critical conversation and help ensure that all members of the community build shared language, experiences, and expectations.

The focus of a learning walk can vary to address general or specific needs and topics identified by school improvement goals or college course standards. For preservice teachers at the early levels, the focus is often broad (e.g., teaching and learning, the learning environment, student/teacher interaction, or democratic education practices). Learning walks continue to support preservice teachers as they move through the education program by providing observations specific to classroom management, instructional strategies, or course standards. Similarly, focus areas for school and university faculty might include school culture, an identified content area, a specific instructional strategy, or identifying strengths and needs in curriculum articulation or behavioral expectations.

To prepare for a learning walk, a focus is established, an agenda is created, and a schedule is determined. The amount of time for the entire process can range from one to two hours. The schedule may also include time for an extended observation following the guided classroom visits. This selection could be based on the grade level, the content area, or on something interesting noticed during the short visits. Figure 3 shows the components included on a typical learning walk agenda used with preservice teachers.

To begin a learning walk, participants are welcomed and an overview is provided. The overview communicates what a learning walk is, the protocol followed, and the parameters for visiting the classrooms. Participants are provided with context for the visits and guided to make and record observations rather than judgments. Because a learning walk team can include from 6 to 24 or more participants, the process for entering classrooms, beginning the observation from the perimeter, and watching for the signal to leave, are also discussed.

Following this overview, classroom visits begin. The amount of time spent in each classroom might range from one to ten minutes. The length of time is determined by the facilitator and depends on what is happening. For example, the team might spend four minutes observing classroom instructions, but spend just one minute looking around the environment

| | UW Lab School Learning Walk |
|---|---|
| | **Focus – The Learning Environment** |
| 1:00–1:10 | Welcome/Overview of learning walks |
| 1:10–2:00 | Classroom visits (K-8)<br>• K-Rooms 126 and 128<br>• 1$^{st}$/2$^{nd}$ – Rooms 125 and 109<br>• 3$^{rd}$/4$^{th}$ – Rooms 120 and 103<br>• 5$^{th}$-8$^{th}$ – Rooms 204, 205, and 206<br>• Spanish – Rooms 219<br>• Art Room 21<br>• PE-Gym<br>• Music Room 11 |
| 2:00–2:30 | Additional observation |
| 2:30–2:40 | Individual reflection |
| 2:40–3:00 | Shared reflection of learning walk team members |

Figure 3: UW Lab School Learning Walk Agenda.

if a classroom is empty. If a learning walk focuses on a specific instructional strategy, more scheduling work is necessary to select classrooms in which the strategy will be evident and each observation might be up to ten minutes. In all cases, the learning walk emphasizes a broad approach with observations in multiple classrooms. Participants are provided with an observation form to take notes and jot down questions during the learning walk. Figure 4 provides an observation form used for observing in classrooms with a focus on specific math criteria linked with a school improvement goal and discussed as part of a book study.

After the classroom visits, learning walk team members individually complete a reflection sheet. The reflection sheet might ask participants about commonalities they noticed; what they expected to see but didn't; new insights and understandings; and questions, wonderings, or surprises. The reflective questions can be adjusted to support the identified focus area. Finally, during the whole group reflection time, participants share their ideas, questions are answered, and additional information is discussed to reduce assumptions and misconceptions. The process promotes learning from one another as it allows participants to see how others are

- The power of mistakes and struggle
- Rich mathematical tasks
- Assessment for a growth mindset

| Grade and Room | Observations<br>Use phrases such as:<br>I noticed . . . I saw . . . I heard . . . | Wonderings |
|---|---|---|
| K<br>126 | | |
| 2<br>125 | | |
| 4<br>102 | | |
| 5<br>102 | | |
| 6<br>205 | | |
| 8<br>206 | | |

Figure 4: Learning Walk Observation Form: Math.

applying ideas in their classrooms, helps with considering vertical articulation across grade levels, and encourages future interactions and follow up to learn more about instructional resources and pedagogy.

*Lessons learned.* Learning walks promote teacher leadership through collaboration, reflection, and articulation of the decisions involved in the complex and dynamic process of teaching and learning. They serve as an effective tool for professional development, which provides an avenue for spreading the vision and culture of a school as well as connecting theory and practice. Through learning walks, areas of teacher strength are identified and teacher leadership is encouraged as teachers become resources for helping one another improve instruction to increase their impact on student learning. In this way, learning walks foster a spirit of continuous learning that can be aligned to school improvement goals, professional development areas, instructional strategies, and educational practices. When teachers open their doors to preservice teachers, colleagues, and university faculty in this way, trust is built and opportunities for leadership and learning result.

### *Co-Teaching Strategies*

As early as 1997, Darling-Hammond outlined the role teacher leaders play in school improvement efforts. According to Darling-Hammond, teacher leaders improve the quality of the profession by mentoring new teachers and sharing knowledge of effective practices. Izadinia (2015) found that mentor teachers are believed to have a significant influence on the professional development of preservice teachers. Despite the vital role that mentors play in the development of future teachers, Ambrosetti (2014) reported that few teachers receive adequate training or preparation for mentoring. Providing professional development and coaching in mentoring skills increases the positive impacts that mentoring can have on the growth of skills and knowledge of mentees (Hudson, 2013). Through mentoring workshops, coaching, and reflection, mentor teachers learn to make their instructional delivery, assessment strategies, and classroom management approaches more explicitly visible and accessible to preservice teachers. Additionally, mentor teachers learn how to provide preservice teachers with specific feedback concerning their teaching strengths and struggles (Heck, Bacharach, & Dahlberg, 2008).

Developing skills and strategies for effective collaboration is another critical piece of the mentoring process. A growing body of research concluded that successful collaboration between mentor teachers and preservice educators leads to better outcomes for students and preservice teachers (Bacharach, Heck, & Dahlberg, 2010). Evans (1996) suggested that opportunities to collaborate and build knowledge enhance job satisfaction and performance. When mentor teachers provide increased support and collaboration, preservice teachers gain a deeper understanding of the curriculum, develop more effective teaching and classroom management strategies, and build professional relationships (Heck et al., 2008).

Mentoring preservice educators is part of the UW Lab School's mission and is a well-established part of the school culture. Teachers at the school share their classrooms and serve as mentor teachers (also known as cooperating teachers) for multiple field experience placements, supporting hundreds of preservice teachers each year. In this role, lab school teachers regularly explain, clarify, and defend the curriculum, instructional practices, and assessments being implemented in their classrooms, as well as the approaches used to create and maintain effective classroom management and a positive culture of learning. To further enhance their knowledge and skills and increase their effectiveness as mentors, teachers at the school have been supported by professional development provided through the school–university partnership to incorporate co-teaching practices during student teaching. The co-teaching model involves two or more educators working together to plan, organize, instruct, and assess a group of students in a classroom. According to Bacharach, Heck, and Dahlberg (2010),

> In a co-teaching experience, the cooperating teacher and teacher candidate collaboratively plan and deliver instruction from the very beginning of the experience. Cooperating teachers are taught to make their instructional decisions more explicit in order to make the invisible workings of the classroom more visible to the teacher candidate. As the experience continues, the pair seamlessly alternate between assisting and/or leading the planning, teaching, and evaluation. As this occurs, the cooperating teacher partners with the student teacher rather than giving away responsibility for the classroom. This enhances the learning opportunities for students, combines the knowledge and strengths of both teachers, and models a positive adult working relationship. (p. 1)

Co-planning and co-teaching during student teaching increases the variety of pedagogical and assessment strategies used in the classroom.

From the beginning to the end of the field experience, the preservice teacher is actively engaged in preparing and implementing curriculum and assessing its effectiveness through evaluation of student learning with scaffolded guidance and support from the mentor teacher. Co-teaching pairs participate in reflective practice using assessment information to provide a variety of grouping strategies that help meet the diverse learning needs of students. In addition, the implementation of co-teaching decreases typical problems such as isolation and inadequate mentoring (Bacharach et al., 2010).

Recently, teacher leaders at the UW Lab School joined College of Education faculty in reviewing research literature related to fully implementing a co-teaching model during student teaching. A group of school and college faculty attended a co-teaching train-the-trainer workshop hosted by researchers at St. Cloud State University to further develop the knowledge and skills necessary to support teaching teams in implementing co-teaching strategies. These efforts were applied in the school setting to train co-teaching pairs in using seven co-teaching strategies: one teach, one collect; one teach, one assist; station teaching; parallel teaching; supplemental teaching; differentiated teaching; and team teaching (Bacharach et al., 2010). The co-teaching strategies provide structure for supporting teaching and learning, value the contributions of both teachers, and help provide for the differentiated needs of students.

Learning about and implementing the co-teaching strategies has supported UW Lab School mentors in furthering their teacher leadership abilities while helping preservice educators excel in their preparation toward becoming certified teachers. A variety of tools have been developed from the research literature to support implementation and evaluate the effectiveness of the model. Mentor teachers are encouraged to reflect on their use of co-teaching versus traditional mentoring practices through use of the form shown in Figure 5. Several times a year, mentors use this information as a self-reflection and goal-setting tool to ensure continued progress toward effective implementation of a co-teaching environment.

During professional development sessions and collaborative team meetings, mentor teachers and preservice educators are encouraged to share classroom examples of the co-teaching strategies they have explored, along with the impact the strategies had on student learning. Consistent messages about utilizing all adults to impact student learning and the critical role of co-planning are conveyed and reinforced. Self-reflection sheets, such as the one shown in Figure 6, focus on personal and professional characteristics as well as components of effective implementation

| | Co-Teaching | Traditional Mentoring | Continuum |
|---|---|---|---|
| Preparation | Training and discussion on implementation of co-teaching strategies | Little or no training support for implementation of co-teaching strategies | 1.....2.....3.....4.....5<br>Co-Teaching  Traditional |
| Introductions | Introduced as teacher candidates and start working with students immediately | Introduced as student teachers and observe for weeks with minimal participation | 1.....2.....3.....4.....5<br>Co-Teaching  Traditional |
| Involvement | Both teachers actively engaged in teaching from beginning to end experience | One teacher is often passive while the other leads instruction | 1.....2.....3.....4.....5<br>Co-Teaching  Traditional |
| Relationship building | Purposefully build and nurture professional trust and respect throughout experience | Little opportunity or structure to support building a relationship | 1.....2.....3.....4.....5<br>Co-Teaching  Traditional |
| Communication and collaboration | Guidance and practice on communication and collaboration skills | Little guidance and practice on communication and collaboration skills | 1.....2.....3.....4.....5<br>Co-Teaching  Traditional |
| Planning | Planning times identified to focus on how, when, and which co-teaching strategies to use | Lessons planned in isolation then approved by cooperating teacher | 1.....2.....3.....4.....5<br>Co-Teaching  Traditional |
| Modeling and coaching | Teachers model, coach, and make invisible skills visible in instructional and management strategies | Teacher candidates expected to be skilled in instructional and management strategies after minimal experiences | 1.....2.....3.....4.....5<br>Co-Teaching  Traditional |
| Leading and full-time instruction | Role of the lead teacher is shared from beginning to end of experience | Amount of teaching time varies | 1.....2.....3.....4.....5<br>Co-Teaching  Traditional |

Adapted from Bacharach, Heck, and Dahlberg (2010)

Figure 5: Co-Teaching/Traditional Mentoring Continuum.

C = Consistently  F = Frequently  S = Sometimes  R = Rarely

*Planning*

1. Mentor teacher and preservice teachers plan together for co-taught instruction    C  F  S  R
2. Mentor teacher and preservice teachers coordinate tasks    C  F  S  R
3. Preservice teachers assume leadership in planning lessons    C  F  S  R
4. When planning to lead instruction, preservice teachers assign tasks and responsibilities to mentor teachers and other adults    C  F  S  R
5. Mentor teacher and preservice teachers work together to make explicit instructional decisions    C  F  S  R

*Communication*

1. I communicate honestly with co-teaching partners even when it is difficult    C  F  S  R
2. I actively listen to suggestions, feedback, and instruction from co-teaching partners    C  F  S  R
3. I bounce ideas off co-teaching partners for genuine feedback and input prior to implementation    C  F  S  R
4. As co-teaching partners, there is a lot of give and take in conversations between us    C  F  S  R
5. As co-teaching partners, we intentionally address communication strategies    C  F  S  R
6. I attend to my co-teaching partners' body language and nonverbal cues    C  F  S  R
7. My co-teaching partners effectively articulate/explain/describe/demonstrate pedagogical practices to make them accessible for me    C  F  S  R

Adapted from Bacharach, Heck, and Dahlberg (2008)

Figure 6: Elements of Successful Co-Teaching.

of co-teaching strategies. This form is completed to identify strengths, determine goal areas, and guide further professional development.

*Lessons learned.* Teachers require professional development in best practices for mentoring and benefit from a distributed model of leadership that encourages and supports teachers learning from and with each other. These practices not only strengthen teachers' abilities to mentor, but also provide opportunities for teacher leadership. Sending a group of lab school and College of Education faculty together to the train-the-trainers workshop helped ensure full support for the implementation of co-teaching as well as common vocabulary and expectations for supporting co-teaching teams in the classroom. Mentors and preservice teachers have shared the significant impact that implementing co-teaching strategies has had on their ability to meet the diverse needs of students at the lab school. Therefore, these strategies will be included in the coming years as part of the school's continuous improvement plan. Through this process, mentors have shared their need for more information about providing preservice teachers with targeted feedback, and this will become a focus for future professional learning. Additionally, because of the strong research base and the initial success in implementing co-teaching strategies during student teaching, the lab school faculty will discuss how to effectively incorporate these strategies during all field experience placements.

## Conclusion

Research shows that the most important factor in a child's education is having a good teacher (Hattie, 2009). By inviting expert teachers to serve as teacher leaders and assist in improving learning conditions throughout the school, Scherer (2007) noted that rather than removing our best teachers from the classroom, we extend their reach. According to Poekert (2012), investing in the development of teacher leaders not only provides short-term gains in student achievement scores, but also provides lasting gains in a school's capacity to learn and adapt to the dynamic circumstances faced each year.

The investment in developing teacher leaders at the UW Lab School, as part of a school–university partnership, contributes to student success and consistently results in strong student growth and achievement. This is evident in assessment data such as the Measures of Academic Progress (MAP) results (Figure 7). Additionally, leadership capacity has been built and lab school teachers effectively adapt to and address the constant changes that take place in both the K-12 and university educational systems.

|  | Percentage of K-9 Students Meeting or Exceeding Fall to Spring Growth Targets (%) | Percentage of K-9 Students at or Above National Mean Score (%) |
|---|---|---|
| Math | 70.8 | 82.3 |
| Reading | 59.7 | 85.0 |

Figure 7: UW Lab School MAP Data: 2015–2016.

A culture fostering teacher leadership through a shared commitment to professional development and service to the education profession can be strengthened through a school–university partnership such as the one described in this chapter. The UW Lab School–UW partnership presents a consistent, deliberate approach to continuous learning for students, pre-service teachers, and school–university faculty. The commitment to helping prepare future educators enhances and enriches the UW Lab School while supporting the notion of a community of teacher leaders as learners and change agents.

# References

Ambrosetti, A. (2014). Are you ready to be a mentor? Preparing teachers for mentoring pre-service teachers. *Australian Journal of Teacher Education, 39*(6), 32–42.

Bacharach, N., Heck, T. W., & Dahlberg, K. (2008). What makes co-teaching work? Identifying the essential elements. *College Teaching Methods and Styles Journal, 4*(3), 43–48.

Bacharach, N., Heck, T. W., & Dahlberg, K. (2010). Changing the face of student teaching through co-teaching. *Action in Teacher Education, 32*(1), 3–14.

Corrigan, D. (2000). The changing role of schools and higher education institutions with respect to community-based interagency collaboration and interprofessional partnerships. *Peabody Journal of Education, 75*(1), 176–195.

Crowther, F., Ferguson, M., & Hann, L. (2009). *Developing teacher leaders: How teacher leadership enhances school success.* Thousand Oaks, CA: Corwin Press.

Darling-Hammond, L. (1997). *Doing what matters most: Investing in quality teaching.* New York, NY: National Commission on Teaching and America's Future.

DuFour, R., DuFour, R., Eaker, R., & Many, T. (2006). *Learning by doing: A handbook for professional learning communities at work.* Bloomington, IN: Solution Tree.

Elmore, R. (2000). *Building a new structure for school leadership.* Washington, DC: Albert Shanker Institute.

Evans, R. (1996). *The human side of change.* San Francisco, CA: Jossey-Bass.

Fisher, D., & Frey, N. (2014). Using teacher learning walks to improve instruction. *Principal Leadership, 14*(5), 58–61.

Fullan, M., Hill, P., & Crevola, C. (2006). *Breakthrough.* Thousand Oaks, CA: Corwin Press.

Goodlad, J. I. (1984). *A place called school.* New York, NY: McGraw-Hill.

Hattie, J. (2009). *Visible learning: A synthesis of over 800 meta-analyses relating to student achievement.* New York, NY: Routledge.

Heck, T. W., Bacharach, N., & Dahlberg, K. (2008). *Co-teaching: Enhancing the student teaching experience.* Eighth Annual IBER & TLC Conference Proceedings, Las Vegas, NV (pp. 1–11).

Heflebower, T., Hoegh, J. K., & Warrick, P. (2014). *A school leader's guide to standards-based grading.* Bloomington, IN: Solution Tree.

Hudson, P. (2013). Mentoring as professional development: "Growth for both" mentor and mentee. *Professional Development in Education, 39*(5), 771–783.

Izadinia, M. (2015). Talking the talk and walking the walk: Pre-service teachers' evaluation of their mentors, mentoring and tutoring. *Partnership in Learning, 23*(4), 341–353.

Learning Forward. (2011). *Standards for professional learning.* Oxford, OH: Learning Forward.

Marzano, R. (2003). What works in schools: Translating research into action. Alexandria, VA: ASCD.

Poekert, P. E. (2012). Teacher leadership and professional development: Examining links between two concepts central to school improvement. *Professional Development in Education, 38*(2), 169–188.

Scherer, M. (2007). Playing to strengths. *Educational Leadership, 65*(1), 7.

Vernon-Dotson, L. J., & Floyd, L. O. (2012). Building leadership capacity via school partnerships and teacher teams. *The Clearing House, 85,* 38–49.

York-Barr, J., & Duke, K. (2004). What do we know about teacher leadership? Findings from two decades of scholarship. *Review of Educational Research, 74*(3), 255–316.

Chapter 10

# National Board Certified Teachers as Bridges for Teacher Candidates Entering the Profession

*Anna M. Quinzio-Zafran and Elizabeth A. Wilkins*

### Abstract

National Board Certified Teachers (NBCTs) are highly accomplished teachers who have learned to deprivatize their teaching practice, and hence provide a valuable model for teacher leadership. This chapter, which focuses on NBCTs as mentors of teacher candidates in a professional development school (PDS) setting, blends the National Board for Professional Teaching Standards' Five Core Propositions, Teacher Leadership Exploratory Consortium Standards, and National Council for Accreditation of Teacher Education PDS Standards to operationalize teacher leadership among four NBCTs. Utilizing multiple case-study research methods, data were gathered using prereflections, weekly e-mail prompts, and end-of-semester interviews. Six common threads focus on NBCTs serving as bridges from preservice to in-service teaching and creating distributed leadership opportunities.

*Keywords:* Accomplished teaching; distributed leadership; mentoring; standards crosswalk; collaboration; distributed leadership

National Board Certified Teachers (NBCTs) represent what accomplished teachers should know and be able to do based on a set of rigorous standards. Through their certification process, NBCTs are developed to be highly effective teachers who have learned how to deprivatize their teaching practice. Their skills and influence on others within the profession constitute a form of leadership. York-Barr and Duke (2004) define teacher leaders as those who influence their colleagues and other members of the school community to improve teaching and learning practices in order to enhance student learning and achievement. Using this definition, NBCTs set themselves apart as leaders due to their completion of a rigorous certification process and successful demonstration of teaching proficiency based on five core propositions (NBPTS, 2016). In support of this process over the past decade, several educational entities have begun to operationalize what it means to be a teacher leader by delineating the knowledge, skills, and competencies teachers need to assume leadership roles in schools (e.g., Teacher Leadership Exploratory Consortium [TLEC] Standards, 2008; The Teacher Leadership Competencies, 2014). Common attributes held by teacher leaders include assuming a wide range of roles to support teachers and students and modeling what it means to be a leader by serving as a formal and informal mentor.

Being a mentor to beginning teachers aligns with the view that "teacher leadership is a powerful strategy to promote effective, collaborative teaching practices…[and] a dynamic teaching profession." (TLEC, 2008, p. 3). In agreement, the National Board for Professional Teaching Standards (NBPTS) advocates for expanding the influence of teacher leaders, including support for beginning teachers. However, being a mentor to a beginning teacher does not only automatically make one a teacher leader. A mentor becomes a teacher leader when he or she positively influences the beginning teacher's practice (Feiman-Nemser, 2012; NBPTS, 2014; York-Barr & Duke, 2004).

In this chapter, beginning teacher is defined as a teacher candidate seeking initial licensure under the guidance of an NBCT serving as a cooperating teacher (referred to by some as mentor teacher, clinical faculty, or school clinical educator). According to the Council for the Accreditation of Educator Preparation (CAEP, 2015), preparing teacher candidates to enter the field entails a structured setting most often referred to as a professional development school (PDS). This setting is similar to teaching hospitals where learning occurs in a hands-on, authentic environment. As defined by CAEP, the university and P-12 school clinical educators work collaboratively to fulfill four elements:

> (1) provide practicum, field experience, clinical practice, and internship experiences; (2) support and enable the

professional development of the educator preparation provider (EPP) and P-12 school clinical educators; (3) support and enable inquiry directed at the improvement of practice; and (4) support and enhance P-12 student achievement. (CAEP, Glossary, p. 19)

When structured in this way, P-12 school clinical educators have the opportunity to serve as mentors to teacher candidates in embedded experiences that occur well before student teaching. In particular, Elements 2–4, provide a unique opportunity for assigned mentors to learn about themselves and to influence teacher candidates. Although implicit, the hands-on, authentic experience provided in a PDS setting allows the mentor to activate teacher leader knowledge, skills, and competencies as identified by the Teacher Leadership Exploratory Consortium (TLEC) and the NBPTS, while working with teacher candidates.

In support of this approach, one large Midwestern university initially operationalized its PDS program with National Council for Accreditation of Teacher Education (NCATE) standards and more recently with CAEP standards. The goal of the PDS program was to create collaborative synergy between the university and P-12 school clinical educators to benefit all children, teacher candidates, school clinical educators, and university personnel. The university subsequently established formal partnerships between the university and selected school districts, allowing teacher candidates extended immersion into the life and work of schools to help them gain greater understanding of diverse learners, develop strong classroom management skills, and grow more confident as teachers. These formal partnerships allow the teacher candidates to take their education courses at their assigned school site (not on campus), join teachers in professional seminars, and get involved in school committees and the local community. In exchange, the university offers support to P-12 school clinical educators by helping to facilitate their professional development needs, which extends to NBCTs serving as classroom teachers and mentors in the PDS setting.

In the past decade, growing attention about teacher leadership has been evidenced by the creation of new standards/competencies as well as the establishment of CAEP. This chapter specifically focuses on NBCTs as bridges for teacher candidates entering the profession through the context of a PDS. First, a literature review with a crosswalk of standards about teacher leadership is presented. Then, a study of NBCTs who completed a clinical practice supervision course and served as mentors to teacher candidates in a PDS is detailed, followed by a description of the findings framed around three sets of standards. The chapter ends with a discussion of the findings and recommendations for practice.

## Literature Review

Since 2008, both national reports and standards related to teacher education programs, specific to clinical preparation and practice have been released. All directly tie in some capacity to PDSs and to the mentoring of teacher candidates. In 2010, for example, NCATE released a report written by the Blue Ribbon Panel on Clinical Preparation and Partnerships for Improved Student Learning. In that report, NCATE specifically called for clinical preparation that allows candidates to be supervised and mentored by effective clinical faculty. Then, in 2012, the Council of Chief State School Officers (CCSSO) report followed suit, but in a more prescriptive manner, by stressing that preparation programs should train all P-12 teachers who serve as mentors in clinical practice, requiring their preparation as part of the program approval process.

Both reports support past studies showing that clinical faculty play a critical role in supporting teacher candidate learning because they provide immediate mentoring and ongoing feedback about practice. Unequivocally, the quality of the field experiences is strongly influenced by various clinical faculty (Boyd, Grossman, Lankford, Loeb, & Wyckoff, 2009; Grossman, 2010; McIntyre & Byrd, 1998; Zimpher & Howey, 2005). Sadly though, teacher education research has shown that lack of preparation for clinical faculty, especially cooperating teachers, has been problematic and chronic (Gall & Acheson, 2010; Ganzer, 2002; Killian & McIntyre, 1987; Killian & Wilkins, 2009; Wilkins-Canter, 1996, 1997).

Collectively, the NCATE and CCSSO reports call for a reexamination of clinical preparation in teacher education, especially since past research has pointed to persistent challenges related to supervision being a weakness in the design of field experiences (American Association of Colleges for Teacher Education, 2010; Zeichner, 2010). Hence, education preparation providers (EPPs) are being called to recognize that high-quality supervision entails a critical link between the university and the school (Council of Chief State School Officers [CCSSO], 2012; National Council for Accreditation of Teacher Education, 2010). The PDS setting lends itself to addressing and studying that critical link. Keep in mind, variation in clinical practice can also come from program type, accredited or nonaccredited (Darling-Hammond, Chung, & Frelow, 2002). For example, accredited programs through CAEP must ensure high-quality field placements, including the expectation to prepare, evaluate, and support clinical faculty (CAEP, 2014).

Because clinical faculty members have such a profound influence on the professional development of teacher candidates, it has been widely advocated that they be carefully selected and trained for their mentoring and supervisory roles (CCSSO, 2012; Killian & McIntyre, 1987; McIntyre & Byrd, 1998; Wang, 2000; Zimpher & Howey, 2005). In order to create this type of collaboration and preparation, Zeichner (2010) proposes creating hybrid opportunities in teacher education programs that bring together school and university-based faculty to enhance learning, which is possible in a PDS setting.

Wenner and Campbell (2017) provide the most recent theoretical and empirical review of teacher leadership literature since the seminal release of aggregated research by York-Barr and Duke (2004). After an initial review of 634 research abstracts, the researchers chose to review a final set of 72 articles in depth. They uncovered four themes to describe the impact of teacher leadership roles on the individuals who assume these roles: (1) stresses/difficulties, (2) changing relationships with peers and administration, (3) increased positive feelings and professional growth, and (4) increased leadership capacity. Wenner and Campbell (2017) also recognize the heightened interest in teacher leadership that has emerged over the past decade through various teacher leadership standards. Because such standards "stimulate dialogue among stakeholders…[as to] what constitutes the knowledge, skills, and competencies that teachers need to assume leadership roles in their schools, districts, and the profession (TLEC, 2008, p. 3)," this study is framed around blending three sets of standards that collectively codify thinking specifically about teacher leadership and indirectly about mentoring in school settings: (1) NBPTS Five Core Propositions, (2) TLEC Standards, and (3) NCATE PDS Standards.

We acknowledge that the NCATE PDS standards do not represent a consensus conception about the use of the more recent CAEP Standard 2, Clinical Partnerships and Practice (2013), or the Nine PDS Essentials proposed by the National Association for Professional Development Schools (2008). Selection of the NCATE PDS standards was purposeful for two reasons: (1) they informed the thinking that emerged from the NCATE 2010 Blue Ribbon Panel on Clinical Preparation and Partnerships for Improved Student Learning and (2) they are more granular than other choices due to being data-driven, developmental, and focused on the unique nature of PDS work.

A crosswalk of the three chosen standards reveals an overlap of five key constructs (see Table 1). First is a commitment to student learning as the central purpose in education. Such commitment encompasses knowledge

Table 1: Crosswalk of Teacher Leadership Standards.

| Key Constructs of Teacher Leadership | NBPTS | TLEC | NCATE |
|---|---|---|---|
| Commitment to student learning | Standard 1 | Domains I, II, and VII | Standard 1 |
| Subject area knowledge, pedagogy, and use of inquiry to impact student learning | Standard 2 | Domain II | Standard 1 |
| Student differences and responding through instruction, assessment, and interpretation of data | Standard 3 | Domains III–V | Standards 3 and 4 |
| Systematic reflection on practice | Standard 4 | Domain III | Standard 2 |
| Collaboration with peers, parents, and community | Standard 5 | Domain VI | Standard 5 |

of students, issues of equity, and teaching the whole child. Second, subject area knowledge, pedagogy, and the use of inquiry are collectively taken into consideration in order to impact student learning. Third, the blended standards value student differences and how to respond to varying student needs through instruction, assessment, and interpretation of data. Fourth, systematic reflection on practice, both alone and with others, provides an effective means for teachers to expand their range of strategies and deepen understanding of their work. Finally, collaboration with others, from peers to parents, enriches the learning community whereby all participants can grow individually and collectively.

NBCTs are highly accomplished teachers who have learned to deprivatize their teaching practice, and hence provide a valuable model for teacher leadership. The remainder of this chapter describes a research study that examined how NBCTs as clinical faculty mentors were prepared through a supervision course as part of a PDS partnership to enhance communication with teacher candidates, using a framework of systematic preparation, delivery of feedback, and collaboration between school and university-based faculty. The focus of the study supports Wenner and Campbell's (2017) call to explore how teacher leadership is enacted (in this case through NBCT mentors as teacher leaders) and how teacher leaders influence improved teaching practice and increased student learning, specifically among beginning teachers.

## Methods

### Participants

Four elementary-level NBCTs agreed to participate in the study: Julia, Pam, Renee, and Debbie (all pseudonyms). All four completed the clinical practice supervision course, which was offered as part of the professional development for cooperating teachers hosting teacher candidates in their respective PDS settings. The course was designed around past research on cooperating teachers' need for systematic preparation in communication skills related to conferencing, feedback, and writing evaluations (Colton & Sparks-Langer, 1993; Grossman, 2010; Hauwiller, Abel, Ausel, & Sparapani, 1988–1989; Killian & Wilkins, 2009; McIntyre & Killian, 1986). All four NBCTs were studied for one academic year as they worked with an assigned teacher candidate.

Collectively, the NBCTs had taught for an average of 14 years and mentored a mean of ten teacher candidates. Utilizing multiple case study research methods (Creswell, 2009; Yin, 2014), particular attention was given to their behaviors as teacher leaders, the mentoring they provided based on the content and skills learned in the clinical practice supervision course, and how they communicated with their respective teacher candidates.

### Clinical Practice Supervision Course

The clinical practice supervision course, TLCI 595, is designed for cooperating teachers and offered to the university's PDS Network. The course is available in the summer for 3-credit hours and focuses on developing (1) an understanding of the three phases of clinical supervision: planning conference, classroom observation, and feedback conference, (2) knowledge and skill in using specific techniques in conferences with teacher candidates,

(3) understanding issues and problems in clinical supervision, peer coaching, and mentoring, and (4) insight into and practice using the skills of systematic observation and analysis of instruction for occasions requiring documentation of practice. The four goals are met using course activities such as discussion, simulation, role playing, and experiential practice with skills inherent in clinical supervision. Differences in curricular and pedagogical philosophies (i.e., models and strategies taught to teacher candidates in the university program to use in field experiences, which could differ from clinical faculty philosophical beliefs) are also addressed, with the expectation that teacher candidates follow district guidelines.

The course involves learning about clinical placements and practices expected by the university as well as observing teacher candidates teaching at different stages in the program. This creates an authentic opportunity for cooperating teachers to better understand teacher development levels, data-driven observation techniques, and the three-part conference cycle. To accomplish this, content is taught during morning sessions and applied in the afternoons as teacher candidates deliver lessons. The overall goal is for skills learned in the course to be transferred and used during the year by cooperating teachers in their respective PDS settings with teacher candidates.

## *Data Collection and Analysis*

Data were gathered from the NBCTs throughout the year using a variety of tools. At the beginning of the semester, the NBCTs were asked to complete a written pre-reflection and share initial perceptions about their interactions with their assigned teacher candidates. Then, during the semester, they were asked to use the Supervisory Effectiveness Continuum (SEC), a formative assessment tool created, validated, and published by Killian and Wilkins (2009) to guide their communication with teacher candidates. The tool is part of the TLCI 595 course content and includes constructs of quality supervision using gradations utilized by the cooperating teacher. Next, to gauge their use of the continuum, the NBCTs received weekly e-mail prompts that read as follows:

> Please take 5 minutes to reply. In thinking about this past week with your teacher candidate, reflect on your interactions with him/her (i.e., kind of conferencing techniques used, when, how often, and type of feedback shared). The Supervisory Effectiveness Continuum is attached for your review.

At the end of the semester, the NBCTs were individually interviewed about their mentoring and teacher leadership as well as their overall perceptions of the clinical practice supervision course. Data collected from the pre-reflections, weekly e-mail prompts, and end-of-semester interviews were used to develop themes using a three-stage process (Corbin & Strauss, 2014; Creswell, 2009). Additionally, triangulation of data was utilized to help confirm the findings and enhance internal validity and strengthen reliability (Merriam, 2009). The rationale for analyzing the data in this way was to develop a deeper understanding about NBCTs as bridges for teacher candidates entering the profession using the three sets of standards.

## Findings

Six themes emerged from the data collected, which related to the influence of the NBCTs as teacher leaders. The study's framework – the blending of NBPTS, TLEC, and NCATE standards – was used to guide theme development.

### *NBCTs are Committed to Advanced Learning*

The first theme indicated that NBCTs are teacher leaders committed to advanced learning (NBPTS 1, TLEC IV, VII, and NCATE 1, 4). In their role as cooperating teachers, the NBCTs displayed a deep commitment to their own students' learning as well as to developing the growth of their assigned teacher candidate. For example, when faced with a struggling teacher candidate, Renee's colleagues suggested that she needed to allow the candidate to come to grips with failure by experiencing it. She replied to them, "It is a really hard thing to do. Unfortunately, my children [in the classroom] have to suffer, and I'm just not willing to do that. I'm the one who is accountable for them, not her." For that reason, Renee chose to intervene during lessons to support and advance the teacher candidate's learning. When Debbie noticed that her teacher candidate was foundering, she too shared a similar approach: "I would step in and team with her when I saw things going south." Pam took a different approach. She spoke of the importance of offering truthful yet encouraging feedback to her struggling teacher candidate: "With your typical student teacher, I think the more pinpointed conversations are better because you can encourage them and provide them with suggestions." These actions evidenced the cooperating teachers' commitment to advance learning for their teacher candidates by supporting them through co-teaching or constructive conversation. The NBCTs modeled best practices on an as-needed basis or by making suggestions to motivate the candidates to stretch themselves.

### NBCTs Display a Command of Content and Pedagogical Knowledge

The second theme to emerge found that NBCTs display a command of content and pedagogical knowledge in their role as teacher leaders (NBPTS 2, TLEC II, III, and NCATE 2). An important aspect of any clinical experience is to assist teacher candidates in making connections between theory and practice. In their role as cooperating teachers, the NBCTs often spoke about ongoing conversations they had with their teacher candidates regarding content and pedagogy. For instance, Pam characterized the importance of complete lesson planning with her teacher candidate by sharing this feedback with her: "Think it all the way through...almost as if you were playing the movie in your mind. What is it going to look like when you're actually standing there giving the lesson?" She wanted her teacher candidate to anticipate potential flaws and consider how differentiation would play out for students. Whereas Renee's teacher candidate was good at designing activities, she struggled to connect to the learning task. To support her teacher candidate in developing better pedagogical knowledge, Renee shared this with her: "Before you start planning anything, you have to think about what you want the kids to learn. That should always be your initial focus." The goal for Renee was to help her teacher candidate reflect and improve her instructional decision-making, while keeping knowledge of students at the center of that thinking process.

When it came to command of content and pedagogical knowledge, some of the NBCTs found that their teacher candidates displayed a false sense of efficacy. Pam, manifesting her understanding of stages of teacher development, noted that at the beginning of student teaching it is typical for teacher candidates to come in very confident. "The first couple of times they attempt to manage the whole class, they realize it is not quite as easy as it superficially appears when someone else is doing it." They also view lesson planning in a similar way. The candidates say they have "gone over" lesson planning in class and understand how it is done. But, when they are actually teaching the lessons planned, they begin to get a more realistic view of the classroom. At this point, the questions the teacher candidate asks begin to change. Their focus moves from the learning to the learners. "[Questions asked by the teacher candidates] become more targeted toward the group of children, like, why is Mason constantly laying on the table and crawling on the floor?" The candidates come to realize that planning cannot take place without first considering the strengths and needs of the students. They learn that one cannot blindly follow a lesson from a teacher's manual or simply link together activities that sound like fun without deliberating on how they support learning goals.

Julia's teacher candidate would constantly go home and research a topic they had discussed, then return the next day offering her new found, elevated understanding of that topic. Julia said, "Man, did I feel uncomfortable when she came back if I felt like she knew more than I did. It was a little condescending at times." This caused Julia to feel that the teacher candidate was trying to show, that as a candidate, she was more knowledgable than a licensed professional. Often teacher candidates try to appear to be more confident than they really are. Pam expanded the conversation about content and pedagogical knowledge efficacy when she described teacher candidates coming into student teaching self-assured that they can do it all. "They come in very confident, then there is a dip, and then they have to build their confidence which is a much more 'realistic' confidence." As cooperating teachers, NBCTs need to be skilled in how to support and respond to teacher candidates when strong efficacy exists. Teacher candidates' sense of efficacy becomes more authentic as they gain skill in classroom management, use of instructional strategies, and promoting student engagement.

### NBCTs Understand How to Direct and Oversee Learning

The third theme revealed that NBCTs are teacher leaders who understand how to direct and oversee learning (NBPTS 3, TLEC III, NCATE 4). Teacher candidates tend to learn one strategy at a time, practicing, so that they can become proficient in its use. Subsequently, they learn how to transfer that strategy to other contexts, which allows them to begin thinking systematically about their work and to apply research-based practices. All of the cooperating teachers took interest in their teacher candidates' progress using this lens of instructional delivery no matter the level of the clinical experience (i.e., early, middle, or capstone). For example, Julia worked with a nontraditional student (i.e., older than 24 years of age) who was in her first clinical experience. When Julia encouraged her to teach a lesson, she repeatedly declined. Then, the university supervisor requested an appointment to see the candidate teach. Julia explained, "She e-mailed me in a panic, so she did teach a lesson." In a similar way, Debbie was concerned that her teacher candidate was quite timid. She stated, "This [timidity] is in her not having completely transitioned from being a student to being a teacher." She was "still on the path of receiving information and doing things when she was asked to do them instead of really stepping up and taking initiative." Pam related that the early days of her teacher candidate's time in the classroom were spent "working the room together. For the first few days, Katelynn was like my aide and then as time went on, I became more of her aide." Use of the gradual release of responsibility model builds in a safety net where the teacher candidate is confident that she can count on an appropriate level of support until she is ready to assume a larger role in the classroom. This approach allows the NBCTs to direct and oversee learning of both the teacher candidate and the students in the classroom.

Unlike the other three NBCTs, Renee was anxious because her student teacher had too much on her plate and was not devoting herself faithfully to her clinical experience. She told her teacher candidate, "You have to make it a priority for you. This is your time to shine and prove what you can do." In her role as cooperating teacher, Renee was direct in overseeing the growth of her teacher candidate by placing herself in the position to be a truth speaker. She communicated the professional expectations of what it means to be a teacher. Sadly, her teacher candidate continued to struggle. In cases where the teacher candidate does not grow, the cooperating teacher and university supervisor create a context where the teacher candidate can recognize, accept, and learn from her mistakes. In this study, NBCTs were cognizant of the importance of guiding, coaching, and providing opportunities for reflection to assist teacher candidates in their growth.

### *NBCTs Seek Participation in Learning Communities*

The fourth theme indicated that NBCTs are teacher leaders who seek participation in learning communities (NBPTS 5, TLEC I, and NCATE 3). Teachers are part of many different communities within their schools (e.g., grade level teams, professional learning communities, and content area committees). Belonging to a learning community was best exemplified when Renee spoke of the isolation that confronts educators and how that can affect the teacher candidate-cooperating teacher relationship. "It is nice to have somebody else in the room to talk to, that you tend to do a lot of personal and professional talking with." According to the NBCTs, the relationship between the cooperating teacher and teacher candidate is both important and opportune. Pam explained the relationship in this way: "You're supposed to be their guide, the next teacher for them, moving them along and helping them perfect their craft before they end up in a classroom of their own." This is a weighty responsibility. Given cooperating teachers receive little formal preparation for the role of school-based teacher educator, they would benefit from increased interaction and support in how to mentor teacher candidates. For example, Debbie suggested that cooperating teachers would benefit from taking the supervision class and discussing issues that relate to being cooperating teachers. "I see those as possibilities, but I don't know to what extent stuff like that is bound to our contract. It becomes an issue of time and things that relate to these responsibilities." By its very nature, the PDS setting lends itself to a collaborative school–university community where cooperating teachers can be supported in learning mentoring strategies that promote effective teaching practices. Protected spaces need to be given to cooperating teachers to participate in professional learning communities focused on developing teacher candidates.

### *NBCTs are Reflective and Grow their own Practice*

The fifth theme revealed that NBCTs are teacher leaders who are reflective and grow their own practice (NBPTS 4, TLEC III, and NCATE 4). In this study, the cooperating teachers reflected on how they supported their teacher candidates when using the SEC. Debbie described the experience: "I believe that one of my responsibilities is to constantly seek input that would help me [be a better mentor]." She appreciated having the supervisory tool because, "it helps me stay focused on the things I need to." Renee also expressed that the tool helped her focus on professional talk. "I did actually talk to [my teacher candidate] in detail about anything that had to do with teaching." Moreover, Renee felt the tool helped her articulate "why" questions with her teacher candidate. Pam, who prized oral feedback over written feedback, claimed, "The piece that is strongest is that daily conversation both before they teach and in the middle of the day when changes can still be made." In their role as cooperating teachers, the NBCTs were themselves reflective about their use of the SEC and how it assisted them in providing detailed feedback with their teacher candidates. The chance to grow their practice as mentors using the continuum appeared to be valued.

### *NBCTs are Cognizant of and Skilled in Delivering Feedback*

The sixth and final theme is woven throughout the five previous themes: NBCTs are teacher leaders who are cognizant of and skilled in delivering feedback. The coaching and support of the teacher candidates by the four NBCTs could not have been possible without regular, effective communication. More specifically, the construct of communication emerged by examining the NBCTs' exchanges, and it was operationalized in this way: (1) evidence of brief and in-depth feedback, (2) evidence of oral and written feedback, (3) evidence of sustained feedback over the field experience, (4) feedback supported by multiple, specific examples, (5) emphasis on teacher candidate growth and independence, (6) communication with the teacher candidate when problems arose, and (7) feedback and questions that encourage reflection. The fact that these NBCTs were teacher leaders who sought a graduate course on supervision and mentoring might explain their heightened awareness of, and skill in, delivering feedback. They were aware of the teacher candidates' development levels such as knowing they would need help with command of content and pedagogical knowledge, reflecting on experiences to grow their practice, and taking advantage of being part of a learning community. To make that possible, their support was facilitated by sustained delivery of feedback.

## Discussion

PDSs are designed to engage school-based educators in their own professional growth while taking on more meaningful roles as teacher leaders in support of the next generation of teachers. This study has identified the role and influence NBCTs have as mentors in building a seamless transition from preservice to in-service teaching. That is, NBCTs working in a PDS setting can serve as a bridge from preservice to in-service teaching because of their mentoring and communication skills. As teacher leaders, NBCTs in their role as cooperating teachers are well positioned to cultivate distributed leadership where collaboration, feedback, and reflection is modeled and encouraged. Operationally defined, distributed leadership entails university and P-12 school clinical educators who are collaboratively responsible for teacher candidates not only when they are preparing to be teachers but also as they enter the profession. This vision of distributed leadership extends Spillane's (2005) original definition by focusing on how collaborative partnerships like those found in PDSs are designed and communicated to facilitate a bridge of leadership between universities and P-12 school clinical educators. In order to build distributed leadership within a PDS setting, NBCTs as both mentors and teacher leaders have the ability to bridge the needs of teacher candidates in five actionable ways.

First, NBCTs in PDS settings can provide input in shaping the coursework for teacher candidates. For instance, the program of study should include content-specific pedagogical courses allowing for application of content knowledge through critical thinking, problem solving, and analytical tasks. This will prepare teacher candidates for the challenges in the classroom. Collaboration between university-based teacher educators and school-based NBCTs would determine how coursework and fieldwork could coordinate. Ideally, this coursework should be aligned with integrated, supervised fieldwork that offers teacher candidates increasingly complex teaching structures as they progress through the education program. Teacher candidates need to be exposed to coursework that will help them succeed with high-need students who would benefit from differentiation and hands-on learning. Pre-service teachers need to become proficient in managing student learning in a variety of classroom structures and learn basic work skills such as planning and time management. NBCTs, based on their experience with teacher candidates, could collaborate with university teacher educators to plan simulations, classroom-based cases, student work protocols, data analysis exercises, laboratory-based experiences, and incorporation of technology that support teacher candidates' learning. Additionally, they could identify or create tools that would assist the teacher candidate in observing the cooperating teacher so as to identify best practices.

Second, EPPs can use the Architecture of Accomplished Teaching (AAT) (National Board for Professional Teaching Standards [NBPTS], 2005) as the model for planning coursework. Sprinkled throughout the findings of this study were grains of how accomplished teachers plan for instruction. As one example, Pam and Renee found that their teacher candidates struggled with setting goals and writing objectives for lessons that take into account students' needs. The AAT begins with the knowledge of and assessment of students. It tasks the teacher to determine the strengths and range of student need and identify goals for the entry point into a sequence of lessons along with meaningful supports for the class, groups, and individuals. The teacher then implements planned instruction and evaluates student learning (formative, summative, and student self-assessment). Then, useful feedback can extend student learning by making them cognizant of correcting errors and debunking misconceptions. Finally, the teacher reflects on the effectiveness of the instruction, including how it met the needs of students before beginning the cycle again. Case in point, many teacher candidates complete a performance assessment as a capstone for licensure. Having the AAT as the planning model teacher candidates work with throughout their preparation would create greater depth of experience to draw upon as teacher candidates construct their culminating portfolios. The AAT is appropriate for any content area, allowing teacher candidates to focus on content by using a familiar process.

Third, NBCTs can mentor teacher candidates to construct new knowledge about the process of teaching and learning, content, and pedagogy. For example, NBCTs can lead teacher candidates toward making their own professional decisions by asking appropriate questions and encouraging reflection. The NBCTs in this study mentored in a number of ways. Some used modeling as a means to expose teacher candidates to new knowledge. Others used a variety of co-teaching models followed by reflective questioning. All four NBCTs worked to build trusting relationships with their teacher candidates so that they could have meaningful conversations about teaching and learning. They used multiple measures to identify effective evidence-based teaching and successful student learning. Also, the NBCTs worked with teacher candidates to identify specific needs for growth and planned how to address those needs with the goal of developing more effective teaching strategies focused on increased student learning.

Fourth, NBCTs as mentors can collaborate with other school professionals such as content area specialists and instructional coaches to support teacher candidates in learning how to work within a professional community. Teacher candidates also can be encouraged and coached on how to build positive professional relationships with parents, colleagues, and other school professionals to best support student learning.

Fifth, NBCTs and university-based teacher educators should work together to help teacher candidates recognize the importance of developing knowledge about students in order to drive instruction. For example, NBCTs can assist teacher candidates in acquiring knowledge about students as learners and as individuals through use of surveys, interviews, and data analysis. Both Renee's and Pam's teacher candidates would have benefited from greater focus on learning about students' strengths and needs. Teacher candidates need to understand the expected growth and development for an age group, how to use data from nationally normed tests like Measure of Academic Progress, and how formative assessment data can be a factor in shaping instructional design. The PDS setting can provide opportunities for teacher leadership and collaboration to intertwine, thereby leading to stronger partnerships between teacher preparation programs and PK-12 schools. The use of distributed leadership strengthens this opportunity. For instance, additional opportunities for networking, professional development seminars, and discussions about needed instructional and assessment skills become possible. Of course, this is all dependent on allowing partnerships to evolve over time with input from both parties that is valued and encouraged. Also, relational trust among all PDS educators (i.e., both university and PK-12) is critical to building and sustaining a bridge to support the teacher pipeline and the development of teacher leaders. Critical constructs (or bridge beams) that emerge from such a setting include communication, teamwork, empowerment, goal setting, and respect for others within the profession and for the profession.

Furthermore, viewing the study's findings through the blended lens of NBPTS, TLEC, and PDS gave insight to essential leadership qualities such as ongoing teacher reflection, developing into a contributory member of the learning community, seeking collaborative conversations, and enhancing one's role and responsibilities as a teacher leader. In doing so, NBCTs in PDS settings can augment the bridge and create distributed leadership when there is a well-defined and purposeful school–university community. However, policy changes at both the school and university levels are needed that specifically speak to this, along with more definitive language in the aforementioned professional education standards. Acknowledging teacher leaders for the curricular and pedagogical role they play at both the preservice and in-service levels would make their roles and influence more transparent. Finally, recognition by national and state accrediting bodies, as well as superintendents and principals as to the importance of distributed leadership would recognize NBCTs and the teacher leader roles they bring to the profession, developing a stronger bridge between preservice and in-service teaching within PDS settings.

## Conclusion

Teacher preparation must be shared responsibility between P-12 and higher education. The university alone cannot prepare teachers without understanding the needs of the schools where their graduates will work, nor can schools expect that new teachers will be ready from the start unless the university has an understanding of what "ready from the start" looks like. Each time a cooperating teacher supports a candidate on the bridge from being a student to becoming a novice teacher, a bit of that person's practice is a legacy to the next generation of educators. Accomplished teachers need to be willing to make this investment in the next generation of teachers. PK-12 schools need to offer support along with structures that allow them to lead from the classroom. NBCTs, through their board certification process, are highly accomplished teachers who have learned how to deprivatize their practice. This can lead to increased collaboration and more dialogue with their peers. Universities need to be willing to be open to accepting their input on matters of teacher education. To provide for well-prepared teacher candidates, stakeholders should shape policy that would allow for NBCTs and university-based teacher educators to design curriculum for cooperating teachers rooted in the Five Core Propositions (NBPTS, 2016). It would be valuable to create hybrid roles for NBCTs that would allow them to continue to have direct impact on students for part of the day and focus their skills on teacher education, mentoring, teacher leadership, and coaching for the remainder of the day. When P-12 and higher education come together to support future teachers (i.e., strengthen the bridge), this sets a tone of mutual respect with a shared vision that values student learning as the central focus.

## References

American Association of Colleges for Teacher Education. (2010). *Reforming teacher preparation: The critical clinical component*. Washington, DC: American Association of Colleges for Teacher Education.

Boyd, D. J., Grossman, P. L., Lankford, H., Loeb, S., & Wyckoff, J. (2009). Teacher preparation and student achievement. *Educational Evaluation and Policy Analysis, 31*(4), 416–440.

Colton, A. B., & Sparks-Langer, G. M. (1993). A conceptual framework to guide the development of teacher reflection and decision making. *Journal of Teacher Education, 44*(1), 45–54.

Corbin, J., & Strauss, A. (2014). *Basics of qualitative research: Techniques and procedures for developing grounded theory* (3rd ed.). Thousand Oaks, CA: Sage Publications.

Council for the Accreditation of Educator Preparation. (2013). *CAEP standards*. Washington DC: Author.

Council for the Accreditation of Educator Preparation. (2014). *Standards*. Retrieved from http://caepnet.org/standards/

Council for the Accreditation of Educator Preparation. (2015). *CAEP accreditation standards*. Washington DC: Author.

Council for the Accreditation of Educator Preparation. (2015). *Glossary*. Retrieved from http://www.caepnet.org/glossary?letter=P

Council of Chief State School Officers. (2012). *Our responsibility, our promise: Transforming educator preparation and entry into the profession*. Washington, DC: Author.

Creswell, J. W. (2009). *Research design: Qualitative, quantitative, and mixed methods approaches* (3rd ed.). Thousand Oaks, CA: Sage.

Darling-Hammond, L., Chung, R., & Frelow, F. (2002). Variation in teacher preparation: How well do different pathways prepare teachers to teach? *Journal of Teacher Education, 53*(4), 286–302.

Feiman-Nemser, S. (2012). Beyond solo teaching. *Educational Leadership, 69*(8), 10–16.

Gall, M., & Acheson, K. (2010). *Clinical supervision and teacher development: Pre-service and in-service applications* (6th ed.). New York, NY: John Wiley & Sons, Inc.

Ganzer, T. (2002). How teachers compare the roles of cooperating teacher and mentor. *Educational Forum, 66*(4), 380–385.

Grossman, P. (2010). *Learning to practice: The design of clinical experience in teacher preparation.* Policy brief. Washington, DC: Partnership for Teacher Quality, National Education Association and American Association of Colleges for Teacher Education.

Hauwiller, J., Abel, F., Ausel, D., & Sparapani, E. (1988-1989). Enhancing the effectiveness of cooperating teachers, *Action in Teacher Education, 10*(4), 42–46.

Killian, J., & McIntyre, J. (1987). The influence of supervisory training for cooperating teachers on pre-service teachers' development during early field experiences. *Journal of Education Research, 80*(5), 277–282.

Killian, J., & Wilkins, E. (2009). Characteristics of highly effective cooperating teachers: A study of their backgrounds and preparation. *Action in Teacher Education, 30*(4), 67–83.

McIntyre, D. J., & Byrd, D. M. (1998). Supervision in teacher education. In G. R. Firth & E. Pajak (Eds.), *Handbook of research on school supervision* (pp. 409–427). New York, NY: McMillan.

McIntyre, D. J., & Killian, J. E. (1986). Students' interactions with pupils and cooperating teachers in early field experiences. *Teacher Educator, 22*(2), 2–9.

Merriam, S. (2009). *Qualitative research: A guide to design and implementation.* New York, NY: John Wiley & Sons, Inc.

National Association for Professional Development Schools. (2008). *What it means to be a professional development school.* Waco, TX: Author.

National Board for Professional Teaching Standards. (2005). *Architecture of accomplished teaching.* Retrieved from https://nbrc.illinoisstate.edu/downloads/nbrc/AbouttheNBPTSDocuments.pdf

National Board for Professional Teaching Standards. (2014). *The Teacher Leader Competencies.* Retrieved from http://www.nbpts.org/sites/default/files/teacher_leadership_competencies_final.pdf

National Board for Professional Teaching Standards. (2016). *What teachers should know and be able to do.* Arlington, VA. Retrieved from http://www.nbpts.org/sites/default/files/what_teachers_should_know.pdf

National Council for Accreditation of Teacher Education. (2001). *Standards for professional development schools.* Washington, DC. Retrieved from http://www.ncate.org/Accreditation/AllAccreditationResources/ProfessionalDevelopmentSchools/PDSStandards/tabid/499/Default.aspx

National Council for Accreditation of Teacher Education. (2010). *Transforming teacher education through clinical practice: Report of the blue ribbon panel on clinical preparation and partnerships for improved student learning.* Washington, DC: Author.

Spillane, J. P. (2005). Distributed leadership. *The Educational Forum, 69*(2), 143–150.

Teacher Leadership Exploratory Consortium. (2008). *Teacher leader standards.* Retrieved from http://teacherleaderstandards.org/downloads/TLS_Brochure.pdf

Wang, J. (2000). Contexts of mentoring and opportunities for learning to teach: A comparative study of mentoring practice. *Teaching and Teacher Education, 17*, 51–73.

Wenner, J. A., & Campbell, T. (2017). The theoretical and empirical basis of teacher leadership: A review of literature. *Review of Educational Research, 87*(1), 134–171.

Wilkins-Canter, E. A. (1997). Providing effective cooperating teacher feedback. In D. J. McIntyre & D. M. Byrd (Eds.), *Preparing tomorrow's teachers: The field experience. Teacher Education Yearbook IV* (pp. 169–177). Thousand Oaks, CA: Corwin Press.

Wilkins-Canter, E. A. (1997). The nature and effectiveness of feedback given by cooperating teachers to student teachers. *Teacher Educator, 32*(4), 235–250.

Yin, R. (2014). *Case study research: Design and methods* (5th ed.). Los Angeles, CA: Sage.

York-Barr, J., & Duke, K. (2004). What do we know about teacher leadership? Findings from two decades of scholarship. *Review of Educational Research, 74*(3), 255–316.

Zeichner, K. (2010). Rethinking the connections between campus courses and field experiences in college- and university-based teacher education. *Journal of Teacher Education, 61*(1–2), 89–99.

Zimpher, N. L., & Howey, K. R. (2005). The politics of partnerships for teacher education redesign and school renewal. *Journal of Teacher Education, 56*(3), 46–56.

Chapter 11

# Teacher Leader Reflections: Definitions, Structures, and Cultures that Promote Teacher Leadership

## Abstract

This chapter features four personal reflections written by practicing teacher leaders from Indiana, Connecticut, Nevada, and New Jersey. The first two reflections describe the transition from teacher to teacher leader through active engagement in leadership roles related to teacher preparation, internships, and field experiences. The third reflection compares teaching in a professional development school (PDS) to teaching at a non-PDS site; and the fourth reflection considers the many benefits of teaching in a PDS, including the support of a professor in residence. The chapter concludes with five questions for discussion and reflection.

*Keywords:* Teacher leadership; teacher preparation; internship; host teacher; TOTAL; charter school; school–university partnership; professional development school; professor-in-residence

## Total Teacher Leaders

*Ashley Bennett*

TOTAL teaching is a program implemented by Indiana State University in Terre Haute, Indiana. This professional preparation experience occurs, most times, in the first semester of a preservice teacher's senior year. It immediately precedes a student teaching placement. In this endeavor, preservice teachers are immersed in schools for entire days and help their host teachers with tasks important and vital for becoming productive teachers. TOTAL interns also teach each general education subject for a week, along with performing a running record, creating a bulletin board of student work, communicating with parents, observing special area teachers, and attending after-school meetings and activities. Through this journey, TOTAL interns learn how to deal with a multitude of learning styles and common challenges that teachers face every day. This is an all encompassing experience that provides real-life preparation that can only be found in a classroom day to day.

My involvement with the TOTAL program is the role of a host teacher at Davis Park Elementary School in Terre Haute, Indiana. Our school is a Title I school with a large special needs population. Our demographic is high poverty as well. As many educators know, these factors create special challenges for teachers. However, schools like mine are also areas where some of the most rewarding work is done.

At this point in time, I have had six TOTAL interns come into my classroom. Each one has arrived timid and quiet. The first day has always been very eye opening and overwhelming for these students as they witness what a real classroom is like from bell to bell, instead of just a few hours at a time. They see and become a part of behavior management, differentiation, scheduling, grading, testing, and different teaching styles; but most of all, they build relationships and connections with students.

TOTAL is a time where preservice teachers get the chance to handle an entire classroom with the support of their host teacher. I have personally seen TOTAL interns struggle, reflect, and then grow as young professionals. As with many preservice teachers entering a classroom for the first time, each one struggles with behavior and time management. I make it a goal to have students model their behavior plan after my own. I believe in giving clear, concise rules and being extremely consistent with consequences and rewards. This way, my students know what to expect each day. This approach also makes it easier for beginning teachers to learn to set a plan in place. TOTAL interns often have trouble accepting that students may get angry with them when given a consequence. My first TOTAL intern refused to reprimand students, so I gave her an assignment. That day, she was to give out one consequence. She was very uncomfortable at first, but soon learned that discipline is a necessary part of classroom teaching. She then became a much more effective teacher.

In this program, host teachers are required to conference weekly with the TOTAL interns. In my classroom, this is a daily practice. We talk about what went well and what could be improved, and then brainstorm ideas to make the needed changes. This process has also helped me to reflect on myself as a classroom teacher. I have to explain to an intern exactly why I am teaching a subject in a specific way. This forces me to decide whether I am truly being effective. As most people do, the TOTAL interns tend to learn much more from their missteps than from their successes. My job as their host teacher is to help them recognize both their achievements and their weaknesses. This prepares them for life not only as a teacher, but also as a teacher leader.

As a teacher leader myself, I believe that I must teach my TOTAL interns what it means to be a good leader. First, they must learn to be flexible. No two days in teaching are alike. Second, they must always look ahead. Becoming consumed with the present and not looking at the bigger picture risks that end goals will not be met. Third, they must be able to critique themselves honestly and address issues and shortcomings promptly. Accepting that there is always more work to be done is difficult, but necessary. By teaching and modeling these leadership principles, each of my TOTAL interns has become a confident and professional teacher. It has been a truly wonderful learning experience for not only the TOTAL interns, but for me as well.

## Quiet Opportunity

*P. Erin Lichtenstein*

Shhhhhh...can you hear that? Listen carefully and you will hear a very quiet knocking. You might not recognize it at first, and it might be difficult to locate. Don't give up, because it's there and once you find it, you will realize that what you have been hearing and searching for is OPPORTUNITY! Teaching often lacks leadership opportunities – other than the thirty plus hours a week a teacher spends leading a group of bright-eyed, open-minded sponges, or the rare opportunities to lead a committee or department. Teachers have an enormous charge, yet they are rarely seen as professionals with goals and ambitions beyond the classroom door.

While obtaining my graduate degree at Harvard University's School of Education, my eyes were opened to the idea of teachers as leaders and the "professionalization" of teaching. Professional development school (PDS) relationships can have a significant impact on teachers' work in the classroom. More importantly, they can quench the thirst that many teachers have to pursue leadership positions. Such is the case at my small, independent pre-kindergarten through eighth grade charter school in Norwalk, Connecticut.

Nearly five years ago, Side by Side (SBS) Charter School partnered with Quinnipiac University in Connecticut to build upon a common mission to prepare our students for a world where social justice is more important than ever. At the time, neither the university nor SBS could imagine the auxiliary benefits that this partnership would afford students and staff. We simply thought we were strengthening our mission and staying true to our charter, which promises two qualified adults in every classroom, and to support developing teachers. Little did we know of the breath of fresh air that would blow through our corridors with the arrival of these young, innovative educators. Little did we know how their fresh perspectives would invigorate our own veteran practices. Little did we know that we would become – and help create – LEADERS.

Over the course of this collaboration, our PDS relationship has evolved. It began as a traditional student teaching model: a 10-week cycle during which cooperating teachers would gradually release to developing teachers the responsibilities of planning and preparing lessons, instructing and assessing learning, and making data-driven decisions. This new partnership created a residency model that we now hope will inspire other teacher preparation programs. Instead of the traditional 10-week student teaching model, our residents are placed in home-base classrooms and submersed in the day-to-day function of the classroom from the first day of school until the last day of school, five days a week, six hours a day. In addition to the positive impact on student learning due to the consistency of two qualified adults in each classroom, the residents have the unique opportunity to collaborate and grow in a way that may not be afforded to student teachers in more traditional models. Reciprocally, SBS's veteran teachers are now collaborating and co-teaching in a way that has revitalized our own practices! The co-teaching model encourages cooperating teachers to share the task of using data to drive instructional decisions, it requires a collaborative process that enables instruction to meet the unique needs of all learners, and it empowers a consistent reflective practice that hones aspiring teachers' developing expertise. As a result, our residents are more prepared, more confident, and more seasoned on the practical nature of teaching and learning.

Just like this partnership, my role as liaison for this program has evolved. In addition to my daily obligation to my third grade students,

I am responsible for the oversight of our residents. I have developed a model that allows residents to become submersed in their home base, while providing the opportunity to make rounds into other classrooms to observe the expertise of our school's seasoned teaching staff. In addition, the residents are offered a safe venue to practice the skills that will (hopefully) be required of them when they enter the workforce. Specifically, residents are placed in a co-teaching classroom where they are offered specific and reflective feedback from colleagues. Using a professional growth model, residents are not only able to observe and be observed but also part of a team that uses feedback to set professional growth goals. Through this process, our residents not only grow philosophically and pedagogically, they also grow professionally, developing a sense of leadership that will resonate with them and follow them throughout their careers.

Personally, the partnership has strengthened my leadership skills by allowing me to reach for goals beyond the classroom. Acting as the liaison between university and school enables me to hone my own administrative skill set and provides me with experiences relative to my own professional aspirations. I have enhanced my ability to negotiate scheduling and coverage, developed my evaluation practices, and worked as a coach for teams of residents and cooperating teachers. Equally important, this opportunity has forced me to refine my own time management and organizational skills. As a mother of two young boys, a classroom teacher, and a PDS liaison, I rely on support systems that I have built to do each job well. I dedicate one night each week to working late in an effort to ensure lessons are planned and prepared, and on these late nights, I schedule weekly meetings with residents to check in and reflect on problems of practice. I also try to take a minimal amount of work home other days of the week so that when I am home I am able to dedicate 100% of myself to my family. My days are packed and my weeks are full, but with careful planning and scheduling, I manage to fulfill all of my obligations with confidence, diligence, and grace.

This partnership has not just had an impact on the leadership potential for everyone involved, it has shifted the paradigm of who is teaching whom. The partnership has offered my colleagues and me an opportunity to lead tenured university faculty in developing an understanding of the evolving world of public education. Practitioners are now teaching theorists, teachers are now researchers, and novices are supporting the growth of veterans. What started as a quiet knock at the door is now a robust opportunity that is appreciated by both communities. For teachers like me, being part of a PDS is being part of a team of leaders.

## Bridges

*Suzanna Nelson*

When I think about preservice teacher education, I think of islands forming. Each new classroom experience forms an island of knowledge in a sea of uncertainty. As teaching and learning experiences occur, those islands continue to grow, but in isolation. Once teachers begin their first year of stand-alone teaching, they start to revisit those islands of knowledge and experience, but must tread water as they do. Wouldn't it be much easier if, instead of treading water, new teachers had bridges?

As a relatively new teacher who has taught at both a PDS and in a traditional school, I am able to share my experiences with both models. I began my teaching career at John C. Fremont Professional Development Middle School in Las Vegas, Nevada, which is where I concluded my student teaching experience through a partnership with the University of Nevada, Las Vegas (UNLV). I completed my second year of teaching at a school without a PDS model. While at the traditional school, I constantly felt as if I were treading water to survive. I desperately missed the bridges of community, support, and empowerment that I had at Fremont.

Unlike most new teachers, I had a sense of calm in the days leading up to my first year of teaching. Since I was hired at the PDS where I had completed my student teaching, I knew I was not going into the stormy waters alone; I had bridges. I had an established relationship with my mentor who would be there to answer any questions I had. I knew the layout of the building and where the copy room was. I knew those who would go out of their way to help me, and those who would not. I knew the two UNLV cohort members who were hired along with me in addition to several other staff members. I knew the principal, the dean, the custodians, the office manager, the registrar, and the campus monitor. All of these bridges lifted me out of the water and allowed me to focus on the most important part of teaching: my students.

The constant support I received at Fremont allowed me to succeed, particularly in regard to leadership. I am a reserved person who generally does not like to lead, but all of the bridges of support at Fremont invigorated me with a sense of empowerment that I used to seek out leadership opportunities. Fremont practices teaming, and I willingly took on the role of team captain. While many of the peers whom I graduated with were struggling to stay afloat, I was able to navigate my first year of teaching and leadership with relative ease while also beginning my master's program in curriculum, instruction, and assessment.

Unfortunately, toward the end of my first year I was informed that because of projected student enrollment and funding, I would be involuntarily transferred for the next school year. I was absolutely crushed. It felt like I was being thrown overboard into the sea of uncertainty. Although upset, I was determined to go into my second year of teaching with a positive attitude. I realized I still had students to teach and I wanted to do right by them, no matter where I wound up.

The school where I was placed was not a PDS, and I felt a drastic difference from day one. The professional development program at Fremont creates a sense of unity that cannot be duplicated at a non-PDS school. Nearly one-third of Fremont's teachers are PDS graduates who completed their student teaching right at Fremont. Teachers who normally would have nothing in common have this commonality that unites them. Many of the teachers took the same college courses, were taught by the same professors, and worked with the same mentor teachers. This bridge of community is invaluable.

Not only did I lose that sense of community at the non-PDS school, but I also lost the bridges of support that helped me succeed during my first year. Because of the constant flow of preservice teachers and the Fremont staff's experience working with them, I felt an incredible amount of support all throughout my first year. While at the non-PDS school, however, I felt a lack of support. That is not to speak poorly of the school itself because they did put forth effort. I just believe their lack of experience working with new teachers is to blame.

The sense of empowerment and leadership that I felt as a first-year teacher at Fremont vanished during my second year of teaching. I lost all of those important connections that held me above water. At my new school I did not have those bridges of community or support, which led to a loss in self-confidence. While at Fremont, I worked through my master's program with ease but struggled greatly to complete the coursework at my new school. I was able to complete my degree, but the process was much more difficult without the assistance that I enjoyed previously. I did not seek out leadership opportunities because I was working so hard just to keep my head above water.

At the end of my second year, a teaching position opened up at Fremont for the next school year. I immediately applied and was welcomed back with open arms. Now, as I approach the end of my third year as a teacher, I can't help but look back on my experiences with gratitude. As a first-year teacher, I knew Fremont was special because of the PDS program in place, but I had no basis of comparison. Now that I have the ability to compare, I truly understand how beneficial the PDS model is for creating successful, happy teacher leaders. Ralph Ellison once said, "Education is all a matter of building bridges." I could not agree more!

## The Best PDS Perk

*Azaria Cunningham*

Paterson Public Schools in Paterson, New Jersey, is part of the William Paterson University (WPU) PDS Network. At the beginning of my educational journey, I did not understand what the title professional PDS encompassed or truly meant. Now, after teaching at a PDS in the district for four years, I can clearly pinpoint major advantages. Paterson Public Schools and WPU have created a partnership that provides my school with many perks. The best perk is our professor in residence (PIR).

A PIR is a professor employed at a university who travels to the public school to provide clinical interns, instructional support, and free resources. My school's PIR is beyond amazing. Each year that I have taught, I have felt the teaching profession becoming harder due to the demands not only from the state, but also from the administration. My PIR provides resources for lessons, teaching techniques, and a positive attitude that outshines the gloomy demands. For instance, the PIR traveled across several classes within my building and provided fun interactive ways to increase student engagement. In my bilingual class, my students were having difficulty with the states of matter. As a result, the PIR and the students created a musical rhythm that allowed students to kinesthetically memorize the scientific content. Observing my students grasp the concept and their love for learning changed my perception on education. I truly experienced an aha! moment when my students not only learned the content but also how to apply it to real-world tasks. Having this interactive moment with a PIR gave my students the opportunity to have an authentic learning experience. The students were highly engaged in their own learning.

The relationship between my PIR and myself has allowed me the opportunity to grow within my building as a teacher leader. Our partnership provides teachers with free educational workshops. Other surrounding schools must pay for the workshops that our schools receive for free. There are also opportunities to facilitate workshops through the university and to provide teachers with year-round support. For example, my colleagues and I conducted a paid professional development workshop through the university on interactive note-booking. This type of implementation provides teachers with differentiated instructional strategies and a portfolio to track students' progress. Participating in these opportunities has paid off in two specific ways. First, when my school principal sent teachers to summer conferences and needed teachers to conduct school-based professional development, I was chosen based on my PIR's recommendation. If I had not been afforded the opportunities to present at the university level, I believe I would not have been prepared to present to my colleagues. Second, when a few colleagues and I realized we had become stagnant in our profession, we began looking at graduate programs to further our education. Our PIR took notice and provided information to fuel the fire for our learning. Then, she initiated a meeting between the director of the WPU educational leadership program and us. As a result, I am now a graduate of WPU's Higher Education Administration master's program and a member of the American Association of Colleges for Teacher Education Holmes Master's Program! These types of teacher leadership experiences have transformed my thinking and inspired me to develop my teaching craft and share my expertise with others in the field.

After attending a few conferences, I realized that this type of PDS relationship and institutional structure does not exist everywhere. Our PIR program allows continued school–university communication, builds relationships, and offers opportunities for growth, both professionally and personally. I believe it is important to formulate relationships between schools and educational institutions. Our PIR is more than a colleague within our building. She is an inspiration to all staff members who value the worth of children. The opportunities that are provided through the PIR model help develop and strengthen our educational community.

## Questions For Further Reflection

*Jana Hunzicker*

1. In the first two reflections, Ashley and Erin explore school–university partnerships from the perspectives of a classroom host teacher and a resident program liaison. Both teacher leaders describe how they contribute significantly to the preparation of preservice teachers in the schools where they teach. To what degree are similar teacher leadership opportunities available at schools not partnered with a university? In your opinion,

what structural or cultural advantages do school–university partnerships offer in terms of preservice teacher preparation?
2. In "Quiet Opportunity," Erin wrote, "Teachers have an enormous charge, yet they are rarely seen as professionals with goals and ambitions beyond the classroom door." To what degree is serving beyond one's classroom a defining characteristic of teacher leadership? Can a teacher whose work is confined to his or her classroom be considered a teacher leader? Why or why not?
3. Suzanna uses a bridge metaphor to illustrate how PDSs provide a comprehensive support system for early career teachers, whereas other schools may require new teachers to tread water. Can you identify with this sink-or-swim approach to teaching? In schools where structures and supports for new teachers are limited, what can teacher leaders do to build bridges of community, support, and empowerment?
4. In the third and fourth reflections, early career teachers Suzanna and Azaria reflect on the advantages of teaching in a PDS, yet in most states PDSs remain special rather than commonplace. Why do you think there are not more PDSs across the United States? What role might teacher leaders play in initiating and promoting PDS relationships and other school–university partnerships?
5. Based on the reflections and chapters in this section, what are some definitions, structures, and cultures that can promote teacher leadership in PDSs and other school–university partnerships? Considering your first-hand experiences and prior knowledge on the topic, what other definitions, structures, and cultures can you add?

Chapter 12

# Definitions, Structures, and Cultures that Promote Teacher Leadership: Making Sense of Section Two

*Michael N. Cosenza*

### Abstract

This chapter synthesizes Chapters 8–11, and discusses various definitions, structures, and cultures of teacher leadership. It also describes how the professional development school model supports various teacher leader roles, responsibilities, and initiatives, including liaisons-in-residence, professional learning communities, learning walks, co-teaching, and mentoring. Recognizing that even amidst rich and authentic examples, a common definition for teacher leadership still does not emerge, the chapter concludes on the note that by not declaring a one-size-fits-all definition of teacher leadership, the concept remains open to various potential leadership roles and responsibilities.

*Keywords:* Teacher leadership; professional development school; liaison-in-residence; professional learning communities; learning walks; co-teaching; National Board Certified Teachers; mentoring; collaboration

Many teachers and administrators in schools view teacher leadership through the lens of specific and formal roles that are officially appointed, elected, or assigned in some manner. Some examples of this are when a teacher is elected department chair, grade level representative, or union leader by his or her peers. These types of positions can also be appointed by an administrator, further clarifying that the role is formal. Though there is no doubt that these are positions of leadership, teacher leadership is not restricted to these roles. In fact, we discover through this book and beyond that teacher leadership can also emerge informally in various ways.

## Understanding Teacher Leadership

The term teacher leadership is one that is challenging to define. The literature about this topic does not provide us with a common definition. Instead we discover that there are many ways in which to be a teacher leader. Wenner and Campbell (2017) discovered that a great deal of literature was generated in the past decade suggesting a growing awareness about teacher leadership as well as an increased desire to understand it. Their review of 74 different studies attempted to seek further clarity on the topic. Within the same time period, we also saw the development of the Teacher Leader Model Standards (TLMS; Teacher Leadership Exploratory Consortium, 2008), which promote the importance of teacher leadership while providing guidance regarding what it should look like in action. The TLMS redirect the focus from top-down models of leadership to actions that are grounded in collaboration, along with the larger idea that teachers are key players in leading schools and students to success (Cosenza, 2015). Greenlee (2007) proposed that teachers are more effective in their classrooms when they believe that they are leaders at the school. Danielson (2006) suggested that teacher leadership is not about the role itself, but about the skills that permit a teacher to exert influence beyond the confines of their classrooms. As we continue to unfold the concept of teacher leadership and consider these varied descriptions, it makes great sense that teacher leadership can be seen in an assortment of actions, interactions, and roles.

## The Potential for Teacher Leadership in PDSs

The different roles of teacher leadership that emerge can influence schools, teaching, and students in various ways. For example, a teacher who voluntarily shares her materials and lesson plan ideas with colleagues is typically viewed as a good team player or a pleasant person to work with. However, in this example the teacher sharing her ideas is a leader whose actions positively impact the way others do their work. This type of leadership, though subtle, has great potential to improve the quality of teaching at the school. This teacher is as much of a leader as the teacher who is a department chair because of the positive influence she has on her colleagues. Sharing best practices may not be a formal role in the school, but it is one that can emerge and be just as valuable – and perhaps even more valuable – than the formal jobs to which teachers are appointed.

The nature of the professional development school (PDS) model is such that it brings together veteran teachers, teacher candidates, and university faculty in collaborative partnership. When PDSs are done well, great collaboration takes place to improve both teaching practice and student achievement. In a PDS, the opportunities for the emergence of both formal and informal leadership roles increases greatly because of the additional number of people available for collaboration. From liaisons-in-residence to mentoring teacher candidates, the chapters in this book bring to light some of these leadership roles and tell stories of how each one positively impacts the school community.

## Liaisons-in-Residence

In Chapter 8, Snow, Anderson, Cort, Dismuke, and Zenkert take a strong look at the role of a liaison-in-residence in a PDS partnership and tie it to democratic leadership theory as described by Woods (2004) and the idea that the position emerged to serve the needs of others. Although it may be known under different terms in other school–university partnerships, the liaison-in-residence role is common in the PDS model and one that is very much needed for any partnership's long-term success. In most PDS environments, the duties of the liaison position entail being the primary contact for teacher candidates, cooperating teachers, and university supervisors. The PDS liaison typically is charged with managing all issues that may come up among these groups of stakeholders. As described in Chapter 8, the liaison-in-residence also serves as a supervisor for teacher candidates in which the leadership role of mentoring becomes a prominent part of the position.

At the schools described in this chapter, the liaison-in-residence position emerged based on the necessity for someone to do the work of providing teacher candidates and P-12 (preschool through twelfth grade) students with the best possible learning opportunities. There was also a need to have a leader at each site who retained the identity of classroom teacher. Having teacher leaders come forward to take on this type of role instead of an administrator or a university faculty member has multiple benefits. First, when a classroom teacher holds a liaison role, she has significantly more credibility with colleagues and teacher candidates because she shares the experience of being a practitioner in the trenches. Second, administrators are often transferred or choose to move about from school to school with much greater frequency than classroom teachers. Having a teacher in the liaison role provides long-term stability to a partnership. When a teacher leader assumes a liaison role, the partnership can carry on uninterrupted even when there is a change in principal. Third, when an administrator holds the position of liaison, what he or she says can be misinterpreted as a directive because of the formal supervisory position they hold.

Another key concept discussed in Chapter 8 revolves around tensions that develop when a teacher takes on the role of a liaison. Because the liaison-in-residence is still teaching in the classroom but has additional duties for the PDS partnership, balancing the workload becomes challenging. Tensions can arise when peer teachers question the liaison's priorities. Concern develops when the needs of teacher candidates occasionally distract them from meeting the needs of the P-12 students. Although these tensions existed among the teachers described in Chapter 8, they did not disturb the spirit of those in the liaison role. Overall, these teacher leaders seemed to feel validated by the trust that was placed in them.

Chapter 8 demonstrates the importance of having PDS liaisons-in-residence because they manage the everyday nuances of the partnership while providing mentoring and leadership for all the stakeholders. In reading the chapter, we learn a valuable lesson that a PDS partnership is much stronger and better positioned for long-term sustainability when PDS liaison roles exist. Because of funding challenges, PDSs throughout the country struggle to figure out ways to support liaison roles, even though they are known to be important. If it is believed that this teacher leadership role has great value, then it becomes necessary to find ways to support the position with additional funding and/or release time. Chapter 8 brings the issue of supportive structures back to the forefront and makes it clear that there is a need for policymakers to better understand the value of the PDS model in teacher education.

## PLCs, Learning Walks, and Co-Teaching

In Chapter 9, Hudson and Hellenberg explore professional development practices that impact the emergence of teacher leadership in a K-8 (kindergarten through eighth grade) university laboratory school. This unique partnership, located on the grounds of a university, creates an environment where all teachers are viewed as leaders just by virtue of the type of school it is. When such a culture exists, and all teachers are validated as leaders, everyone has buy-in and commitment to the mission of the educational program. The key structures of Chapter 9 are professional learning communities (PLCs), learning walks, and co-teaching. All three structures require a great deal of time commitment for people to work together in different ways while providing more opportunities for teachers to be leaders in their school. Collaboration is not often viewed as leadership, but when one ponders the level of commitment and professionalism needed to work together effectively, we begin to see how important it is to leadership. When one looks at the TLMS, one can see the value that is placed on collaboration as a characteristic of teacher leadership.

PLCs as described by DuFour, DuFour, Eaker, and Many (2006) are highly collaborative groups of professionals working together to improve the school, teacher practice, and student achievement. The PLC model clearly demonstrates the teacher leadership that emerges when collaboration takes place. Chapter 9 demonstrates both the reliance on and effectiveness of the PLC model for continued reflection about school improvement. What is especially noble is the realization that using the PLC model is an ongoing learning process requiring both commitment and trust.

Learning walks (Fisher & Frey, 2014), which are like instructional rounds (Roberts, 2012), offer another collaborative opportunity for colleagues to improve professional practice. In a medical school, physicians and interns make rounds together to evaluate patients, discuss their symptoms, and propose both diagnoses and treatments. Similarly, learning walks allow the onlookers to observe classrooms and reflect on the lesson and about whether students were engaged and learning goals were achieved. If done in a nonjudgmental way, this type of collaborative activity can be instrumental in helping teachers reflect on their practice and learn best practices from one another. In a school–university partnership, this is especially valuable for preparing teacher candidates because they can see a variety of teachers using different strategies in the classroom and decide what they would adapt to improve their own practice.

Co-teaching has gained a great deal of momentum over the years, since the grant-funded work of St. Cloud University demonstrated through its research the benefits to both teacher candidate preparation and P-12 student achievement. St. Cloud University (2017) describes co-teaching as two teachers working together with groups of students; sharing physical space and the planning, organization, delivery, and assessment of instruction. Co-teaching is a collaborative opportunity for candidates and their mentors to learn from one another, improve teaching practice, and improve student achievement. The PDS model is ideal for co-teaching since cohorts of candidates typically work with cooperating teachers for an extended period. Chapter 9 calls to attention that co-teaching is an excellent opportunity for both school and university partners to learn from one another, develop strong rationale for lesson choices, and reflect on results to inform future practice.

## Mentoring Teacher Candidates

In Chapter 10, Quinzio-Zafran and Wilkins explore the relationship between National Board Certified Teachers and the teacher candidates they mentor in PDS settings. The chapter highlights the teacher leadership that emerges when experienced teachers mentor teacher candidates. Connections to the TLMS (2008) and Council for the Accreditation of Educator Preparation (CAEP, 2014) standard 2 for clinical practice demonstrate how teachers who mentor candidates positively influence the profession by preparing the next generation of classroom teachers. There can be no argument that mentoring teacher candidates is a critical leadership role within the profession and a way to authentically prepare the future generation.

Chapter 10 also puts at the forefront the notion that it is no longer appropriate for universities to prescribe in isolation the manner in which teachers are prepared. Instead, it is clear that practitioners need to be at the table to provide real-world input regarding the blending of theory and clinical practice so that new teachers are truly ready for their first teaching position. This idea supports the concept put forward by CAEP (2014) that the responsibility to prepare aspiring teachers falls on both universities and the P-12 schools. The PDS model provides the best opportunity for this type of collaboration because university faculty and P-12 teachers are already working together to meet common goals.

## Teacher Leader Reflections

Chapter 11 contains reflections that provide a variety of perspectives regarding teacher leadership. Bennett, Lichtenstein, Nelson, and Cunningham openly share about the various roles that make them feel like leaders. Mentoring teacher candidates, sharing best practices, modeling success, collaborating with others, and reflecting on practice were all major themes of their stories. One reflection that resonated talks about a teacher who worked in both PDS and non-PDS schools and described how the comradery was stronger at the PDS. This author's perception was that the PDS model united the staff across grade levels, which provided more opportunity to collaborate with colleagues who might not have anything in common at a non-PDS. This is an interesting perspective because it implies that in non-PDS schools, collaboration might only take place among those within a common grade level or academic department. The idea that the PDS model unites all teachers through partnership with the university and mentoring teacher candidates is powerful affirmation for the potential of PDSs in developing teacher leadership.

## Making Sense of Section Two

It is clear that the chapters in this section affirm that teacher preparation is no longer just the responsibility of colleges and universities. Instead, it is a shared charge between schools and institutions of higher education with clinical practice at the core of the experience. The PDS model, which is based on the relationship between a medical school and teaching hospital, is best suited to bring together school and university partners to achieve this common goal. It is through the PDS model that both schools and universities have a platform to collaborate with one another to truly take on the responsibility of preparing new teachers while simultaneously reinvigorating the practice of veteran teachers.

Another common theme in this section of the book is the idea of collaboration as a primary characteristic of teacher leadership. Whether teacher leaders engage in co-teaching, mentoring, coaching, sharing best practices, PLCs, or learning walks, at the root of it all is collaboration. In Chapters 8–11, we see multiple examples of teachers, teacher candidates, university professors, and administrators collaborating with one another to achieve common goals. This sends a clear message that teacher leadership is less about formal roles such as being the department chair or union representative, and more about influencing the profession beyond the daily duties of teaching. Throughout all the chapters in this section, the common theme of collaboration demonstrates the power teachers have to improve schools and student achievement by influencing both teaching practice and curriculum design. When teachers collaborate, the culture of the school changes and less reliance is placed on top-down leadership. The lasting effect teacher mentors have on teacher candidates is another example of how leadership through collaboration influences the profession.

The teachers and candidates written about in this section clearly view their roles as something that takes place beyond the confines of their classrooms. They demonstrate leadership not because a role or responsibility was assigned to them, but rather rise to the occasion, to fill a need, to provide support, or to improve their schools. Even after reading these chapters, it can be recognized that a common definition for teacher leadership still does not emerge. Perhaps this is a good thing. By not declaring a one-size-fits-all definition of teacher leadership, the concept remains open to various potential leadership roles and responsibilities that can continue to influence the profession in a positive way.

## References

Cosenza, M. (2015). Defining teacher leadership: Affirming the Teacher Leader Model Standards. *Issues in Teacher Education*, *24*(2), 79–100.

Council for the Accreditation of Educator Preparation. (2014). *Standards*. Retrieved from http://caepnet.org/standards/

Danielson, C. (2006). *Teacher leadership that strengthens professional practice*. Alexandria, VA: ASCD.

DuFour, R., DuFour, R., Eaker, R., & Many, T. (2006). *Learning by doing: A handbook for professional learning communities at work*. Bloomington, IN: Solution Tree.

Fisher, D., & Frey, N. (2014). Using teacher learning walks to improve instruction. *Principal Leadership*, *14*(5), 58–61.

Greenlee, B. J. (2007). Building teacher leadership capacity through educational leadership programs. *Journal of Research for Educational Leaders*, *4*(1), 44–74.

Roberts, J. E. (2012). *Instructional rounds in action*. Cambridge, MA: Harvard Education Press.

St. Cloud University. (2017). The academy for co-teaching and collaboration. *Co-Teaching Research and Resources*. Retrieved from https://www.stcloudstate.edu/soe/coteaching/research.aspx

Teacher Leadership Exploratory Consortium. (2008). *Teacher leader standards*. Retrieved from http://teacherleaderstandards.org/downloads/TLS_Brochure.pdf

Wenner, J. A., & Campbell, T. (2017). The theoretical and empirical basis of teacher leadership: A review of literature. *Review of Educational Research*, *87*(1), 134–171.

Woods, P. A. (2004). Democratic leadership: Drawing distinctions with distributed leadership. *International Journal of Leadership in Education*, *7*(1), 3–26.

# Section III

# Teacher Leader Preparation and Development

Chapter 13

# Cultivating Teacher Candidates' Passions into Leadership for Tomorrow: The Gift that Keeps on Giving

*Vail Matsumoto, Jon Yoshioka and Lori Fulton*

### Abstract

Teacher preparation programs (TPPs) in the professional development school model can serve as a valuable channel for teacher leadership opportunities. Using the distributed leadership perspective, this chapter explores how one school–university partnership focused on developing teacher leaders rather than simply teacher candidates. Viewing the TPP as an incubator for teacher leaders primes candidates to not only teach in the classroom, but to also seek out leadership opportunities based on their passions. This chapter highlights components of the TPP, such as assignments and innovative practices, and provides two specific examples of teacher candidates following their passions to leadership.

*Keywords:* Professional development schools; school–university partnerships; teacher leader development; teacher preparation program; distributed leadership; community involvement

Teacher leadership can take many forms, but in essence, it is a gift that keeps on giving. This chapter focuses on the role that teacher leadership plays in a professional development school (PDS) partnership and the benefits experienced by each stakeholder, including the school–university partnership, the teacher preparation program (TPP), the PDS, and the teacher candidates (TCs). Readers will be privy to the scope of work and learn about the successes and struggles TCs experienced as they began seeing themselves not as novice teachers, but as teacher leaders who actively contribute to a PDS–university–community partnership.

The University of Hawai'i at Mānoa's (UHM) Master of Education in Teaching (MEdT) program began its formal PDS partnership with Waipahu High School in 2012. The PDS' student-centered motto, "My Voice, My Choice, My Future," extends to faculty, staff, and the TCs who are placed there. This focus not only helps the high school students prepare for success in the twenty-first century, but also makes the school an ideal learning community where TCs can flourish.

The MEdT program subscribes to and upholds the UHM College of Education's mission of preparing educators who, through their sense of purpose and place, contribute to a just, diverse, and democratic society. Directly connected to this mission are the MEdT program's four guiding principles: (1) integrating theory and practice, (2) inquiry-based learning, (3) collaboration, and (4) reflection. When combined with a focus on developing teacher leaders, these principles, along with the Nine Essentials of a PDS (National Association for Professional Development Schools, 2008), formed the basis for a collaborative partnership wherein TCs have a multitude of opportunities to develop as teacher leaders in the classroom, school, and community.

## Conceptual Framework

### Teacher Leadership

Teacher leadership has been conceptualized in many different ways, such as teachers taking on roles outside of the classroom, supporting school-based professional learning, informing decisions on policy, improving student learning, and working toward school-based change (Wenner & Campbell, 2017). The roles teacher leaders play can vary greatly. York-Barr and Duke (2004) defined teacher leadership as "the process by which teachers, individually or collectively, influence their colleagues, principals, and other members of school communities to improve teaching and learning practices with the aim of increased student learning and achievement." (pp. 287–288). Stemming from this view, we define teacher leaders as individuals who use their gifts and talents to create a positive impact on student learning and school/community culture inside and/or outside of the classroom.

The concept of teacher leadership has been embraced by classroom teachers for over two decades (York-Barr & Duke, 2004). Accepted by progressive administrators and reformists, the concept has now trickled down into the realm of teacher preparation (Bond, 2011; Holland, Eckert, & Allen, 2014) and to PDSs (Gonzalez & Lambert, 2001). Therefore, the successful TC in today's PDS must possess skills not only in the areas of curriculum development, classroom management, and assessment, but in a number of other arenas as well. Specifically, PDS TPPs must prepare TCs to be leaders (Bond, 2011; Carver & Meier, 2013; Katzenmeyer & Moller, 2009) in all facets of teaching so that they are prepared to pursue leadership roles in the schools where they observe, learn, and teach.

The value of teacher leadership can be revealed in many ways at the school level and in the school's community, including action that improves the school as well as the community (Crowther, Ferguson, & Hann, 2009). Seeing the value of teacher leadership, more classroom teachers are assuming leadership roles on multiple levels within a school (Carpenter & Sherretz, 2012; Wenner & Campbell, 2017; York-Barr & Duke, 2004). The majority of these teacher leaders receive training focused on specific content knowledge, pedagogical strategies, and leadership skills through professional development or university-based degrees, certificates, or endorsements (Wenner & Campbell, 2017). However, the specifics related to these different leadership paths are often not clear or decipherable (Wenner & Campbell, 2017; York-Barr & Duke, 2004). While most teachers have access to information, resources, and opportunities related to teacher leadership, once they become classroom teachers (Carver & Meier, 2013; Katzenmeyer & Moller, 2009; Ross et al., 2011) we believe the path to leadership should be accessible and navigable for TCs as they prepare for the profession, especially with the unique levels of support and opportunities that are possible in a PDS model.

## *Distributed Leadership Perspective*

The collaborative, interactive participation that is a hallmark of a successful PDS structure also forms the basis for our theoretical perspective. Spillane, Halverson, and Diamond (2004) conceptualized the distributed perspective of leadership as taking place in a sociocultural context, in which leadership is an interaction between leaders, followers, and situations. In this model, leadership is "stretched out" over multiple individuals rather than a single person taking the lead. Harris (2004) further described distributed leadership as "engaging expertise wherever it exists within the organization rather than seeking this only through formal positions or roles." (p. 13). Distributed leadership theory lends itself to the idea that anyone, at any level, can serve as a leader by sharing their expertise in order to make a positive impact on the students, school, and community. This approach to meaningful and authentic leadership should be introduced and modeled during the TPP (Bond, 2011; Snyder, 2015). When teachers begin their careers in education with a teacher leadership mindset that drives their decisions and shapes their choices, the path and destination become clear.

This chapter examines how TCs were supported in their journey to become teacher leaders using a distributed leadership perspective within a TPP and a school–university partnership. TCs' paths to teacher leadership are laid out in chronological order to document the process by which they were supported by the partnership. This focus is based on the lack of literature in this area (Wenner & Campbell, 2017). We also explore how TCs worked to internalize teacher leader mindsets and find their personal paths to leadership. Called to action by their TPP, TCs were encouraged to use their unique skill sets and follow their passions, which created possibilities that led to leadership roles across the PDS.

## TPP Components

In 2012, the UHM MEdT program coordinator stated that

> We've moved away from being the kind of traditional program that drops off candidates in several schools just so they can fulfill the program requirements. Most of the time in that model, it is a one-way relationship where programs just take, take, take from the host school. We want to be the kind of program that gives as much or more than it takes. We want a mutually beneficial, reciprocal relationship with our partners. This is why we constantly ask the question, "What can we do for you?" when we work with our PDS partner.

While prior iterations of the program included a leadership component in the curricula, it was often demonstrated through planned service learning projects, individual pursuits, or random opportunities. All this changed when the "What can we do for you?" philosophy became the driving force behind the TPP–PDS relationship and for the cohort groups of TCs. Leadership became one of the foundational pillars for the partnership, and leadership expectations were woven through each semester's assignments and into the field work at the PDS.

With leadership as a pillar, the PDS raised both the expectations for the TCs and their privileges on campus. Whereas previous cohorts had been politely welcomed onto the partner school's campus, these budding teacher leaders were embraced within the PDS community. At the same time, the warm welcome was paired with the uncompromising expectation that these TCs would, from day one, become participating members of the school community, make contributions, and conduct themselves as teacher leaders. Clearly, part of the conception of giving back as a TC manifested itself through embracing leadership and was modeled by all who worked within the PDS partnership.

## *Placements*

The university's support of the teacher leadership model was evident in the innovative structures that were put in place at the PDS sites. The mutual and cohesive understandings and agreements between university faculty and the PDS administration served as the foundation upon which the structures were built. One of the structures that became essential to TC success was focused on selective placement within the partner school. By considering the gifts and talents TCs brought with them, the PDS team had the requisite information to purposefully make informed placements, matching TCs with mentor teachers or within teams or academies, which complemented their gifts or had the potential to develop their gifts further. Additional structures at the school level included an open-door policy, encouragement of pitching new ideas, and powerful mentor teacher role models.

## *Alumni Pipeline*

The mentor teachers were not the only ones who served as teacher leader role models for the TCs. An additional TPP structure that helped TCs see the possibilities and grasp the potential of their own gifts revolved around the teacher leader alumni pipeline. Recent TPP graduates were invited back to share their leadership stories and expound upon the challenges they had encountered, thereby illustrating how they became role models and mentors for the next wave of teacher leaders entering the profession.

These alumni not only supplied real-life examples of teacher leadership, but exemplified TPP expectations toward which TCs could aspire. Stories from the teacher leader pipeline helped demonstrate the diverse gifts that TCs brought with them, and how the school–university partnership and the innovative program structures shaped the TCs into leaders, thereby allowing every partner in the PDS to flourish.

The components of the TPP–PDS partnership and its structures, along with the teacher leader pipeline stories, illustrate the possibilities that exist for every TPP and for every TC. Next, we share the experiences that TCs engaged in to develop their leadership skills. Assignments and innovative practices serve as starting points for creating a roadmap that demonstrates the possibilities for the future of teacher leadership when TCs are born, raised, and shepherded through TPPs that are preparing not only teachers, but future teacher leaders.

## *Assignments*

Four assignments were designed to allow TCs to hone their skills as leaders from day one in the TPP program.

**Seeing themselves as leaders.** To set the stage for the teacher leadership journey, TCs were given an open-ended writing assignment, which was focused on documenting the unique gifts and skills they brought to the PDS partnership. After spending a day within the PDS partnership to gain an understanding of its background, each TC was asked to think carefully and deeply about how s/he might contribute to the school. This question was posed through a writing prompt: What gifts do I bring to my PDS community? The TCs struggled with this assignment on many levels. While they may have understood the premise behind the question, they were challenged to see how they fit into the spirit of giving.

Recognizing that even the newest TCs possessed gifts that would benefit the school community was a difficult concept for the candidates to grasp. They had officially been TCs for less than 24 hours and were already being asked to jump higher and reach farther than traditional TCs because they were now seen as budding teacher leaders. This cognitive disequilibrium was a jarring experience for some TCs, but the process of resolving it allowed them to accommodate new ideas and experiences by restructuring their previously held beliefs about teaching, the teaching profession, and their contributions as teacher leaders. The new ideas and experiences provided them with opportunities for growth over the long term as they discovered their paths toward teacher leadership.

**Broadening their views of leadership.** After all the TCs' fears were assuaged, the result of the simple question, "What can we do for you?" laid a strong foundation and the groundwork for a two-year journey. Each TC brought a varying degree of leadership skill, but all were mentored, encouraged, supported, and expected to grow. While expectations were the same for every candidate, each TC's journey, and thereby learning, was personalized.

After asking TCs to think about the gifts they brought to the school, we expanded their perspective to think about what others brought. We asked each TC to have conversations with five different PDS community members other than their mentor teachers. They were encouraged to step outside their content areas to speak with a variety of faculty, staff, and administrators. While their conversations were not scripted, many of the interviewees spoke about teacher leadership and TCs came away with examples that were shared with the entire cohort. These examples proved to be some of the most influential forces that changed the way the TCs viewed themselves and served as a stepping stone for leadership possibilities. Candidates not only gained authentic examples of PDS classroom teachers as leaders, but also resource teachers, custodial staff, and support personnel stepping up to the task of being leaders within the PDS community, all demonstrating the concept of distributed leadership (Spillane et al., 2004). Providing role models and authentic examples of teacher leadership in the schools where TCs were placed was a powerful influence on the continuum from TC to teacher leader.

**Developing a roadmap to leadership.** After learning about the varied and numerous teacher leaders at the PDS partner school, TCs were better able to formulate ideas about the type of leadership they could pursue. Each TC put pen to paper and delineated these ideas into first steps, which became their professional growth plan. The professional growth plan was a living document meant to be a tool that TCs used throughout the program and into their professional careers.

Introduction to the professional growth plan included the reminder to TCs that teacher leaders demonstrate their leadership in a variety of ways (Harris, 2004, Spillane et al., 2004). They were also asked to remember that each TC's journey would likely be different, based upon skills, interests, dispositions, and gifts, along with goals and opportunities. Irrespective of what they chose, all TCs were expected to seek out leadership opportunities that allowed for growth and boundary spanning. Since some had already been participating in activities that were considered teacher leadership, they were encouraged to continue with those activities and take an additional step out of their comfort zone. Such opportunities for growth were continuously encouraged.

As a roadmap with a desired destination, the professional growth plan asked TCs to consider five prompts:

1. What are your professional goals? Please include at least two. If you are having difficulty fleshing out your professional goals, imagine where you'd like to be in your career 5 or 10 years from now.
2. Think about someone who might be willing to serve as a mentor who can guide you toward your goals. This person does not have to be in the position that you are working toward, but s/he should be able to provide support and feedback as you work toward your goals. Who would this be? How do you envision them helping and mentoring you?
3. What resources or supports will you need to reach your goals?
4. For each of your goals, what are specific, actionable steps that you will take? Consider skills that you need to acquire or gaps in your experience or knowledge.
5. Create a timeline connected to your action steps.

The professional growth plan was not devised as an assignment to be checked off, but one that would grow and change with the TCs to meet their evolving needs and abilities as teacher leaders. Candidates referred to their plans throughout the four semesters in the program, making revisions often as they executed the steps they had designed.

**Supporting one another on the journey.** An ongoing component of teacher leadership within the cohort structure revolved around making mistakes and taking calculated risks. One of the recurrent exercises the cohorts undertook was a two-part reflective assignment called Help and Here's Something that Works. In formal class discussions, TCs were asked to recall an event in their field experience that they wanted to celebrate along with an occurrence that they considered a mistake. While it was somewhat easier for candidates to share celebratory instances, the real pockets of learning came from discussing their mistakes using the four Ds: dissection, deliberation, discussion, and debate.

After several rounds of discussion, TCs began seeing their mistakes as opportunities for growth rather than as representations of failure. They began to understand that good leadership often involves taking risks and being innovative and that while one could choose a safer route, it would not necessarily translate into success or leadership.

## Innovative Practices

In collaboration with the PDS, the TPP was able to incorporate innovative practices that promoted TCs' development as teacher leaders, including personalized learning, an open-door policy, and a community contribution project.

**Personalized learning.** In the second semester of the program, TCs were asked to reflect metacognitively about teacher leadership. Key issues that were covered included personal definitions of leadership, a gauge of readiness to pursue teacher leadership, challenges encountered, supports necessary, and a cyclical look at the initial assignment about the gifts they brought to the PDS.

While it was important for the TCs to learn about leadership, see examples of leadership in their field experience, and make plans for themselves, it was equally critical for them to think about whether their own definition of leadership had changed over time. The TCs' reflections on leadership were critical because their perceptions of their own abilities as leaders influenced whether their transformation would accelerate, decelerate, or disappear. The TCs who saw their leadership potential, however fledgling, saw growth earlier and made larger strides than the TCs who did not. If TCs did not see any leadership potential in themselves, it became the mission of all the stakeholders in the partnership to help them discover their potential. The reflection was developed as a quick and effective way to ascertain each TC's self-perception, and the resulting data worked in a number of ways for the TCs, TPP, and PDS.

The data gathered from the reflections accompanied another innovative strategy that was born out of necessity. Each TC had a different perspective on teacher leadership, a variety of goals, and a different place on the leadership spectrum, requiring a significant amount of personalized learning. A one-size-fits-all approach would not work. Once the TCs started on their individual leadership journeys, it would have been counterproductive to rein in those who wanted an accelerated route or force those who were just getting their feet wet to dive into things head first.

While a personalized approach was more time-consuming and demanding on the school–university partnership personnel, the alternative would have crushed many of the TCs' leadership dreams. The personalized goals and steps to TCs' chosen leadership destinations were not born out of a textbook or state standard. They were created by the TCs themselves within the contexts of their partner schools and the needs that emerged there. Candidates found meaning in the leadership goals they pursued as they were filling roles that often had immediate effects on student learning and the PDS community.

**Open-door policy.** An innovative practice that worked in tandem with personalized learning was the open-door policy in place at the PDS. This policy applied especially to candidate-generated ideas and creative solutions to challenges on campus. Instead of feeling intimidated by their inexperience, the budding teacher leaders were encouraged to pitch their ideas, no matter how far-fetched they might seem. For example, one improbable, place-based idea, which we will share in detail later, involved building a fire, butchering a wild pig, and having students stay at the school overnight. This idea, and many others that seemed out of the realm of possibility, came to life once they were brought to the PDS administration through the open door.

The TCs' naiveté, enthusiasm, and innovation were celebrated rather than rebuffed. The administration at the PDS held the TC-driven projects as examples of what teacher leadership in action could look like. When veteran teachers needed their fires reignited, administration often pointed to the TCs' ideas as a means for inspiration. Having TCs influence and inspire veteran teachers was only possible because of the open-door policy instituted by the PDS.

The TCs' confidence as teacher leaders was also boosted by the open-door policy. Once they mustered the courage to pitch an idea, the TCs started looking at themselves and the other members of their cohort as teacher leaders whether the idea crystallized into a full-fledged project or was sent back for revision or additional information. The TCs were reminded repeatedly that although many teacher leaders' ideas do not come to fruition, the process and the willingness to take the risk of pitching an idea is often what set a teacher leader apart. Those TCs who found success through the open-door policy often became the strongest members of the teacher leader pipeline, as will be demonstrated through the examples of two TPP graduates who not only exemplified the qualities of teacher leaders, but continued to hone their leadership skills as new teachers in the profession.

**Community contributions.** As part of their introduction to the PDS, TCs were taken on a tour of the surrounding community. One of their stops was a community center, Safe Haven, in an economically challenged neighborhood. The TCs were introduced to various programs provided by the center, such as the after school tutoring program for elementary students. After this visit, TCs were inspired to volunteer at the center in order to give back to the community in which they taught. Within a month, they had put together a holiday fair with educational games and crafts for the children who lived there. This was the beginning of the community contribution cohort assignment.

Each TC was asked to develop an individual or group project that culminated in a contribution to the school or community. This innovative practice directly connected to the distributed leadership theory as each TC relied on his/her expertise to find a way to give back to the PDS community. No one from the university or PDS directed these projects; each TC took the lead for his/her project. As part of the PDS, TCs' community contributions included hosting the annual school safety fair, creating interactive booths at an arts and communications family night, serving as coaches and senior project judges, and improving facilities within the school.

## Two Examples: From TCs to Teacher Leaders

Throughout the two years of the program, TCs developed their leadership skills, styles, and capabilities by putting their words into actions. In this section, we share two examples of teacher leaders who emerged from the program, Robert Bruce and Arthur Joseph.

### *Robert Bruce*

Robert Bruce's road to teacher leadership began with his love for sports. As a TC, Robert knew that he wanted to pursue leadership both in the classroom and on the playing field. However, he also tempered this desire with the reality he was experiencing as part of the PDS partnership. He was well aware of the time commitment required of a coach and the infrequent openings on the coaching staffs across the PDS. What resulted from his careful consideration of passion, commitment, and reality was a slow and steady showing of his extracurricular interest within the PDS.

Robert made it known early and often that coaching was his passion and route to teacher leadership. He shared this through his course assignments, in his professional growth plan, in class discussions, and in informal conversations with university faculty. The most significant way he shared his vision of teacher leadership was through his day-to-day interactions and exchanges with PDS faculty, administration, and students.

By sharing his love of basketball with his students and showing rather than telling the PDS coaching staff about his interest, Robert made a strong statement in very few words. This quiet persistence and dedication attracted the attention of the boys' varsity head coach who began to take notice of Robert's work ethic, success in the classroom, and leadership potential. By the beginning of the basketball season, Robert had been invited to serve as a volunteer coach.

The love of the game was not Robert's only draw to leadership through athletics, as he shared:

> Getting involved in extracurricular activities like coaching basketball…was so appealing to me…because basketball is an opportunity to reach the kids from a different angle. I don't pretend to think that all thirty kids that sit in my classroom are passionate about English, but I do know that all twenty kids that step onto the court love to play basketball, so really to reach them from that angle has been just a great experience. (Class Assignment, 2013).

This indirect line toward improving student achievement was a purposeful strategy, not one of chance. Robert knew, as stated, that there are many avenues to reach students and this was definitely one that fit his gifts.

Robert's leadership goals have extended and transformed through the years since he graduated from the TPP. From serving as a volunteer coach, Robert was promoted to the position of assistant coach in his second year of coaching. Two years later, his leadership responsibilities increased again when he transitioned into the head coach position for the junior varsity boys team.

Robert's slow and steady advancement through the coaching ranks at the PDS was the result of a number of things. His passion for the game was already present, but through the TPP, he was provided with an outlet for that passion. Moreover, that outlet was focused and channeled to a specific destination: teacher leadership. Through his placement in the PDS, Robert had multiple opportunities to showcase his passion and skills.

### *Arthur Joseph*

Arthur Joseph began as a TC fresh out of his undergraduate science program. With a bachelor's degree in environmental science, Arthur didn't know much about being a teacher, except that he wanted to be one. The idea of incorporating leadership as part of his journey never crossed his mind. He worried about interviewing to be admitted to the program, then worried about where he would be placed, and he even worried about getting all of his course assignments done. The one thing he never once worried about was being a leader, as he never envisioned it as part of being a teacher.

When asked to write about the gifts he was bringing to the PDS, Arthur humbly made mention of his extensive place-based educational experience working with natural resources like watersheds and native Hawaiian ecosystems. He, like many TCs, focused on surface level skills and experiences as opposed to talents or hobbies about which they were passionate but seemed to have no connection to schooling or education. What Arthur failed to include as part of his gifts was his upbringing on a Big Island farm that practiced the traditional art of the imu or underground oven. It was only by chance that this gift was brought to his cohort coordinators' attention.

During a class when TCs were sharing snacks, Arthur's contribution was homemade beef jerky. When several people raved about it, he revealed that it was a product of his family's farm and that his grandfather still worked as a butcher. He shared that he often hunted for pigs and that they cooked what they caught in the imu that they had been using for generations. While this seemed like simple conversation, it became the basis for what would become Arthur's legacy as a teacher leader at his PDS.

The passing conversation struck Arthur's cohort coordinators as a shining example of a TC turning a passion into an opportunity for leadership. After being encouraged to design and build an imu on campus with the Natural Resources Academy in the PDS, Arthur began seeing the possibilities for his role as a teacher leader. He admitted to being incredulous at first, wondering how a "wild and crazy" idea that involved students, working with fire, and staying overnight on campus would ever come to fruition. But the passion behind this gift overcame any insecurities and doubts Arthur held.

The imu project had a simple and clear connection to the Natural Resources Academy goals, the science standards, and the sense of place that is vital to honoring Native Hawaiian practices. Over the course of three years, Arthur implemented a plan that involved not only designing the imu, but also having the students take ownership of it, which eventually resulted in them teaching underclassmen to carry on the art. This plan has been realized many times over and is now an indispensable piece of the curriculum that impacts hundreds of students each year.

A key element of Arthur's success with the imu project and his progression into the role of a teacher leader was the support he received through the open-door policy implemented on the PDS campus. His "wild and crazy" idea was received by the PDS administration not as an unrealistic or preposterous idea by a TC with inadequate classroom experience, but as a proposal to increase student engagement and achievement developed by a teacher leader.

While enjoying the success of the imu project, Arthur proceeded to develop and launch other projects that were direct results of the confidence and leadership that emerged from his experience with the imu. He established a partnership with a community group that oversaw part of an ahupua'a (Hawaiian watershed) and began taking his students on monthly field trips there to learn and help preserve the environment.

The true test of teacher leadership, especially when cultivated as a TC, is longevity. While we try to instill teacher leadership as a way of life and philosophy that is deeply rooted and enduring in our TPP and the PDS partners we work with, in the end, it is the TC's choice to continue in the profession as a teacher or a teacher leader.

## Closing Thoughts

Working under the premise that anyone at any level can lead (Harris, 2004; Spillane et al., 2004) makes it possible for TCs to grow and flourish into teacher leaders. This is especially true within a PDS model. This chapter has documented how one school–university partnership created a path to teacher leadership for TCs, and two examples of preparing TCs to be not only teachers, but teacher leaders as well. Based on these examples, we put forth the idea that developing teacher leaders within a PDS can create capacity within the PDS partnership.

### *Developing Leaders at the Partnership Level*

While challenging for those involved, encouraging, guiding, and helping TCs embrace teacher leadership as part of their daily routine is the epitome of the gift that keeps on giving. Developing TCs as leaders is truly a worthwhile and effective means to the long-term successful growth of schools and the greater community. Teachers who enter schools as teacher leaders have the potential to change their students' lives from the very first day of their careers within their classrooms and beyond. In addition to that impact in the classroom, the connection to the distributed leadership perspective allows for any teacher to use his or her expertise and gifts to benefit the school and community, thereby widening the pool of potential leaders.

Since change for both TPPs and TCs can be slow and time-consuming, beginning teacher leadership development from the inception of a TC's interaction with school–university partnership stakeholders offers a better chance of success. The distributed leadership perspective provides an almost limitless wealth of opportunity for these chances of success. Equally important is longevity as a teacher leader because consistency over time helps develop the critical pathways and relationships necessary for success.

### *Growing Your Own: Creating Capacity in the PDS partnership*

A connection to future work involving teacher leadership within the PDS can be found in the ranks of mentor teachers who work with TCs. Because preparing teacher leaders rather than classroom teachers is a recent phenomenon (Bond, 2011; Holland et al., 2014), we are not sure where this trend will lead. While it may not be feasible at the present time, the next generation of mentor teachers could come from the graduates who were raised in the PDS and are now blazing trails as teacher leaders in their own right. This "grow your own" philosophy builds teacher leader capacity within the school–university partnership. This step will undoubtedly take time as teacher leaders gain experience and establish themselves in their schools. These new teacher leaders will be steeped in the philosophy shared by the TPP and the PDS, ready to contribute immediately to the school community. The idea of giving back to a new generation of teacher leaders is part and parcel of this upbringing and a vital component of building a strong, sustainable PDS.

## References

Bond, N. (2011). Preparing preservice teachers to become teacher leaders. *The Educational Forum, 75*(4), 280–297.

Carpenter, B. D., & Sherretz, C. E. (2012). Professional development school partnerships: An instrument for teacher leadership. *School–University Partnerships, 5*(1), 89–101.

Carver, C. L., & Meier, J. M. (2013). Gaining confidence, managing conflict: Early career conceptions of teacher leadership during graduate coursework. *The New Educator, 9*(3), 173–191.

Crowther, F., Ferguson, M., & Hann, L. (2009). *Developing teacher leaders: How teacher leadership enhances school success.* Thousand Oaks, CA: Corwin Press.

Gonzalez, S., & Lambert, L. (2001). Teacher leadership in professional development schools: Emerging conceptions, identities, and practices. *Journal of School Leadership, 11*(1), 6–24.

Harris, A. (2004). Distributed leadership and school improvement: Leading or misleading? *Educational Management Administration & Leadership, 32*(1), 11–24. doi:10.1177/1741143204039297

Holland, J., Eckert, J., & Allen, M. (2015). From preservice to teacher leadership: Meeting the future in educator preparation. *Action in Teacher Education, 36*(5–6), 433–445.

Katzenmeyer, M., & Moller, G. (2009). *Awakening the sleeping giant: Helping teachers develop as leaders.* Thousand Oaks, CA: Corwin.

National Association for Professional Development Schools. (2008). *What it means to be a professional development school.* Retrieved from http://napds.org/wp-content/uploads/2014/10/Nine-Essentials.pdf

Ross, D., Adams, A., Bondy, N., Dana, N., Dodman, S., & Swain, C. (2011). Preparing teacher leaders: Perceptions of the impact of a cohort-based, job embedded, blended teacher leadership program. *Teaching and Teacher Education, 27*(8), 1213–1222.

Snyder, J. (2015). Teacher leadership and teacher preparation: A personal narrative. *The Educational Forum, 79*(1), 5–11.

Spillane, J. P., Halverson, R., & Diamond, J. B. (2004). Towards a theory of leadership practice: A distributed perspective. *Journal of Curriculum Studies, 36*(1), 3–34. doi:10.1080/0022027032000106726

Wenner, J. A., & Campbell, T. (2017). The theoretical and empirical basis of teacher leadership: A review of the literature. *Review of Educational Research, 87*(1), 134–171. doi:10.3102/0034654316653478

York-Barr, J., & Duke, K. (2004). What do we know about teacher leadership? Findings from two decades of scholarship. *Review of Educational Research, 74*(3), 255–316.

Chapter 14

# Developing Teacher Leaders Using a Distributed Leadership Model: Five Signature Features of a School–University Partnership

*Brianne W. Morettini, Kathryn McGinn Luet, Lisa J. Vernon-Dotson, Nina Nagib and Sharada Krishnamurthy*

### Abstract

This chapter describes the development of a teacher leader preparation program that emerged from a partnership between a university and a local high-needs district. Using a sociocultural approach, researchers conducted a needs assessment for teachers in the district. Drawing on this data and extant literature, researchers designed a program aimed at increasing opportunities for distributed leadership. The Beginning Teacher Project is built around five signature features, including targeted professional development, ongoing dialog, turnkey training, instructional decision-making, and community engagement. The chapter traces the development of the program and describes the signature features in detail.

*Keywords:* Distributed leadership theory; sociocultural theory; targeted professional development; turnkey training; instructional decision-making; community engagement

This chapter outlines how three university researchers used an external grant to design The Beginning Teacher Project, a teacher leader preparation program, using aspects of sociocultural theory as a framework. The Beginning Teacher Project leverages the power of a partnership between Hillside Public Schools (all names of places and people are pseudonyms) and a nearby university to support teacher leaders and, by extension, beginning teachers and ultimately students. Over 10 years ago, Hillside Public Schools joined the university's professional development schools (PDS) network; three out of nine schools in the Hillside district are part of the PDS network. In this way, the university remains inherently invested in the success of Hillside teachers and students.

The university researchers established the signature features of The Beginning Teacher Project during year one of the project in consultation with the district administrators. Analysis of data gathered from a needs assessment of teacher leaders and novice teachers related to school climate and culture, areas of strength, and challenges for professional practice. The researchers also drew upon their knowledge of extant literature on beginning teacher attrition, effective professional development, and signature pedagogies for the teaching profession. Using this research and data as a framework, the project unfolded as a sustainable, tiered model of support for beginning teachers.

Together, the university and Hillside Public Schools agreed on their shared commitment to the goals as outlined in the notice of grant opportunity: (1) developing a high-quality program of professional learning to prepare teacher leaders to support beginning teachers, (2) implementing mentor training for a cadre of teacher leaders, (3) creating and implementing high-quality professional learning opportunities for district and school leaders, and (4) examining and upgrading district mentoring programs and other policies and practices that impact teacher leaders' work.

The ultimate aim of this chapter is to illustrate how a sociocultural theoretical framework was used to guide the development of a teacher leader preparation program for teacher leaders working in PDSs in order to address the four goals outlined earlier. To that end, the chapter begins with an overview of relevant literature on school–university partnerships, teacher leadership, and distributed leadership to support teacher leadership. From there, the chapter outlines how a sociocultural theoretical framework was used to guide the analysis of empirical evidence and develop the signature features of The Beginning Teacher Project. While the project spans three years, this chapter focuses on year one – the foundation. After describing the research methods employed to study both the context and the effectiveness of the program, the chapter describes the signature features of The Beginning Teacher Project, which includes targeted professional development, ongoing dialog, turnkey training, instructional decision-making, and community engagement. The chapter concludes by considering directions for future work.

## Literature Review

### School–University Partnerships and PDSs

In 2010, the American Association of Colleges for Teacher Education announced a nationwide call for the increase in formal agreements between university colleges and schools of education and P-12 schools. This school–university partnership was described as a professional agreement imperative to the successful implementation of clinical practice (NCATE, 2010). Burns, Jacobs, Baker, and Donahue (2016) identified seven core ingredients that are essential for the success of school–university partnerships in transforming teacher preparation:

1. A shared, comprehensive mission dedicated to equity for improved PreK-12 student learning and educational renewal
2. Designated partnership sites with articulated agreements
3. Shared governance with dedicated resources that foster sustainability and renewal for the partnership
4. Clinical practice at the core of teaching and learning
5. Active engagement in the school and local community
6. Intentional and explicit commitment to the professional learning of all stakeholders
7. Shared commitment to research and innovation through deliberate investigation and dissemination. (p. 88).

One robust model of school–university partnerships cited as essential to improving teacher preparation is the PDS. The National Association for Professional Development Schools (2008) outlined Nine Essentials, which became the acceptable standard for all PDSs. The Council for the Accreditation of Teacher Preparation (n.d.) defines PDS as

> [a] specially structured school in which Educator Preparation Provider (EPP) and P-12 school clinical educators collaborate to 1) provide practicum, field experience, clinical practice, and internship experiences, 2) support and enable the professional development of the educator preparation provider (EPP) and P-12 school clinical educators, 3) support

and enable inquiry directed at the improvement of practice, and 4) support and enhance P-12 student achievement.

This project's PDS network dates back to 1999. Currently, the university has eight active PDS sites, three in Hillside School District. Each PDS partner has a professor-in-residence and a PDS site-based leadership team. These two elements are the only shared aspects of the PDSs. Although each has a unique plan for professional learning and supports preservice and in-service teachers differently, the seven core ingredients (Burns et al., 2016) are evident. It was the long-standing school–university partnership that led to the initiation and success of The Beginning Teacher Project.

### *Teacher Leadership*

As the needs of twenty-first century learners and educators continue to transform, it is imperative that schools build capacity in their teachers. In recent years, teacher leadership has surfaced in educational policy, practice, and research. While there is no consensus on the definition of teacher leadership (Neumerski, 2013), a key tenet of teacher leadership is grounded in the idea that teachers can influence others to improve school climate and educational practices, with the goal of promoting effective leadership, quality teaching, and student learning (Katzenmeyer & Moller, 2009; York-Barr & Duke, 2004). Therefore, for the purposes of this chapter, teacher leaders may be defined as educators who have teaching responsibilities in a P-12 setting and take on leadership roles outside of their classrooms (Wenner & Campbell, 2016).

Teacher leadership creates opportunities for distributed, schoolwide and districtwide leadership; it allows teachers innumerable opportunities to develop their own practice and the practices of their colleagues (Harris, 2003). Moreover, teacher leadership has been shown to positively influence job satisfaction and retention (Chew & Andrews, 2010; Vernon-Dotson et al., 2009) while also building a pipeline within the profession (Vernon-Dotson & Floyd, 2012). These impacts build a sense of professionalism that attracts others to the field (Beachum & Dentith, 2004).

### *Distributed Leadership to Support Teacher Leadership*

If school improvement is to be constant and effective, all personnel must take responsibility for school reform efforts. By influencing teacher leaders to become competent in their practice and sharing in the responsibility and accountability for ensuring the knowledge and skills of their colleagues, all students benefit. Distributed leadership empowers teacher leaders by inspiring them to collaborate through partnerships both within and beyond the walls of the school (Van Horn, 2006; Vernon-Dotson, 2008).

Although Woods, Bennett, Harvey, and Wise (2007) describe distributed leadership as a term that "attracts a range of meanings and is associated with a variety of practices," (p. 439) it is best understood as "a product of the interactions of leaders, followers, and their situation." (Spillane & Diamond, 2016, p. 148). From this perspective, leadership is performed by the entire educational community and affords daily interactions between formal and informal leaders and other members within organizations. This type of shared leadership allows decision-making to be managed and directed by individuals vested in the education process (Gronn, 2000; Spillane & Diamond, 2016).

Distributed leadership is based on the willingness of school leaders to share their authority and power (Harris & DeFlaminis, 2016). Thus, as the university researchers and Hillside administrators collaborated in the design of The Beginning Teacher Project, an emphasis was placed on providing learning opportunities to help prepare teacher leaders to engage in school-wide decision-making and to serve as instructional leaders in their schools.

## A Sociocultural Approach to Teacher Leadership

That the history of research on teacher leadership tends to lack full theoretical grounding is well documented. As noted by Wenner and Campbell (2016), it is "only partially theoretical as just over a majority of the literature was framed by theory." (p. 161). The Beginning Teacher Project is not a prescriptive approach to teacher leader preparation and development; rather, the project illustrates how school–university partners enacted a sociocultural approach for preparing and developing teacher leaders over time. Drawing on tenets of sociocultural theory as outlined by Vygotsky (1978), the researchers maintain that teachers develop leadership capacity when educational opportunities attend to context, specifically environmental factors and teachers' specific needs. Further, such opportunities progress in logical stages, promoting incremental learning. University researchers, therefore, collaborated with PDS and partnership administrators and teacher leaders to design and implement strategies to increase beginning teacher retention in the district.

## Research Methods

The goal of The Beginning Teacher Project is to build teacher leadership capacity in a district with multiple PDS sites that experience high rates of beginning teacher turnover and low student performance. The related research is primarily qualitative in nature and serves as a case study of both the creation and implementation of this university–district mentoring program (Creswell, 1998).

In developing the project, the university researchers collected and analyzed data from teacher leaders to identify strengths and areas in need of growth with respect to pedagogy, community engagement practices, and mentoring: all of which are important contextual data that helped the researchers build a relevant teacher leader program. In addition, a representative sample of beginning teachers was interviewed to better understand the context for learning among novice teachers in Hillside Public Schools. Using these data, the researchers developed five signature features of the program aimed at improving teacher leaders' skills while supporting beginning teachers in the context of Hillside Public Schools.

To ensure that the program continued to meet teachers' needs throughout implementation, ongoing data were collected to evaluate both successes and challenges encountered with respect to each of the five signature features. Data sources included surveys, interviews, field notes, external evaluator reports, teacher leader evaluations, and teacher leader blog posts. After describing the setting of the project, these are explored more detail.

### *Research Context*

The city of Hillside is 35% African American, 44% Hispanic or Latino, and 19% white. Twenty-four percent (24%) of Hillside's population is foreign born, as Hillside is host to many migrant and seasonal farmworkers, and 44% of the population is nonnative English speakers. Approximately one-third (34%) of the entire documented population of Hillside lives in poverty (U.S. Census Bureau, 2010). Hillside Public Schools serve approximately 5,820 students. Hillside is geographically considered rural but has many indicators of an urban community; the majority of students are Hispanic, and over half the entire student population receives free meals or meals at reduced rates. In this regard, Hillside could be considered an "urban characteristic" school as Milner (2012) outlines in his evolving typology of urban education.

In the first year of this three-year project, district administrators selected 24 teacher leaders to participate in The Beginning Teacher Project. In year two, ten new teacher leaders were added as a second cohort. Applicants for the program were evaluated in terms of their overall effectiveness rating based on the Danielson Evaluation Instrument (Danielson, 2014), their attendance, contributions to the district, and years of teaching experience. The teacher leaders represented a variety of grade levels, subject areas, and schools in the district. In year one of the project, work focused exclusively on developing the skills of the teacher leaders. In year two, first-year teachers were also invited to participate in program activities, and teacher leaders had the opportunity to put their mentoring skills into practice. Because of large-scale layoffs in the district, the beginning teacher population was small in year two; eight beginning teachers were hired, and all participated in the project.

## *Empirical Evidence*

Consent to collect data was obtained from all teacher leaders and a sample of beginning teachers within the district; a representative sample of 14 beginning teachers was interviewed in order to identify areas in which they felt they were progressing and areas where they would like more support. Similarly, survey and interview protocols asked the teacher leaders to discuss their areas of strengths, needed growth, and essential supports. The signature features of the project, therefore, highlight teachers' voices and lived experiences. Building on these data, the project unfolds as a context-specific method to developing teacher leaders in partnership districts with long-standing PDS sites. The focus on context demonstrates the researchers' shared commitment to a sociocultural theoretical framework. As data collection continued throughout year one, it also encompassed participants' assessment of the program itself, including elements the participants found helpful and areas that could be improved.

All interview data were audiotaped and transcribed for analysis. Data were analyzed using open-coding procedures (Emerson, Fretz, & Shaw, 1995) and descriptive statistics, when appropriate, for quantitative data. Specifically, the researchers read through the entire data set of surveys and interviews and developed coding schemes to capture teacher leaders' and beginning teachers' primary areas of strength and areas in need of support. In addition, as per grant requirements, the researchers worked with an external evaluator who provided quarterly updates regarding the effectiveness of the program. Table 1 illustrates data sources and related key findings.

Table 1: Data Sources and Findings.

| Data Source | Number ($n$) | Select Finding(s) |
|---|---|---|
| *Initial data* | | |
| Teacher Leader Surveys | 24 | Strengths include instructional decision-making and institutional knowledge of Hillside Public Schools; areas in need of support include effectively utilizing students' funds of knowledge and community resources |
| Teacher Leader Interviews | 24 | Strengths include instructional decision-making and institutional knowledge of Hillside Public Schools; areas in need of support include effectively utilizing students' funds of knowledge and community resources |
| Beginning Teacher Interviews | 14 | Strengths include feeling accepted by colleagues; areas in need of support include instructional decision-making and whom to ask for assistance |
| *Ongoing data* | | |
| Field Notes from Professional Learning Series | 8 | Teacher leaders would like more preparation in culturally responsive teaching, anti-racist teaching, and CFGs |
| Reports from External Evaluator | 5 | Open and ongoing dialog through the blog is effective at capturing teacher leaders' thoughts and questions |
| Teacher Leader Evaluations from 8 Professional Learning Series | 192 | Teacher leaders prefer professional development facilitators with experience working with communities commensurate with Hillside |
| Teacher Leader Blog Posts | 258 | A culture is being created at Hillside around culturally responsive teaching and viewing students and the community from an asset-based perspective |

## Initial Findings and Resources

All beginning teachers who were interviewed reported feeling accepted by their school and the community of Hillside. More specifically, all 14 beginning teachers said someone within the district, but not necessarily at their school, formally mentored them, while a teacher at their school acted as an informal mentor. This precipitated the beginning teachers' perceptions of acceptance. This finding prompted the researchers to provide leadership support for teacher leaders who are not formally assigned beginning teacher mentees but who continue to support beginning teachers in their school. In addition, all beginning teachers indicated a need for support with implementing effective instructional strategies to meet the needs of the diverse student population in their classrooms at Hillside Public Schools. This finding prompted the researchers to provide support for teacher leaders in assisting beginning teachers with effective instructional decision-making strategies.

The teacher leaders' data showed that while all the teacher leaders were familiar with the basic demographics of Hillside, teacher leaders were unfamiliar with the community assets and resources within Hillside. These findings prompted the researchers to engage teacher leaders with Hillside community leaders. In particular, the researchers tapped into networks of colleagues and community leaders to serve on a community advisory board (CAB), which would engage in open and ongoing dialog with teacher leaders about the assets and how to effectively address the particular challenges that students in Hillside Public Schools face.

The Beginning Teacher Project resulted in the creation of three resources: a teacher leaders' blog, a community resource guide, and mentoring handbook. First, using the Edmodo platform, a secure website was created for teacher leaders to reflect on professional development sessions, raise questions, and share resources. Second, a community resource guide was created after it became apparent that many of the teacher leaders were unaware of all the resources in the Hillside community. The university researchers brainstormed with CAB members during a meeting and determined that a community resource guide with information about resources in Hillside could benefit anyone teaching the students in that community. The community resource guide also included myths about families and guardians in Hillside and reasons why such myths are untrue.

The teacher leader data also revealed the lack of a centralized source or reference book for teacher leaders who mentor beginning teachers. University researchers, therefore, set up a summer institute, which consisted of a two-day workshop after the school year ended following year one of the project. During this summer institute, teacher leaders worked in small groups to develop a mentoring handbook that would serve as a centralized source of information and references for any teacher leader mentoring a beginning teacher in Hillside Public Schools. The mentoring handbook received approval from Hillside's Board of Education and was distributed to all teacher leaders and principals in Hillside.

These three deliverables from the project fortified the sustainability of a sociocultural approach to teacher leader preparation and development; the community resource guide and the mentoring handbook are now official documents distributed to all teachers in the district and as such, will outlive the funding period of the project. Moreover, the blog remains a space where teachers can connect with one another to share ideas and raise concerns.

## Signature Features

Using a sociocultural theoretical framework in conjunction with a distributed leadership model, The Beginning Teacher Project recognizes all members of the education community as sources of knowledge. With a sociocultural theoretical framework, the project builds on five targeted inputs, which were conceptualized in consultation with district administrators and by analyzing teacher leader and beginning teacher data and related research. The five inputs are discussed in depth below, including evidence of effectiveness, as well as challenges that the researchers encountered in implementing each element (see Figure 1).

### *Targeted Professional Development*

The project included eight monthly professional learning series (PLS) sessions for teacher leaders that focused on growth areas as identified from data collection. PLS topics included anti-racist teaching, culturally responsive pedagogy, teacher leadership, and critical friends groups (CFGs). These sessions were led by external facilitators who shared relevant research and invited teacher leaders to reflect on data from their own classrooms. District administrators attended the PLS sessions in order to communicate relevant information to building principals and to build those positive relationships essential to encouraging distributed leadership.

*Developing Teacher Leaders Using a Distributed Leadership Model* 227

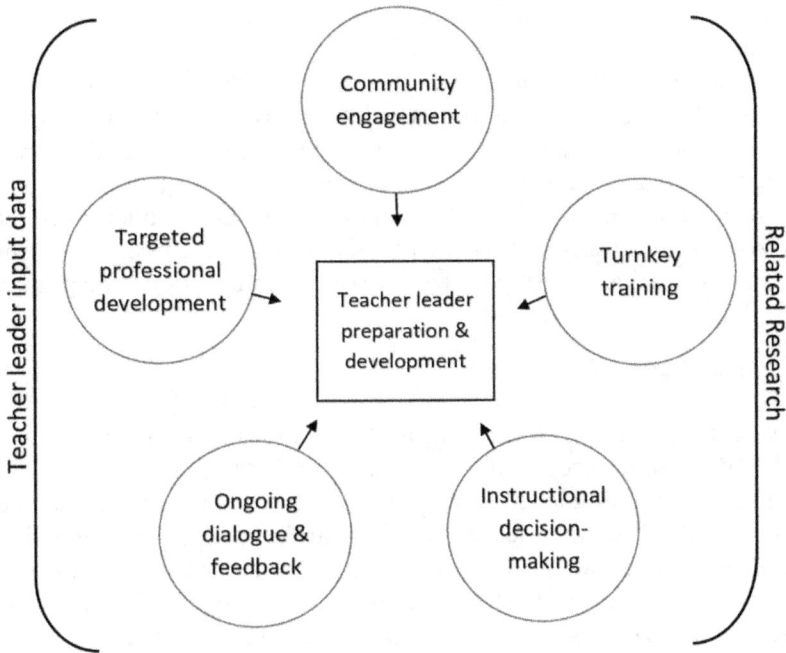

Figure 1: Signature Features of Sociocultural Approach to Teacher Leader Development.

Evidence from the teacher leaders' blog demonstrates the effectiveness of these sessions, particularly in terms of the way they encouraged teacher leaders to think more critically about their classroom practice and their role in the larger school community. For example, after a session about culturally responsive pedagogy, one teacher leader wrote:

> My perception of marginalized groups was altered after our session.... I began to look deeper into all the ways someone can be marginalized. Obviously, this is now a conversation I will bring to the table with new teachers and even current colleagues. We can ally ourselves to children and their families by first recognizing how they may feel marginalized. (Teacher Leader, June 9, 2016)

In addition, surveys administered by the grant's external evaluator after the session demonstrated that 100% of the teacher leaders either agreed or strongly agreed that the PLS session provided opportunities for teacher leaders to work collaboratively with their colleagues to discuss issues relating to mentoring in the district.

One particular challenge of the PLS sessions relates to communication with district administrators and school leaders. While typically at least one district administrator attended each meeting, school principals were not required to attend, and teacher leaders were at times unsure how to implement new strategies or modes of collaboration without building-level support. As a result, researchers began attending monthly school improvement committee meetings to ensure a direct line of communication to all principals.

### *Dialog and feedback*

As teacher leaders worked to improve their leadership capacity, successes and setbacks were recorded on the teacher leaders' blog. In this way, ongoing group dialog and feedback among the teacher leaders served to aid them in enacting their leadership skills and knowledge under a distributed leadership model. After each PLS session, a question was posted on the blog, asking teacher leaders to connect what they had learned to their classroom experiences. At the beginning of each subsequent PLS session, the teacher leaders reviewed key comments posted on the blog relating to the previous meeting, reflecting on how their colleagues' feedback resonated with – or differed from – their own perspectives.

One of the successes of the blog was that it prompted teacher leaders to continue conversations beyond the PLS; further, the blog encouraged districtwide communication, as nine schools comprise the Hillside district. In addition, the blog also served as a forum to share notes and information. For instance, as teacher leaders worked together to construct the mentoring handbook, they often posted resources on the blog, ensuring that everyone had access to the materials.

As time progressed, maintaining consistent participation of all the teacher leaders on the blog became challenging. Therefore, researchers began sending consistent and gentle reminders for participation. Furthermore, typically the researchers – and not the teacher leaders – initiated conversation threads on the blog. Researchers, therefore, began inviting teacher leaders to start conversation topics on issues of particular relevance to them.

### *Turnkey Training*

University-identified experts in the field facilitated the PLSs for the teacher leaders in year one. Then, these teacher leader experts held sessions in year two to prepare other teachers to work effectively with beginning teachers. In this way, The Beginning Teacher Project loosely borrows from the residency model, a signature pedagogy from the medical profession, in which teachers learn by working closely with established experts in the field (Shulman, 2005).

While all of the teacher leaders had extensive P-12 classroom teaching experience, they did not have the same level of expertise in working with adult learners. Teacher leaders reported they were sometimes unsure regarding the appropriate level of rigor to build in their sessions, and they were hesitant in managing a class of their peers. At times, conversations were off-topic or occurred simultaneously, and teacher leaders did not know how to respond. In retrospect, a co-teaching model – in which the researchers and teacher leaders delivered material together – may have been a useful approach as the research team transitioned control to teacher leaders.

### *Instructional Decision-Making*

Positive change is best achieved when a school culture supports instructional decision-making, particularly through the use of CFGs. CFGs are a particular type of professional learning community in which educators convene at least once a month with a commitment to improving their practice through collaborative learning (Burke, Marx, & Berry, 2011; Curry, 2008). CFGs are organic efforts in which teachers facilitate their own reflections with one another, building relationships as they discuss and deliberate instructional choices. Teacher leaders were introduced to CFGs at an early PLS session and encouraged to think about how they could implement them in their respective schools.

Teacher leaders were particularly enthusiastic about the potential of CFGs to provide support and to create positive change in the district. For example, one teacher leader commented on the teacher leaders' blog:

> Critical friends groups are a lifeline. This journey called teaching can be overwhelming and sometimes even the most seasoned professional can feel that they're drowning in an ocean with no saving grace; just imagine what a novice teacher might feel. So a beginning teacher should know that a CFG can help restore their confidence and be the rescue that they need. I suggest to have CFG sessions a part of our regular PD schedule or even staff meetings. (Teacher leader, May 19, 2016)

In fact, one group of teacher leaders approached their building principal, asking to incorporate CFGs into time set aside for teachers to meet in their professional learning communities.

Here, again, one of the challenges associated with CFGs is ensuring that school leaders are receptive to – and knowledgeable about – new practices. After talking with their principal, the teacher leaders expressed the concern that their principal did not entirely understand the purpose of CFGs. While he was willing to let the teachers try to create CFGs at his school, he stressed the importance on data and accountability, which the teacher leaders worried would undermine some of the key tenets of CFGs, particularly the emphasis on shared ownership for problem-solving and supportive collaboration.

### *Community Engagement*

Under the aegis of distributed leadership as defined by Spillane and Diamond (2016), The Beginning Teacher Project emphasized teacher leaders' community engagement with Hillside. To that end, researchers worked with Hillside's teacher leaders and district administrators to establish CAB in an effort to acknowledge the community as a source of knowledge. The CAB served as a space for parents and community members to meet with teacher leaders to discuss community assets that all teachers could incorporate into their teaching practice.

The CAB developed and shared their community resource guide with teacher leaders during the two-day summer institute at the end of year one. In surveys completed at the end of this meeting, teacher leaders described insights they gained about the community. For instance, some teacher leaders indicated their amazement on learning that parents still do not always feel welcome in schools. Several teacher leaders noted that they learned that parents would like to be more involved with the work that teachers do. Other teacher leaders were surprised to find that parents "are thinking about the same things teachers are," such as the heavy emphasis on test preparation in the curriculum (Teacher leader Survey Response, 2016).

One challenge associated with the CAB has been finding time to bring together community members and teachers for sustained dialog. However, the CAB continues to brainstorm ways to approach teachers in order to challenge potential assumptions held about the community without engendering defensiveness.

## The Future: Moving Forward

Based on year one data from an external evaluator, 100% of teacher leaders ($n = 24$) agreed or strongly agreed that their knowledge and skills as teacher leaders were enhanced and improved as a result of participating in The Beginning Teacher Project. Artifacts from year one (i.e., the community resource guide, mentoring handbook) are now official Hillside Public School documents. Further, blog posts provide evidence that a culture was created in Hillside that will outlive the funding period for project.

In developing The Beginning Teacher Project, the researchers collected and analyzed beginning teacher and teacher leader data through a needs assessment and ongoing evaluation efforts and collaborated with district partners and PDS administrators to develop a series of professional development opportunities specific to the needs of Hillside Public Schools. As the project unfolds in year two and beyond, the university researchers continue to consult with district leaders, teacher leaders, and beginning teachers to ensure that the project continues to meet the needs of participants. In this way, a sociocultural approach to distributed leadership proves to be self-sustaining and in the best interest of continued positive school–university partnerships.

This chapter provides a conceptual framework for guiding others who endeavor to leverage a school–university partnership to implement a sociocultural approach for a distributed leadership model. The key idea of teacher leadership is grounded in teachers influencing others to contribute to school improvement or educational practice (Katzenmeyer & Moller, 2009; York-Barr & Duke, 2004) with the goal of promoting effective leadership, quality teaching, and student learning. Based on this promising practice, the researchers are convinced that setting a priority for a distributed leadership model that incorporates a sociocultural approach to teacher leader preparation will support all facets of districtwide and schoolwide teacher mentor programs. In turn, these programs will positively affect beginning teacher retention and ultimately improve student outcomes.

## Acknowledgment

The Beginning Teacher Project (2015-2018) was a Building Teacher Leadership Grant fully funded by *Improving Teacher Quality Partnerships* (ITQP) Title II, Part A, Subpart 3, of the No Child Left Behind Act of 2001 (NCLB), P.L 107-110 (CFDA 84.367B).

# References

American Association of Colleges for Teacher Education. (2010). *The clinical preparation of teachers: A policy brief.* Washington, DC: AACTE. Retrieved from http://edwebsfiles.ed.uiuc.edu/transitions/AACTE-Policy-Brief-March-2010.pdf

Beachum, F., & Dentith, A. M. (2004). Teacher leaders creating cultures of school renewal and transformation. *Educational Forum, 68*, 276–286. doi:10.1080/00131720408984639

Burke, W., Marx, G., & Berry, J. (2011). Maintaining, reframing, and disrupting traditional expectations and outcomes for professional development with critical friends groups. *The Teacher Educator, 46*, 32–52.

Burns, R. W., Jacobs, J., Baker, W., & Donahue, D. (2016). Making muffins: Identifying core ingredients of school–university partnerships. *School–University Partnerships [special issue: What is a PDS], 9*(3), 81–95.

Chew, J. O. A., & Andrews, D. (2010). Enabling teachers to become pedagogical leaders: Case studies of two IDEAS schools in Singapore and Australia. *Educational Research for Policy and Practice, 9*, 59–74. doi:10.1007/s10671-010-9079-0

Council for the Accreditation of Educator Preparation. (n.d.). *Glossary.* Washington, DC: Author.

Creswell, J. W. (1998). *Qualitative inquiry and research design: Choosing among five traditions.* Thousand Oaks, CA: Sage Publications.

Curry, M. (2008). Critical friends groups: The possibilities and limitations embedded in teacher professional communities aimed at instructional improvement and school reform. *Teachers College Record, 110*(4), 733–774.

Danielson, C. (2014). *The Framework for Teaching Evaluation Instrument* (Version 1.2). Retrieved from http://www.danielsongroup.org

Emerson, R. M., Fretz, R. I., & Shaw, L. L. (1995). *Writing ethnographic fieldnotes.* Chicago, IL: University of Chicago Press.

Gronn, P. (2000). Distributed properties: A new architecture for leadership. *Educational Management Administration & Leadership, 28*, 317–338.

Harris, A. (2003). Teacher leadership as distributed leadership: Heresy, fantasy of possibility. *School Leadership & Management, 23*, 313–324. doi:10.1080/1363243032000112801

Harris, A., & DeFlaminis, J. (2016). Distributed leadership in practice: Evidence, misconceptions and possibilities. *Management in Education, 30*(4), 141–146. doi:10.1177/0892020616656734

Katzenmeyer, M., & Moller, G. (2009). *Awakening the sleeping giant: Helping teachers develop as leaders* (3rd ed.). Thousand Oaks, CA: Corwin Press.

Milner, R. (2012). But what is urban education? *Urban Education, 47*(3), 556–561.

National Association for Professional Development Schools. (2008). *What it means to be a professional development school.* South Carolina: The Executive Council and Board of Directors.

National Council for the Accreditation of Teacher Education. (2010). *Transforming teacher education through clinical practice: A national strategy to prepare effective teachers*. Washington, DC: Author.

Neumerski, C. M. (2013). Rethinking instructional leadership, a review: What do we know about principal, teacher, and coach instructional leadership, and where should we go from here? *Educational Administration Quarterly, 49*(2), 310–347. doi:10.1177/0013161x12456700

Shulman, L. S. (2005). *The signature pedagogies of the professions of law, medicine, engineering, and the clergy: Potential lessons for the education of teachers*. Speech delivered at the "Teacher Education for Effective Teaching and Learning" workshop, hosted by the National Research Council's Center for Education, Irvine, CA.

Spillane, J. P., & Diamond, J. B. (2016). School leadership and management from a distributed perspective: A 2016 retrospective and prospective. *Management in Education, 30*(4), 147–154. doi:10.1177/0892020616665938

U.S. Census Bureau. (2010). *QuickFacts*. Retrieved from https://www.census.gov/quickfacts/table/PST045216/00. Accessed on July 12, 2016.

Van Horn, L. (2006). Re-imagining professional development. *Voices from the Middle, 13*(4), 58–63.

Vernon-Dotson, L. J. (2008). Promoting inclusive education through teacher leadership teams: A school reform initiative. *Journal of School Leadership, 18*(3), 543–554.

Vernon-Dotson, L. J., Belcastro, K., Crivelli, J., Lesako, K., Rodregues, R., Shoats, S., & Trainor, L. (2009). Commitment of leadership teams: A district-wide initiative driven by teacher leaders. *International Journal of Teacher Leadership, 2*(2), 34–38.

Vernon-Dotson, L. J., & Floyd, L. O. (2012). Building leadership capacity via school partnerships and teacher teams. *The Clearing House: A Journal of Educational Strategies, Issues and Ideas, 85*, 38–49. doi:10.1080/00098655.2011.607477

Vygotsky, L. (1978). *Mind in society: The development of higher psychological processes*. Boston, MA: Cambridge University Press.

Wenner, J. A., & Campbell, T. (2017). The theoretical and empirical basis of teacher leadership: A review of the literature. *Review of Education Research, 87*(1), 134–171. doi:10.3102/0034654316653478

Woods, P. A., Bennett, N., Harvey, J. A., & Wise, C. (2004). Variabilities and dualities in distributed leadership: Findings from a systematic literature review. *Educational Management Administration and Leadership, 32*(4), 439–457.

York-Barr, J., & Duke, K. (2004). What do we know about teacher leadership? Findings from two decades of scholarship. *Review of Educational Research, 74*, 255–316. doi:10.3102/00346543074003255

Chapter 15

# Growing our Own: Fostering Teacher Leadership in K-12 Science Teachers through School–University Partnerships

Zareen G. Rahman, Mika Munakata, Emily Klein, Monica Taylor and Kristen Trabona

### Abstract

This chapter describes a teacher leadership professional development program for K-12 science teachers constructed through a partnership between a university and five school districts. The development and implementation of the program drew from the literature on teacher leadership, communities of practice, and distributed leadership. The program supports teachers through a two-year fellowship program where they examine their teaching practices, attend professional development workshops, and undertake an independent teacher leadership project in their own schools. The chapter also describes the research conducted by the university to improve the program and shares findings and future implications of this research.

*Keywords:* Communities of practice; reflective practice; distributed leadership; school–university partnerships; teacher fellows; teacher leadership; STEM; simultaneous renewal

It would be cool to be the person [who can help when a teacher asks], "Oh, I'm having a hard time teaching density. Can you help me?" And being like, "Yes! I have this great thing we can do. Let's go!" ... Kind of like a super-hero. (Definition of a Teacher Leader, Fellow, Cohort One).

This chapter describes a school–university partnership program designed to support the teacher leadership development of 60 K-12 science teachers from five local school districts. The overarching goal of the program was to nurture experienced teachers to become teacher leaders by having them reflect upon their practice, collaborate with peers, and develop and implement independent teacher leadership projects. Teachers who participated in the program (hereafter referred to as fellows) come to see themselves as teacher leaders who have the potential to work alongside school administrators and other teachers to make change within their districts, each in a distinct way. In this chapter, we describe our innovative school–university partnership program, highlight the most significant program features, and discuss the salient outcomes of the program. We end with questions that will serve as the focus for our next round of funding and development.

## Overview of the Program

The Wipro Science Education Fellowship (SEF) is a teacher leadership grant program designed to support experienced K-12 science teachers as they improve their teaching practice and develop into teacher leaders within their districts. It is a five-year program funded by Wipro Limited, a global information technology and consulting company with a vested interest in public education, both in India and in the United States. The program was developed by University of Massachusetts, Boston, and is being implemented in similar ways across three universities, each working with five local school districts, with slight variations that accommodate differences in settings. Here, we describe the specific implementation and outcomes associated with the project at one of the three sites: Montclair State University (MSU).

A primary goal of the program was to promote teacher leadership and to improve teachers' instructional practice in schools, with the potential to impact student learning (Crowther, Kaagan, Ferguson, & Hann, 2009). Furthermore, we encouraged our fellows to lead within and beyond the classroom; identify with and contribute to a community of teachers, learners, and leaders; and influence others toward improved educational practice (Katzenmeyer & Moller, 2001). Our hope was that the fellows would view themselves as teachers of both students and peers and would be driven by the desire to influence instructional practice (Danielson, 2006).

Our program at MSU is coordinated by four members of the College of Science and Mathematics and the College of Education and Human Services, a project manager, and doctoral students. Specifically, the project team includes two teacher educators with expertise in teacher leadership, a mathematics educator who works in STEM (science, technology, engineering, mathematics) education, and a science educator and director of a STEM professional development center. The project team at MSU led all monthly professional development workshops, coordinated with the other sites and school districts, and mentored the fellows – both in groups and individually – as they pursued their year one group activities and year two individual teacher leadership projects. In addition to coordinating the program, the faculty and doctoral students on the project conducted research, both to inform revisions and to contribute to the literature on teacher leadership. We relied on interviews, observations, and artifact data, which enabled us to examine the complex work and dynamic relationships of the fellows.

## Teacher Leadership

Teacher leadership is not a new concept, yet the definition is elusive, varied, and emerging. The literature collectively has described teacher leaders through varied lenses: as educators who positively influence their peers by establishing and sustaining collegial relationships for the purpose of affecting and advocating for change (Jacobs & Crowell, 2016; Lieberman & Miller, 2005; York-Barr & Duke, 2004); as individuals who possess a strong sense of purpose (Donaldson, 2007; Lambert, 2003); as those willing to extend their work beyond their respective classrooms to foster collegial interactions that focus on instructional strategies (Fullan & Hargreaves, 1996); and as risk takers (Center for Comprehensive School Reform and Improvement, 2009). As lifelong learners, teacher leaders continually reflect and refine their practice (Day & Harris, 2002). Their informal leadership practice evolves over time, going through several developmental stages (Hunzicker, 2012). Finally, teacher leaders cultivate a positive school environment because they understand how political factors of the school impact their peers' needs (Donaldson, 2007: Frost & Durrant, 2003; Gronn, 2000; Harris, 2010; Muijs & Harris, 2007; Spillane, 2006).

Teacher leaders influence others' instructional practice beyond the scope of their classroom through constant collaboration with teachers, administrators, and university faculty (Ackerman & Mackenzie, 2006; Burns, Yendel-Hoppey, & Jacobs, 2015; Chrispeels & Martin, 2002; Rogers, 2002). This involves collaborating with various stakeholders to help them shape their pedagogy, while simultaneously changing and refining their own teaching practice. As one of our fellows explained, teacher leadership does not occur in isolation: "You have to build those teams of people that will do it together or help each other out or work toward the common goal not ... you know the leadership that is really one person just running the show." Thus, it is essential to support teacher leaders' work toward improved instructional practice, understanding teacher leaders' experiences when enacting and supporting leadership.

Our program has been greatly influenced by the distributed leadership framework (Gronn, 2000; Harris, 2010; Muijs & Harris, 2007; Spillane, 2006). This perspective situates a teacher leader's role at the epicenter of improving teaching and learning. In contrast to the traditional leadership roles, teacher leaders emerge spontaneously and organically from the teacher ranks. Teacher leaders are known for taking initiatives to address various areas within their school, where they work directly with peers or colleagues. They have no positional authority; their influence stems from the respect they elicit from their colleagues by means of their expertise and practice (Danielson, 2006; Katzenmeyer & Moller, 2001; Taylor, Goeke, Klein, Onore, & Geist, 2011).

## MSU Wipro SEF Model

Existing research points toward teachers' need for opportunities to examine their practices in the context of their own schools and that connect to the needs of their students (Taylor, Klein, Munakata, Trabona, & Rahman, under review). Most teacher professional development continues to be driven by district agendas and led by outside professionals who may have little understanding of the needs of individual students in specific classrooms (Cochran-Smith & Lytle, 2009; Elmore, 2004; Lieberman & Miller, 2011; Talbert, 2010). The use of videos as an effective means to promote teacher reflections has been documented (Borko, Jacobs, Eiteljorg, & Pittman, 2008). Furthermore, there has been a rise in literature on teacher leadership as a means of improving teaching practices within collaborative groups of teachers working in response to calls for education reform (Muijs & Harris, 2003; Murphy, 2005; Smylie, Conley, & Marks, 2002; Welch, 2000).

This program is built upon the Montclair State University Network for Educational Renewal (MSUNER), a school–university partnership that is committed to the simultaneous renewal of schools and teacher education through collaboration among the university and its partner school districts. It exemplifies a teacher leadership model that builds upon a decade-long partnership and various collaborative school/university models such as professional development schools (Goodlad, 1988; Levine & Trachtman, 2009; Rutter, 2011; Teitel, 2003, 2004). Being university-based, our program existed in a space outside of the district yet within a sphere of influence. We were positioned to both influence and support teachers as we were intimately familiar with their school and district contexts. But we also offered an outside perspective that helped them seek other possibilities for how things might be done.

*Fellow Selection*

School districts from the MSUNER were invited to apply to participate in the Wipro SEF program. Of the eight that applied, we selected five districts based on their demonstrated commitment to the program and alignment of vision for the teachers. These five districts located across three states participated in all five years of the project. All members of the university project team had worked within these districts in other partnerships prior to this grant and thus had a context for understanding the challenges and supports each faced. We knew from literature on partnership work (Levine & Trachtman, 2009; Rutter, 2011; Teitel, 2003, 2004) that this kind of understanding was essential to support change and also required sustained engagement.

Our program involved three cohorts, each comprising 20 K-12 science teachers. Teachers were recruited based on their experience (with most teaching more than three years at the time of recruitment) and written responses to questions related to their understanding of and plans for teacher leadership and content area focus. To support their work on the fellowship, each selected fellow received $10,000 for two years of participation. Over the two years, each fellow was required to participate in 125 hours of Wipro SEF activities.

## Significant Program Features

### Collaborative Work in Year One: Horizontal and Vertical Learning

In the first year of the program, fellows worked in vertical teams (content-based) in the fall semester and then in horizontal teams (grade level-based) in the spring semester. Vertical teams included members across grades from elementary to high school with the understanding that they would share ideas and experiences spanning all grade bands. For example, while an elementary school teacher might learn what is expected of students in the middle school and high school, a teacher in high school might learn about the background knowledge students bring into their classrooms. The intent of the horizontal teams was to facilitate discussion among teachers from the same grade level band to allow for deeper inquiry into the teaching practices and content specific to that grade level. For both models, each team consisted of four or five teachers. This work was premised on the theory that, while we could not prescribe a community of practice, genuine inquiry with similarly motivated teachers around issues of practice would support the growth of a strong learning community.

The purpose of the collaborative work in year one was to provide a structure for fellows to engage in reflective practice around their instruction. Fellows met regularly (about five times a semester) as they discussed each member's instruction, based on viewing of a lesson through video. The program guided the fellows as they navigated the protocol and became accustomed to a process that was unfamiliar to most. Given the sensitive nature of providing feedback on one's own and others' teaching, it became critical that a clear support system and set of norms be in place.

At the beginning of the semester, each team chose a problem of instructional practice to study and a content area upon which to focus. They also selected one research article related to their chosen practice to serve as a framework for their analysis. For example, one vertical team, whose content area was physics, chose to focus on questioning techniques and read a research paper on the role of questioning in the teaching and learning of science (Eshach, Dor-Ziderman, & Yefroimsky, 2014). The first group meeting involved discussing the research article and setting norms for providing feedback on video-recorded lessons. After this initial meeting, each member of the team video-recorded a lesson and shared it with the team. Teams met approximately five times during the semester, using a series of protocols to conduct video analysis. These protocols were developed by the University of Massachusetts, Boston (Center of Science and Mathematics in Context, n.d.), and modified for our context based on our own work with video and teacher leadership professional development. For each teacher observed, the group engaged in a pre-lesson meeting and a debrief meeting. To guide discussions during these meetings, each individual came to the meetings with completed forms that gathered their feedback. To gather feedback, fellows used simple forms to jot down "warm" (positive) and "cool" (for areas in need of improvement) feedback as they viewed the videos. To guide reflection and the debrief meetings, fellows were asked to complete a reflection form on what they learned from the meetings as they thought about their own classroom experiences and teaching practice. The form also encouraged the fellows to connect the observed lesson to research and provide suggestions for future meetings.

Our research points to the value of the fellows' collaborative work in the first year. The vertical articulation in the fall semester benefited teachers of all levels. High school teachers expressed a newfound appreciation for the elementary teachers. As one research participant put it, "The elementary teachers were really doing science...because, sometimes, you don't know because it's not their major." Through the videos, the observing teachers saw the depth of science content in which the students were engaged. Teachers of the higher grades also came to better understand the educational backgrounds of their students: "[It] enlightened me as to what to expect when students arrived." A different teacher noted, "Another interesting thing was I was able to see what kind of curriculum misconceptions teachers and/or the students had from younger grades. This allowed me to clarify when students came to high school."

Regardless of grade level taught, the vertical groups provided insights into the K-12 curriculum as a whole, through the lens of the chosen science content area. For many, this form of professional development was completely novel and participants noted it as particularly powerful, somewhat to our surprise. We realized that few professional development programs for public school teachers are focused on vertical learning, especially between elementary, middle, and high schools. It seems that, especially for the high school teachers, knowing the significant level of conceptual work of elementary students made them re-consider what they were asking of their own students.

### *Monthly Professional Development Workshops: Participating in a Community of Learners*

In addition to vertical (and horizontal) meetings, the entire cohort met monthly with the project team in professional development workshops that focused on such topics as Understanding by Design (Wiggins & McTighe, 2005), classroom discourse, standards-based teaching, teacher leadership, developing effective communication skills, and action research. The purpose of these workshops was to provide ongoing support to the teachers for improving their teaching practice and a space where they could share ideas and experiences. They also laid the foundation for the teachers' independent leadership projects in year two. One session in particular focused on elements of successful professional development workshops. During this session, the fellows were encouraged to think about how they might implement a professional development workshop in year two. Underlying all of our activities were two important goals: (1) to provide teacher leaders the tools they would need to support their work and (2) to build a larger community of practice for their leadership. Fellows reported that this was indeed an important aspect of their development.

The professional development workshops, along with their experiences in the vertical and horizontal groups, provided valuable learning opportunities for the fellows. They shared what they learned at the end of each semester, and in groups, presented their experiences from their vertical and horizontal teams. The teams were charged with framing their work within the context of their research article and with sharing lessons learned from the experience.

The participation in professional development workshops spanning five districts seemed to have a particular benefit. For example, one teacher noted, "They all have the same issues. Different districts show the same problems. We look at problems collectively. We don't have the same prejudices of administrators. It was nice to look at this collectively with outside opinions and without bias." Fellows also appreciated the community built around the program. When asked about the most significant learning experiences in year one, a teacher reported, "Definitely all the connections I made with teachers. We can e-mail, ask for advice…" Camaraderie and a sense of community among the teachers were significant benefits of our regular professional development workshops.

The constant work on building reflective discourse, a feature of numerous meetings, was another big take-away for the fellows:

> We spent a lot of time encouraging reflection and dialogue. I tried new things because I had district support … As far as pedagogy, the most beneficial was the focus on student driven dialogue or discourse as they call it. This became a massive role in how I run my class … Also, the reflective practices that we worked on made a difference. The introduction to SE [science education] practices is helping me teach this year.

Overall, we note the importance of building both pedagogical skills and community in supporting teacher leadership development. Too often, professional development for teacher leaders leaves out the skills teachers need both to improve their own practice and to engage in leadership work. This program sought to fill this gap.

## *Pursuing Teacher Leadership Projects in Year Two*

In year two, fellows designed and implemented a teacher leadership plan in their districts with support from mentors from MSU and their districts, as well as a "buddy" from a previous cohort. The fellows were encouraged to draw from their collaborative experiences and the professional development workshops from year one that were deliberately developed to prepare the teachers to undertake independent teacher leadership projects (e.g., communication, action research, and teacher leadership). The goal of the teacher leadership project was for teachers to strive to meet an individually designed objective and enact positive change in their districts. Fellows were encouraged to take lessons learned from year one activities and propose a project that could be completed between September and June. Fellows submitted project proposals, delving deeply into their inquiries and extending their spheres of influence to lead professional development in their grades, schools, and districts. Some required several iterations of revision and support from the mentors to develop their teacher leadership plans. The whole group met twice a year to share their experiences and problem-solve challenges.

Projects included conducting action research, facilitating teacher study groups, mentoring and coaching teachers, exploring interdisciplinary connections, infusing instruction with meaningful uses of technology, revising curricula, and proposing to de-track first-year science courses. Fellows were encouraged to present their work at state and national conferences and at meetings within their districts. In addition to implementing their leadership projects, fellows were required to lead and video record one professional development activity. The activities ranged from leading multi-district workshops on the implementation of the Next Generation Science Standards to coaching teachers from a single school. Fellows submitted monthly reflection logs chronicling their teacher leadership projects and their work on developing and implementing a professional development activity for their colleagues.

In our research, fellows reported that, in some cases, the most significant support of the year two teacher leadership project was the backing of a university-based program:

> Actually, it gave me the avenue to do this…When I approached them, I asked, "Well, I'm doing this for the

> Wipro program. This is the whole idea if you wanted to participate." If I was doing this on my own, I would have come across as some crazy guy. I don't know how they would have interpreted it, but the whole idea gave me a foundation that [suggested]: "Oh, this is something important, sure I'll help."

Many of our teacher leaders noted the value of the project's backing in the collateral it gave them as they negotiated with districts, schools, and peers. The program encouraged (and even required) them to take risks in reaching out to those who might be able to help them realize a project they had been considering for years.

For others, the time, support, and funding to delve deeply into an area of teaching practice became the most significant feature of the program. One fellow described how it helped her emerge as a leader in implementing the new science standards in her building:

> Because my [teacher leadership project] focus is on Next Gen Standards, it allowed me to jump into that and really understand it. I have an understanding of what they expect of us in the classroom from these standards. From the very beginning it completely changed how I teach science, not so much of the content but more the activities that allow students to be more in control. Actually it's more a facilitator role than a teacher role.

The teacher leadership project in year two opened a space for the fellows to engage in the kinds of activities they had previously been unable to enact, either because the resources did not exist, or they did not feel they had the necessary authority.

### *Differentiated Mentoring of Teacher Leadership*

Meeting the fellows where they were in the process of becoming teacher leaders was a unique feature of our program. Mentoring might involve finding relevant resources or necessary professional development opportunities for the fellow. Other fellows needed help with strategies to navigate the school districts and devise a step-by-step approach to encouraging change. For example, one fellow needed mentoring in developing her conversation skills when working with someone she perceived to be a person in authority. Her university mentor modeled for her how these conversations might sound, and with this support and guidance, by the third year, the fellow was having these conversations on her own.

In terms of facilitating fellows' growth, the program provided mentorship by taking the fellows' feedback into account, guiding them in developing their teacher leadership plans, and encouraging them to continue to seek leadership opportunities within their districts. One fellow noted how his mentor encouraged him to think more ambitiously about his goals:

> She was instrumental in getting me to realize that I could do more than what I was actually going to do for my [teacher leadership project]. On top of that, I got help from [university mentors] in getting funding for better filming equipment. Throughout every step of the way, they were instrumental in getting me to a point where I could do really solid work.

It is worth noting that in many cases, fellows needed support that went beyond ideas and resources. For example, fellows often needed help in re-shaping their notions of what counted as leadership. One fellow who was working on building a girls' STEM initiative (that would eventually incorporate both girls and boys in the entire school) worried that her goals were too modest and that she wasn't doing the "right" kind of teacher leadership, "That was something that I talked to [the faculty mentor] about…I'm just running a club after school…How am I really being a leader?" Many conversations helped this fellow re-define her notion of teacher leadership, which then pushed her to think more expansively about how to build upon the impact of her work.

Additionally, university mentors supported fellows in accessing other opportunities to engage in the profession. For example, fellows were provided funds to attend national conferences to present their work and to network with other teachers. For some, this was their first experience presenting to peers or attending a national conference, an opportunity that allowed them to share their leadership efforts with the wider research community. Many noted the power of attending and presenting at conferences with university mentors since those experiences helped them to see the broader context and impact of their work.

Besides the support provided by the university, school administrators, district coordinators (DCs), and other members of the school also played a significant role in mentoring fellows in the program. They provided tangible administrative support to the fellows as they discovered their own leadership paths and implemented their teacher leadership plans, from mentoring them in designing their leadership plans to helping them enact those plans. The DCs enlisted qualified teachers into the program and helped with the logistics of enacting leadership (i.e., scheduling and planning professional development, providing substitute teachers when needed, and arranging schedules and meetings to facilitate teacher leadership plans). They also attended regular meetings with the fellows and extended their support by acting as a liaison between the fellows and the school administration as the fellows pursued their teacher leadership projects.

## *Extending Teacher Leadership beyond the Program*

Our program has offered fellows multiple and various opportunities to grow as teacher leaders. In addition to the regular professional development workshops and the collaborative work that was put into place, the teacher leaders had opportunities to find a network of professionals beyond the walls of their classrooms.

After year two, fellows were encouraged to apply for a mini-grant to extend their teacher leadership project. For some fellows, mini-grants led to looking for and completing larger grant proposals to support new initiatives. For others the mini-grants allowed other teachers in their schools to become involved in new curriculum development. For example, prior to program participation, a Cohort One fellow noticed that the freshman biology classes in her high school were taught using traditional pedagogy with many students failing and having to repeat the class. Participating in the program led her to reflect on her practice and question why so many students were failing. She spent the first year of the program reading research about different teaching practices and attended a workshop about using cases to teach science.

Encouraged by the effectiveness of this pedagogy, she decided to create an individual project that focused on teaching biology using cases with a team of teachers. She and her colleagues collected data that year and found that they had far fewer failures and many more students being recommended for honors-level tenth grade geoscience. In her third year, with support from a mini-grant, she invited her tenth grade geoscience colleagues to participate in the case study method, and has now impacted the science pedagogy of two grade levels. Demonstrating that changing to a more engaging pedagogy leads to achievement, this fellow's teacher leadership project has led the de-tracking of the ninth grade biology classes. In the future, teachers hope to do the same in the tenth grade geoscience classes. The mini-grants funded more sustainable change in the participating districts and provided fellows with more freedom to take ownership of the changes they were leading in their schools.

Engagement in the program allowed for the fellows to alter their perceptions of their own role as a science teacher. In the process of emerging as teacher leaders, they expanded that role to include more agency into their teaching practice, whether through their independent teacher leadership projects or efforts to sustain their projects (Taylor et al., under review). The program also brought fellows recognition within their districts because their work was viewed as affiliated with an outside source. This helped in giving fellows a voice within their districts and gave their projects credibility. Fellows received recognition in various ways. Some became teacher of the year, and all districts were awarded plaques for their efforts at board meetings. Recognition of the fellows' work allowed them to further their causes and recruit other teachers into their programs.

Their teacher networks naturally extended across three sites, because the implementation of the program is in three states. Each year, one of the sites hosted a conference during which teams from year one presented their work and fellows at the end of year two presented posters of their teacher leadership projects. In addition to workshops led by leaders in the field of science education and teacher leadership, fellows from the three sites had opportunities to share their respective experiences, not just about the program, but about K-12 science education in general.

More than anything, this project provided an opportunity for teachers to be treated as professionals. They attended conferences, presented, and networked with other teachers, both through our program and by meeting colleagues from across the three sites. Many noted that the opportunity to serve as professionals beyond the classroom was central to their growth as teacher leaders.

## Nurturing Teacher Leaders: Our Findings

In addition to the features of the Wipro SEF noted above, this work has given us a unique opportunity to analyze the experiences of teachers as they developed into teacher leaders. We have been conducting ongoing recursive research to inform and to hone our professional development practices, and to disseminate findings at national and international conferences and through peer-reviewed publications in the field.

Four major themes emerged from careful analyses of the data.

## Ownership

Fellows need to have ownership of the direction of their professional development. They are more invested in the examination of practices when their questions and potential innovative practices directly emerge from challenges they face in the classroom or school. Their motivation needs to be both authentic and organic. This was particularly evident when we examined the transcripts of the vertical team debrief meetings. The most in-depth discussions centered around issues that emerged organically from examining the teaching videos in the debrief sessions. Taking ownership of the conversation was an important step in the fellows' journey toward becoming teacher leaders. The move from providing structured responses elicited by the protocols to communicating shared concerns depicted a development of the team from a pseudo-community (Grossman, Wineburg, & Woolworth, 2001) toward a strong learning community. Moving forward, we plan to foster side conversations that develop organically as a way of gaining deeper insights into how teams take ownership of conversations. Conversations are features of authentic communities of practice that emerge as teachers discuss common goals and questions that are relevant to them (Printy, 2008).

## Teachers are the Most Consistent Change Agents

In our extensive experiences of working in partnerships with schools, including prior to this project, we have understood that administrative leadership can have a significant impact on teacher leadership and sustainable school change, and also that administrators are in constant flux and such instability must be anticipated. For example, in one district the superintendent has changed three times in the last four years. The same district eliminated the math/science supervisor position last year. This lack of stability in the upper administration points to the need for classroom teachers, or Wipro Fellows, to be the stable forces that advocate for positive change and lead initiatives in their districts. This finding supports our vision of our fellows' role as teacher leaders. As we mentioned earlier, the Wipro SEF draws from the literature on distributed leadership in which teachers shoulder the responsibilities of change along with school administration to bring about change in their districts (Danielson, 2006; Katzenmeyer & Moller, 2001; Taylor et al., 2011). Teacher leaders are the consistent change agents in their buildings because their leadership work – as well as their leadership identities – emerges from working on issues within their districts.

## Principals as Supports

Fellows feel pressure to address district needs, as outlined by district-level administrators, but often the principal is the most significant administrator in determining both needs and implementation. In year one of the grant, principals were not included in the teams and therefore had not been in positions to support the fellows. We would like to provide increased opportunities for principal involvement – but in a twofold capacity as both an administrator who can help to support the teacher leaders and also as a co-learner who understands the complexities of implementing innovative practices to bring about change. Our hope is that these efforts will allow principals to realize the benefits of distributed leadership (Gronn, 2000; Harris, 2010; Muijs & Harris, 2007; Spillane, 2006).

## Elementary Teachers in Particular Need Support

The fellows in the elementary schools teach a variety of content areas, and hence are naturally interdisciplinary. Furthermore, connecting other disciplines to science is one way to give science adequate instructional time. Our intensive science-focused program allowed the elementary-level fellows further opportunities for reflection about their pedagogical practices in a science content area. The vertical articulation enhanced their understanding of science across the grade levels, enabling them to gain a deeper understanding of the content they teach (Suh & Seshaiyer, 2015).

Supporting elementary science teachers as they become teacher leaders can also encourage recruitment of colleagues to engage in interdisciplinary projects. Many feel isolated without the Wipro community and seek a community of inquiry. Our fellows also sought to build their own communities and transfer what they learned from their experience with the Wipro SEF, developing their own communities for sustained support. This is consistent with the literature, which notes the importance of communities of practice for elementary school teachers (Cook & Buck, 2014; Gellert, 2013).

# Conclusion

Much of the research about teacher leadership examines the ways in which teachers enact leadership in schools and districts with little focus on the best practices for the professional development of teacher leaders. The Wipro

SEF provides a model for school–university partnerships that involves teacher leaders, university personnel, and school administrators collaborating to enhance practice and student outcomes in K-12 science education. While much of what we know about effective professional development holds true for teacher leadership development, we also recognize the unique ways in which teacher leaders need to learn and be supported in their growth. We are continually making efforts to improve our program and the findings from our research guide our efforts and provide insight into the design of other programs aimed at developing teacher leaders.

We realize that much of what we were able to offer teacher leaders in the Wipro SEF was a kind of "in between" space for teacher leaders to network, develop, and "tune" their practice with others. Additionally, university-based mentors were able to work within districts where they had long-standing partnerships to help fellows navigate the inevitable challenges of leadership work. Each fellow needed unique and differentiated support, with consideration given to the context of their school and district – support we were able to structure through the flexibility of the second year of the model.

As we conclude three cohorts of the Wipro SEF, we move into a second phase of the project: sustainability and scale. This next phase will seek to build on the significant base of science teachers in each district who have been members of the program. For the next three years, we will support teachers as they become more independent from the program structures. They will be charged with taking lessons learned from their previous experiences as they involve others in professional development practices such as vertically aligned reflective teaching groups, or as they undertake new or expanded teacher leadership projects. In addition to working within their districts, fellows will work to recruit new teachers into the Wipro SEF, challenging themselves to become spokespeople for the program. In this way, our first cohorts of science teacher leaders will continue to be instrumental as our program develops and grows.

# References

Ackerman, R., & Mackenzie, S. V. (2006). Uncovering teacher leadership. *Educational Leadership, 63*(8), 66–70.

Borko, H., Jacobs, J., Eiteljorg, E., & Pittman, M. E. (2008). Video as a tool for fostering productive discussions in mathematics professional development. *Teaching and Teacher Education, 24*(2), 417–436.

Burns, R. W., Yendol-Hoppey, D., & Jacobs, J. (2015). High quality teaching requires collaboration: How partnerships can create a true continuum of professional learning for educators. *The Educational Forum, 79*(1), 53–67.

Center for Comprehensive School Reform and Improvement. (2009). *Vertical alignment: Ensuring opportunity to learn in a standards-based system. Issue Brief.* Center for Comprehensive School Reform and Improvement. Washington, DC. Retrieved from http://www.centerforcsri.org

Center of Science and Mathematics in Context. (n.d.). University of Massachusetts Boston. Retrieved from https://www.umb.edu/cosmic. Accessed on May 15, 2017.

Chrispeels, J. H., & Martin, K. J. (2002). Four school leadership teams define their roles within organizational and political structures to improve student learning. *School Effectiveness and School Improvement, 13*(3), 327–365.

Cochran-Smith, M., & Lytle, S. L. (2009). *Inquiry as stance: Practitioner research for the next generation.* New York, NY: Teachers College Press.

Cook, K., & Buck, G. (2014). Pre-Service Elementary Teachers' Experience in a Community of Practice through a Place-Based Inquiry. *International Journal of Environmental and Science Education, 9*(2), 111–132.

Crowther, F., Kaagan, S., Ferguson, M., & Hann, L. (2009). *Developing teacher leaders: How teacher leadership enhances school success.* Thousand Oaks, CA: Corwin Press.

Danielson, C. (2006). *Teacher leadership that strengthens professional practice.* Alexandria, VA: ASCD.

Day, C., & Harris, A. (2002). Teacher leadership, reflective practice, and school improvement. In K. Leithwood & P. Hallinger (Eds.), *Second international handbook of educational leadership and administration* (pp. 957–977). Dordrecht: Springer Press.

Donaldson, G. A. (2007). What do teachers bring to leadership? In R. H. Ackerman & S. V. Mackenzie (Eds.), *Uncovering teacher leadership: Essays and voices from the field* (pp. 131–140). Thousand Oaks, CA: Corwin Press.

Elmore, R. F. (2004). *School reform from the inside out: Policy, practice, and performance.* Cambridge, MA: Harvard Education Press.

Eshach, H., Dor-Ziderman, Y., & Yefroimsky, Y. (2014). Question asking in the science classroom: Teacher attitudes and practices. *Journal of Science Education and Technology, 23*(1), 67–81.

Frost, D., & Durrant, J. (2003). Teacher leadership: Rationale, strategy and impact. *School Leadership and Management, 23*(2), 173–186.

Fullan, M., & Hargreaves, A. (1996). *What's worth fighting for in your school?* New York, NY: Teachers College Press.

Gellert, L. M. (2013). Elementary school teachers and mathematics: Communities of practice and an opportunity for change. *Journal of Education and Learning, 2*(4), 113–122.

Goodlad, J. I. (1988). School–university partnerships for educational renewal: Rationale and concepts. In K. A. Sirotnik & J. I. Goodlad (Eds.), *School–university partnerships in action: Concepts, cases, and concerns* (pp. 3–31). New York, NY: Teachers College Press.

Gronn, P. (2000). Distributed properties: A new architecture for leadership. *Educational Management and Administration, 28*(3), 317–338.
Grossman, P. L., Wineburg, S., & Woolworth, S. (2001). Toward a theory of teacher community. *Teachers College Record, 103*(6), 942–1012.
Harris, A. (2010). Distributed leadership. In T. Bush, L. Bell, & D. Middlewood (Eds.), *The principles of educational leadership and management* (pp. 55–69). London: Sage.
Hunzicker, J. (2012). Professional development and job-embedded collaboration: How teachers learn to exercise leadership. *Professional Development in Education, 38*(2), 267–289.
Jacobs, J., & Crowell, L. (2016). Developing as teacher leaders for social justice: The influence of a teacher leadership graduate program. *The New Educator*, 1–27. doi: 10.1080/1547688X.2016.1237693
Katzenmeyer, M., & Moller, G. (2001). *Awakening the sleeping giant: Helping teachers develop as leaders*. Thousand Oaks, CA: Corwin Press.
Lambert, L. (2003). *Leadership capacity for lasting school improvement*. Alexandria, VA: ASCD.
Levine, M., & Trachtman, R. (2009). *Professional development school pathways to teacher quality in urban areas: Linking PDSs to improve teacher induction and alternate routes to certification*. Washington, DC: National Council for Accreditation of Teacher Education.
Lieberman, A., & Miller, L. (2005). *Teacher leadership*. San Francisco, CA: Jossey-Bass.
Lieberman, A., & Miller, L. (2011). Learning communities: The starting point for professional learning is in schools and classrooms. *Journal of Staff Development, 32*(4), 16–20.
Muijs, D., & Harris, A. (2003). Teacher leadership and school improvement. *Education Review, 16*(2), 39–42.
Muijs, D., & Harris, A. (2007). Teacher leadership in (in)action: Three case studies of contrasting schools. *Educational Management Administration & Leadership, 35*(1), 111–134.
Murphy, J. (Ed.). (2005). *Connecting teacher leadership and school improvement*. Thousand Oaks, CA: Corwin Press.
Printy, S. M. (2008). Leadership for teacher learning: A community of practice perspective. *Educational Administration Quarterly, 44*(2), 187–226.
Rogers, B. (Ed.). (2002). *Teacher leadership and behavior management*. Thousand Oaks, CA: Sage.
Rutter, A. (2011). Purpose and vision of professional development schools. *Yearbook of the National Society for the Study of Education, 110*(2), 289–305.
Smylie, M., Conley, S., &, Marks, H. (2002). Exploring new approaches to teacher leadership for school improvement. *Yearbook of the National Society for the Study of Education, 101*(1), 162–188. Retrieved from http://doi.org/10.1111/j.1744-7984.2002.tb00008.x
Spillane, J. P. (2006). *Distributed leadership*. San Francisco, CA: Jossey-Bass.

Suh, J., & Seshaiyer, P. (2015). Examining teachers' understanding of the mathematical learning progression through vertical articulation during Lesson Study. *Journal of Mathematics Teacher Education, 18*(3), 207–229.

Talbert, J. E. (2010). Professional learning communities at the crossroads: How systems hinder or engender change. In A. Hargreaves, A. Lieberman, M. Fullan, & D. Hopkins (Eds.), *Second international handbook of educational change* (pp. 555–571). Dordrecht: Springer Press.

Taylor, M., Goeke, J., Klein, E., Onore, C., & Geist, K. (2011). Changing leadership: Teachers lead the way for schools that learn. *Journal of Teaching and Teacher Education, 27*(5), 920–929.

Taylor, M., Klein, E., Munakata, M., Trabona, K., & Rahman, Z. (under review). Professional development for teacher leaders: Using activity theory to understand the complexities of sustainable change.

Teitel, L. (2003). *The professional development schools handbook: Starting, sustaining and assessing partnerships that improve student learning.* Thousand Oaks, CA: Corwin Press.

Teitel, L. (2004). *How professional development schools make a difference: A review of research* (2nd ed.). Washington, DC: National Council for Accreditation of Teacher Education.

Welch, R. L. (2000). Training a new generation of leaders. *Journal of Leadership & Organizational Studies, 7*(1), 70–81.

Wiggins, G. P., & McTighe, J. (2005). *Understanding by design.* Alexandria, VA: ASCD.

York-Barr, J., & Duke, K. (2004). What do we know about teacher leadership? Findings from two decades of scholarship. *Review of Educational Research, 74*(3), 255–316.

Chapter 16

# Developing Leadership Capacity in PDS Master Teachers

*Somer Lewis, Amy Garrett Dikkers, Lynn Sikma and Katie Fink*

### Abstract

Grounded in the principles of constructivist leadership, the Master Teacher Program at the University of North Carolina Wilmington began as a three-year initiative to highlight and strengthen the extraordinary work and leadership potential of teachers in a multi-district professional development system. Currently in its fifth year, the program has evolved to include an array of collaborative opportunities impacting not only our partnership teachers, but also college faculty, professional development school beginning teachers, and the students they serve. This chapter shares the experiences of program participants and a multitude of ways in which each has engaged in practices meant to enhance and promote teacher leadership in our partnership.

*Keywords:* Constructivist leadership theory; school–university partnerships; teacher leadership; master teacher; STEM; teacher leader development

The simultaneous renewal of teacher education programs and P-12 schools has served as the ongoing vision of the professional development school (PDS) movement since the mid-1980s. While organizational structures have shifted over time, a shared dedication to reciprocal growth, teacher candidate preparation, and the examination of educational practice to support student achievement continue to be mainstays in school–university collaborations (Cozza, 2010; Darling-Hammond, Bullmaster, & Cobb, 1995; Goodlad, 1988; Teitel, 2004; Trachtman, 2007). These commitments reveal the need to not only alter teacher education programs to support the professional growth of preservice teachers in the field, but also to create support systems for improving the practice of teachers on site, where educators take on new leadership roles and engage with university faculty to rethink practice (Cozza, 2010; Lewis & Walser, 2016; Teitel, 2004). According to Darling-Hammond et al. (1995), these interactions create "an opportunity for the profession to expand its knowledge base by putting research into practice and practice into research." (p. 88). Purposeful interactions and partnerships supported by the design of a PDS allow for the development of new instructional models, re-examination of teaching and learning, and growth of teacher leaders.

In 1993, the Watson College of Education (WCE) at the University of North Carolina Wilmington (UNCW), signed its first partnership agreement with two local school districts. Since then, our professional development system has grown to include 12 districts, 146 schools, and over 2,000 partnership teachers. It is currently structured using a flexible, tiered system for partnership. Tier 1 schools and university faculty participate in mutually beneficial professional development opportunities aimed at building capacity in our partnership schools. Tier 2 teachers, administrators, and faculty collaborate to support the growth of preservice teacher candidates. Tier 3 school–university partners engage in research and other more in-depth initiatives that help to inform the design of our teacher education programs. While our PDS system hosts an array of initiatives aimed at impacting teaching and learning throughout our partnership, the Master Teacher Program serves as our most intentional, innovative example of mutually beneficial collaboration that works to develop and promote teacher leadership at various levels.

Our school–university partnership supports master teachers as constructivist leaders (Lambert, 2005; Lambert et al., 2002) impacting their own classrooms and schools by providing opportunities to learn, explore, and face challenges; inspiration to create, design, and discover; encouragement to try again, do their best, do it better, work harder, and never give up; connections to the world beyond the classroom and community; nurturing relationships with a caring adult; and cooperative engagement to work with peers, challenge others, and evaluate learning.

To further support this program, we utilize a working definition of teacher leadership that emerged from Wenner and Campbell's (2017) review of the teacher leadership literature where teachers are

> working beyond the classroom walls, supporting professional learning in their schools, and being involved in

policymaking and decision making at some level with the ultimate goal of improving student learning and success and seeking improvement and change for the whole school organization. (p. 157)

Grounded in leadership as a socially constructed paradigm, the Master Teacher Program began as a three-year initiative that served to highlight and strengthen the extraordinary work and leadership potential of our partnership teachers.

## Evolution of the Master Teacher Program

Initially, the Master Teacher Program supported the collaboration of P-12 professional educators to reflect on current practice and impact the educational environment by creating a safe, comfortable, and nurturing environment where all children can learn; making decisions based on what is best for all students; engaging children in interesting and meaningful ways; fostering the "whole" child to build connections that address their social, emotional, and physical needs; and reflecting on current and past practices to continually improve the learner's experience (University of North Carolina Wilmington, 2016). The initial 2012–2015 cohort of master teachers represented the spectrum of P-12 grade levels and a variety of content areas. Teachers were nominated by college faculty and the 12 teachers who were chosen participated in 30 hours of professional development in a hybrid learning environment. As part of the professional development, teachers shared recordings of themselves conducting one lesson and completed a series of self-reflections that described their journey toward mastery in teaching. Master teachers received a stipend for each year of participation. Upon completing their extended professional development, they supported field experience students and interns in their classrooms, provided lesson demonstrations in college methods courses, served as guest speakers or panelists at selected college professional development opportunities, and served as advisory board members to the university PDS office at one meeting per year.

Teachers from our initial cohort reported feeling "inspiration and encouragement" when leaving their bi-annual master teacher meetings. They enjoyed the opportunity to collaborate with colleagues across schools and looked forward to returning to their schools to share the ideas discussed at their master teacher meetings. They identified collaboration among fellow master teachers as the greatest accomplishment of the program, but also expressed interest in working more closely with teachers in their schools, faculty in the college, and P-20 students to have a greater impact on our school–university partnership at large.

Although our first cohort experienced success and satisfaction as teachers in instructional practice, a goal of our second cohort's program design focused on enhancing opportunities for leadership beyond the scope of each teacher's individual classroom. We sought to further engage teachers in the principles of constructivist leadership, "the reciprocal processes that enable the participants in an educational community to construct meanings that lead toward a shared purpose of schooling." (Lambert et al., 2002, p. 42). Our PDS partnership supports opportunities to collaborate with teachers in a dynamic process. As a result, cohort two has experienced a more intentional, extended program design. Our current Master Teacher Program includes an array of collaborative leadership and professional development opportunities impacting not only our master teachers, but also college faculty, PDS beginning teachers and, as always, the students they serve (see Figure 1).

This new model of professional growth enhances the development of school-based teacher leadership that is integral to the success of our school–university partnership and to the growth of P-20 students and teachers. Members of our second master teacher cohort take part in more than 30 hours of face-to-face professional development alongside Watson College faculty master teacher associates (MTAs) on topics self-selected by master teachers and their faculty partners. In addition, master teachers collaborate with MTAs to design and implement one or more professional

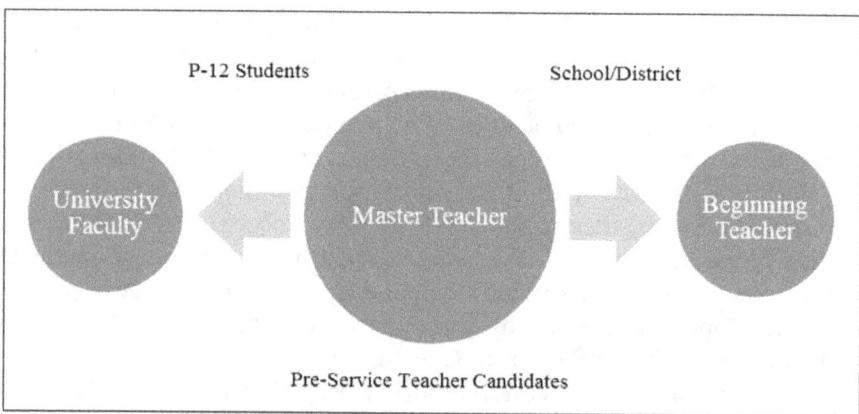

Figure 1: Master Teacher Program Design. The figure illustrates master teacher collaboration with faculty and beginning teachers impacting P-12 students, pre-service teacher candidates, schools and districts within our school–university partnership.

growth and enrichment opportunities in their classrooms, schools, or district. Growth opportunities are not restricted, and may include action research, designing professional development for teachers, or co-planning coursework, to name a few. One master teacher and MTA, for example, are implementing an inquiry model in the teacher's fifth grade classroom. This master teacher's students are now moving from guided inquiry to a student self-guided approach, and the teacher and her faculty partner are developing an inquiry mini-lesson catalog for teachers at the school, as well as leading professional development for teachers across our 12-district partnership. Another pair is researching strategies for maintaining a STEM (science, technology, engineering, mathematics) mindset in high school students. Together, this team will survey students and their families to better understand strategies for keeping students motivated and engaged in STEM learning with the intention of sharing and implementing these strategies in the master teacher's classroom and throughout the school.

During their three-year term, in addition to their collaboration with faculty MTAs, cohort two master teachers serve as mentors to beginning teacher Promise of Leadership (POL) Award recipients. These beginning teachers are dispersed throughout our school–university partnership, often working in a school and/or district not the same as the one in which our master teachers are employed. Our POL Award recipients are teachers in their second or third year who have already begun to demonstrate leadership in their classrooms or schools. The program pairs master teachers with POLs who are then supported in designing and delivering professional development for other beginning teachers. The relationship between master teacher and POL is further supported by the faculty MTA, if needed.

Also, similar to our initial cohort, master teachers are called upon to host more intensive field experiences, provide lesson demonstrations to WCE classes, serve as guest speakers and panelists at select WCE events and meetings, and/or serve as advisory board members to the PDS office or dean. The Master Teacher Program seeks to lift the voices of our partnership teachers, empowering them as formal leaders "growing and changing in concert with others," (Lambert et al., 2002, p. 40) leading in their schools, districts, and as essential members of our teacher education programs and larger learning community. Table 1 provides a brief timeline of the two-year partnership between master teachers and MTAs.

The followings are the experiences of two program participants, a faculty MTA and a master teacher, both co-authors of this chapter. Their stories reflect not only the intentional design of the program, but also the unintended occasions that manifest when teachers are provided the

Table 1: Master Teacher Timeline.

| Meeting Dates | Year 1 (2016–2017) | Year 2 (2017–2018) |
|---|---|---|
| September (MTs and MTAs) | Discuss common interests, personal and professional goals, and decide on professional growth opportunity | Revisit shared goals, implementation and progress monitoring; renew research review protocols; consider NAPDS Conference and other PDS initiatives |
| November (MTs and MTAs) | Share implementation plan with group and decide how to monitor progress, what supports are needed; develop research review protocols | MTs and MTAs report progrss to group, discuss opportunities to share initiatives |
| February (MTs and POLs) | MTs report progress to group; meet with POLs to plan May professional development | MTs report progress to group; meet with POLs to plan May professional development |
| April (MTs and MTAs) | MT and MTA group updates and report, identify support needs for following year; readjust goals, implementation and progress monitoring | MT and MTA group updates and final reporting, evaluations, feedback |

opportunity to learn, grow, and lead with others, central to constructive leadership.

## A Master Teacher Associate's Story

Nikki and I began working together in January 2016 when I was supervising student interns at her school. Nikki served as both a partnership teacher and site coordinator at her school, and because of these dual roles, we had frequent interactions with each other. As the semester progressed, I learned about Nikki's love and enthusiasm for teaching science (despite not feeling confident in her science content knowledge), which is unusual to find in an elementary teacher. Since the focus of my teaching and research is elementary science teaching, I knew I wanted to work with Nikki in some capacity. Later that spring, my university's PDS office put out a call for proposals for a Partnership in Action Award, $2,500 to be awarded to a faculty-teacher pair working on a project together within our professional development system. I immediately approached Nikki, asking her whether there was any project she wished she could do if she had the money and resources. She expressed a desire to create a STEM resource lab; STEM activities and resources that would be available to teachers at all grade levels to check out. At the time, I knew Nikki was going to be asked to be a master teacher and would need a faculty MTA. The award would serve as a jumpstart for her master teacher project.

When we received the award, Nikki and I met several times to discuss her major and minor goals for the STEM lab and to develop a long-term implementation plan. From there, we discussed the research aspects of the project, both my plan and interests and her role as researcher. This was pivotal, as it was the first time Nikki considered being "more than just a classroom teacher." She was nervous at the prospect of doing research and questioned her own abilities. Adopting the role of coach, I assured her she could and would be successful and that I would help each step of the way. This has been a pattern throughout our work together, and one of the reasons I think our partnership has been so successful; I am constantly encouraging Nikki to step out of her comfort zone with the promise of being her safety net.

Implementation of the STEM lab began in September 2016, and is ongoing. Nikki has reported growth in both her students and herself. At the start of the project, she quantified her own confidence level in teaching STEM at about 50%, and midway through the year that had improved to 70%. Her students began the year generally enthusiastic about STEM, but without a solid understanding of the processes involved in doing STEM. A few months in, the students' enthusiasm for STEM was so high that Nikki had to constantly force them outside for recess because they wanted to carry on with the STEM activities. The activities provided students with a much better understanding of the processes involved in STEM and Nikki recounted several instances where students carried out activities outside of school. Teachers in Nikki's school have approached her with increased frequency for lesson plan ideas and to model STEM instruction in their classrooms.

In addition to implementing the project, Nikki and I have also partnered outside her classroom. We recently presented our work at a national conference, and another presentation is forthcoming. We are working on publishing some of Nikki's STEM lesson plans and reflections, and I recently had Nikki as a guest speaker in my science methods classroom, presenting on how she utilizes standards to create lesson plans and some of the struggles she faces as a classroom teacher. Each of these experiences has had a tremendous impact on Nikki's personal and professional growth. In less than a year of working together, I have seen her confidence improve and watched her evolve from a teacher to teacher researcher and, ultimately, to teacher leader. In a recent master teacher survey, Nikki noted that

> I am learning a lot from [my MTA]. My confidence in the science content that I teach is improving as well as unfolding the components of STEM. I am learning how to complete an action research project and what steps are involved in an IRB (Institutional Review Board proposal). These are things I would have never pursued if it weren't for the partnership. ... I have become more self-reflective and ventured outside my comfort zone, which is necessary to grow professionally. (March, 2017)

As a teacher educator, it has been helpful for me, as Nikki's MTA, to be intricately involved in the schools, as it gives me first-hand, real-time classroom experience that can be applied to my courses. The opportunity afforded by the Master Teacher Program keeps me abreast of what challenges and opportunities exist for teachers in elementary classrooms. However, the most rewarding outcome hasn't been my personal gain, but rather seeing the personal growth made by Nikki in such a short period of time. I am extremely grateful for the opportunity to be part of her advancement as a teacher leader.

## A Master Teacher's Story

When I was in my third year of teaching, I was named a POL Award recipient from the UNCW and received the opportunity to be mentored by a faculty member. As part of that process, I was able to present a professional development session for other beginning teachers with the help of my faculty mentor. I successfully implemented a professional development session and was immediately hooked on designing and facilitating meaningful and relevant professional development. It is rare for a beginning teacher to take on such leadership roles and it truly sparked my journey into educational leadership.

After my experience as a POL, I continued my leadership roles by becoming the lead mentor in my school. I currently oversee the beginning teacher support program mandated by the state and provide professional development to meet the needs of the beginning teachers in my building. In the past five years, I have finished my master's degree, earned National Board Certification, and completed my doctorate in educational leadership. After being named the 2015–2016 County Teacher of the Year, I was nominated to become a master teacher at the university. Once again, I was given the opportunity to work with a faculty member to deepen my experiences in education to enhance my own career.

When nominated to serve a three-year term as a master teacher, I was excited by the opportunity to work with faculty in the WCE to enhance my own professional experiences. When I learned that the faculty partner would be the same person, I knew my experience would be a great one. Over the past year, my MTA has helped me accomplish some of my professional goals. Within the next few years, I would like to make the transition from teaching in a high school to teaching in a university. In order to do that, I need to write an effective curriculum vita (CV), gain experience presenting papers at state and national conferences, and publish my work. Over the past year, working under my MTA's guidance, I have created a CV, presented at three state conferences, and am in the process of getting articles published. My MTA has been enormously helpful in providing me with feedback and keeping me on track to accomplish my professional goals.

The relationship I have with my MTA is symbiotic, because I am helping her conduct research at the same time that she is helping me advance my professional goals. Though it is still in the early stages, we are researching global education initiatives in our region. Given that I have experience creating surveys and analyzing survey data while working on my doctorate in education, I can be more helpful to her than other research assistants.

Another aspect of the master teacher initiative is that I get to mentor a POL as she designs and facilitates a professional development session of her own. Mentoring beginning teachers has been my biggest passion since I was one myself, and it is a rewarding opportunity to see the POL collaboration from both angles. I have had the opportunity to mentor two beginning teachers over the past two years, and I can tell that both of them will continue to develop their leadership skills and be strong teacher leaders. This component of the program makes leadership sustainable within the districts, and the impact will be felt for many years to come.

Besides the benefits of working with a faculty member, being a master teacher has provided me with the chance to build relationships with other teacher leaders throughout the region. High school teachers tend to work in isolation. We go in our classrooms, close our doors, and teach with little to no collaboration. The master teacher initiative provides me with the opportunity in each quarter to meet face to face with teacher leaders from all grade levels and content backgrounds around the southeast region of our state. Though we have only been meeting for a little over a year, we are already developing strong professional relationships which I'm sure will continue long after our tenure as master teachers.

In addition, I have continued to enhance my own leadership experiences since becoming a master teacher. Shortly after being named a master teacher, I was named the 2016–2017 Regional Teacher of the Year, which has provided me with countless leadership opportunities. My master teacher status has resulted in invitations to present at WCU and attend a meet and greet with the local board of education. Between these experiences and my work with my MTA, I know I will continue to be a strong leader and advocate for public education in our state.

## Reflections on the Program Redesign

As part of the renewed effort to enable growth in teacher leadership and establish true partnerships between school and university constituents, we are gathering Master Teacher Program data at several points to check in on the process, understand the impact of the program for all partners, and readjust any aspects of the program, as needed. Survey data gathered in April 2017 (75% response rate) reflect approximately eight months of collaboration between master teachers and MTAs in cohort two. At this stage in the process, 52% ($n = 8$) believe their goals and their partner's goals are very aligned, while 33% ($n = 5$) believe their goals are aligned, and 13% ($n = 2$) believe they are somewhat aligned. In addition, the majority are confident they will achieve most of their goals (53%, $n = 8$) during their two-year partnership. Three participants (20%) believe they will achieve each of their goals, and four (27%) are confident they will achieve at least one of their goals.

Participants in the program see value on many different levels. Similar to the initial cohort of master teachers, the second cohort views collaboration with colleagues and sharing of new instructional strategies and techniques as main benefits of the program. In addition, master teachers cite opportunities for personal and professional growth, mentioning occasions for self-reflection, opportunities to "venture outside of [their] comfort zones," being pushed to implement new strategies, and the possibility of experiencing future career opportunities by engaging with faculty at the university.

One master teacher mentioned the value of working with a faculty partner in a way she never thought possible: "I never saw myself as an equal to a professor, but he quickly made me realize that we are partners in this research." The partnership has elevated this master teacher's perspective of herself as a professional and as a teacher leader. Teachers feel equal to, connected with, and valued by their faculty partners. It is equally affirming when faculty share that there is just as much to learn from the master teachers, citing opportunities for reciprocal growth. Several mentioned the value of having the real-time experience in P-12 classrooms that they would not otherwise be provided. As one MTA stated, a major benefit of the collaboration is

> being able to connect with a teacher who is involved in implementing an innovative change in her classroom. She can speak to the general issues related to the support for innovation, obstacles to innovation, lack of support for sharing innovative practices, etc.

In addition, the opportunity is beneficial for faculty research and scholarship, as one MTA commented:

> One of our goals is for me to mentor [the teacher] as she works to establish her name as an educational researcher. I value partnerships and opportunities such as this. If [she] and I are able to work together to develop, disseminate, and analyze the global education survey, it could help me tremendously.

While the program has yielded many benefits, each individual partnership is messy and depends so much on professional context, individual personalities, and an understanding of each master teacher and MTA's unique roles in the collaboration. Participants note that time has been the biggest challenge, as has working with administrative personnel at the district and school levels to ensure commitment to the value of the partnership and to overcome hurdles such as necessary approvals and paperwork. One MTA noted:

> I think there is great potential in the master teacher-MTA program. Unfortunately, however, the dependence on TWO

individuals means that if any one person cannot dedicate the time and attention, the partnership will end. Where I sit right now in our specific instance, it seems like it would be better if there were a small group of individuals working on a project. Maybe two faculty and two teachers – however, we tried that with [a separate initiative] before, as well, and that was a struggle, too.

In addition to the limitations of time, one MTA noted potential "differences in perspectives on pedagogical practices," which could lead to differences in expectations for the outcomes of their collaboration. One master teacher stated:

I didn't understand my role, necessarily. I thought that I was more of an assistant to him in his research and not a partner, per se. I am glad that he was open with me and direct. That cleared a lot of things up for me and offered me the opportunity to share more ideas. My challenge with [collaboration] has been daily time restraints and teaching at the same time.

Open, frank discussions regarding shared interests and opportunities for mutually beneficial growth seem to be a necessary step in helping partners flesh out opportunities for collaboration and enrichment.

## Looking to the Future

Through the Master Teacher Program, teachers are taking on leadership roles while feeling supported by university faculty and staff. At this early stage in the process, they are already impacting practice in schools, districts, and university classrooms as they share their learning with others. We see mutual benefit and great value in extending collaborations between school–university partners. However, it is clear this collaboration requires additional resources, including time, funding, and organizational support at all levels.

One essential element of constructivist leadership is purposeful learning within a community. The program is designed with quarterly meetings for all participants to come together for shared professional growth. However, because master teachers and MTAs are already very active in their educational communities, they often use these quarterly meetings as an opportunity to plan with each other, rather than sharing ideas and learning together across the group as a whole. In addition, the program is designed for master teachers and MTAs to work in pairs. However, if one member of the pair is unable to continue, this often means the project ends. As one MTA noted, one option is broadening the partnership beyond pairs to include other teachers or faculty to ensure the ongoing implementation of a project.

As we continue to refine the Master Teacher Program, we recognize the need to structure opportunities for greater dissemination of collaborative outcomes, projects, and experiences within and beyond our professional development system. This allows our school–university partnership to enact a shared commitment to innovative and reflective practice, building a broad network of teacher leaders.

## Acknowledgments

The Master Teacher Program in the Watson College of Education at the University of North Carolina, Wilmington, was initiated by former PDS Director Dr. Donyell Roseboro in 2012–2013. Dr. Roseboro supported the initial cohort during the program's first two years of implementation. Because of her vision, the program continues to extend the reach of its initial impact and further the mission of our PDS.

## References

Cozza, B. (2010, June). Transforming teaching into a collaborative culture: An attempt to create a professional development school–university partnership. *The Educational Forum 74*(3), pp. 227–241.

Darling-Hammond, L., Bullmaster, M. L., & Cobb, V. L. (1995). Rethinking teacher leadership through professional development schools. *The Elementary School Journal, 96*, 87–106.

Goodlad, J. (1988). School–university partnerships for educational renewal: Rationale and concepts. In K. Sirotnik & J. Goodlad (Eds.), *School–university partnerships in action: Concepts, cases, and concerns* (pp. 3–31). New York, NY: Teachers College Press.

Lambert, L. (2005). What does leadership capacity really mean? *Journal of Staff Development, 26*(2), 38–40.

Lambert, L., Walker, P., Zimmerman, D. P., Cooper, J. E., Lambert, M. D., Gardner, M. E., & Szabo, M. (2002). *The constructivist leader* (2nd ed.). New York, NY: Teachers College Press.

Lewis, S., & Walser, T. M. (2016). Advancing a professional development system: Evolution and evaluation. *School–University Partnerships*, *9*(3), 130–152. Retrieved from http://napds.org/wp-content/uploads/2016/10/93-lewis.pdf

Teitel, L. (2004). Two decades of professional development school development in the United States. What have we learned? Where do we go from here? *Journal of In-Service Education*, *30*(3), 401–416.

Trachtman, R. (2007). Inquiry and accountability in professional development schools. *The Journal of Educational Research*, *100*(4), 197–203.

University of North Carolina Wilmington. (2016). *Master Teachers*. Retrieved from http://www.uncw.edu/ed/pds/masterteacher.html

Wenner, J. A., & Campbell, T. (2017). The theoretical and empirical basis of teacher leadership: A review of the literature. *Review of Educational Research*, *87*(1), 134–171.

Chapter 17

# Teacher Leader Reflections: Teacher Leader Preparation and Development

### Abstract

This chapter features three personal reflections written by practicing teacher leaders from North Carolina, Kentucky/Missouri, and New Jersey. The first two reflections describe various challenges and successes of instructional coaches working with new teachers and experienced teachers in two different schools. The third reflection recounts one teacher's frustrating experience trying to provide support for his school's Parent and Teacher Organization. The chapter concludes with five questions for discussion and reflection.

*Keywords:* Teacher leadership; instructional coaching; school–university partnership; professional development school; Parent and Teacher Organization

## Knowing and Being Known

*Mark Meacham*

I like to tell the story of my first day as an instructional coach for the North Carolina New Teacher Support Program. It was early September, and I had just been assigned to my first high school in one of the largest school systems in the state. I remember sitting in the front office, waiting for the school's new principal. To my left, a woman stood behind a paneless window in what appeared to be a large closet. As students waited in line to explain their tardies, I listened to stories of broken alarm clocks, dead batteries, and senior citizens who'd failed at the most basic responsibility of getting grandchildren to school on time. As each student approached the woman in the closet, she readied her pen atop a pad of paper.

To my right, a long hallway led to a wall where its path continued at a right angle toward some interior set of offices. "Ms. Smith is ready for you now." In a tone that radiated indifference, a small woman with short white hair pointed toward the hallway. "Last door on the right," she mumbled. The principal's office was exactly what I expected: large desk opposite door, set of bookshelves behind desk, and walls decorated with decades of faculties seated on gymnasium bleachers. What I didn't expect was Ms. Smith's introductory statement. From a conference table in the corner, she announced, "You will not come into my school and bother my teachers."

Whenever I tell this story, I emphasize how Ms. Smith's comment drew from me a realization that perhaps I'd made a serious mistake. I had left the comfort of a familiar classroom and students in a school where I'd taught for the last ten years. I had left my reputation as a hard-working, challenging, yet fair teacher and colleague. I'd taught English to every kind of student one can imagine and had, over the years, gradually increased my teacher leader responsibilities. As a mentor, I had worked to acclimate new faculty to the culture of our particular brand of public high school. Beginning with the first day tour, I drew pleasure in sharing the latest culturally responsive strategies with bewildered beginning teachers, whose own life histories (many would later share) fell opposite the myriad challenges faced by the young people populating their 90-minute blocks.

I remember one beginning teacher confide, "[In my high school] up north, there were no Mexicans. I don't really know how to teach them." I replied, "Ask them what they love. Ask them who they care about. Then, ask them to write." I also suggested that this teacher attend sporting events and choral performances; that he appear during lunch periods and simply ask how his students' days were going. As I reflect on my transition to instructional coach in an unfamiliar high school, I recall fragments of similar conversations and realize that I often longed for what I left behind – a kind of leverage that comes with knowing and being known. With the end of each year and the start of another, I take that realization into each new school partnership. It's a realization of identity as an outsider.

In my role as instructional coach, such an identity poses certain challenges. As Ms. Smith's stark warning suggests, to fully support a beginning teacher it is important that I first build trust. For many, that has meant learning about personal histories – about families and friends, about pre-service preparation (if any), about favorite novels and music and food, about the cultures that frame a beginning teacher's values and beliefs. I know, for example, the sixth grade math teacher I observed last week is a former accountant who enjoys an independent wealth most of her students (and, perhaps, colleagues) will never experience. I know, above all else, that she values order and control, which to her moves and sounds like a predictable gentle breeze. A challenge for her, then, involves recognizing distinctions between compliance and engagement. While building the trust of a beginning teacher is an important aspect of instructional coaching, as an outsider I've also learned I must approach each interaction with pedagogical flexibility. The extent to which I take on instructive, collaborative, and/or facilitative stances depends upon situation and context.

For Alex's first three months as a social studies teacher, he struggled with classroom management. As I got to know him, I approached many conversations with a facilitative and, at times, collaborative stance. I began each observation debriefing with open-ended questions designed as prompts for self-reflection on maintaining consistency and accountability. In this way, we explored successes and challenges associated with each class observation and with each lesson plan Alex shared. Although this approach helped build trust and highlight areas where he'd improved, Alex's progress seemed to stall after three months of collaboratively reflecting on his practice. For some reason, his lesson plans lacked the same careful attention to detail as those he'd implemented earlier in the semester. Entering our final meeting before the winter break, this problem sat like a brick in the back of my mind. While Alex shared his latest frustrations, we took time to commiserate over the poor season his beloved Cincinnati Bengals were having and whether their quarterback would, as Alex put it, "Straighten himself out." Recognizing an opening, I mused, "You know, their issues are not altogether unlike yours." With this segue, I pivoted toward an instructional stance, using direct talk geared toward challenging Alex to examine his approach to planning.

As I reflect on my instructional coaching experiences, I wonder at the incremental progress I made with Alex as well as many of the teachers I have supported in my new work. I've come to realize that in order to support their growth I must maintain pedagogical flexibility. I must also foster professional relationships built on trust and personal understanding. While other aspects of my work may contribute to their success, if I do not come to know (and be known by) the individuals I serve, my work may, as Ms. Smith warned, become a bothersome burden.

## Tools for Successful Leadership

*Stefanie D. Livers*

After nine years of successful elementary teaching, I became an instructional coach for a rural district in Kentucky. My years in the classroom included teaching in a private school for dyslexic students, three years in a Title I school, and five years in a high performing school. Moving from the position of classroom teacher to instructional coach was a transforming process that relied on more than just content expertise.

Providing professional development and, in the field, instructional support to teachers is much like building a plane in the air. There are many variables that a coach must keep in the air to create positive change. The pressures for student achievement are real. Instructional coaches are positioned to increase student achievement; but without fostering positive relationships with teachers, that position loses the opportunity to create change. Building relationships through rapport, trust, and empowerment were the tools I chose to "coach" myself out of a job.

The first tool placed in my toolbox was to build rapport. Coming from the high-performing district next door, I was met with many challenges. I was the outsider. Hired by the district and not by the school increased the skepticism and criticism of my purpose. Who knew that a composition notebook would be the cause for fear and disgust and prevent having rapport with teachers?

As a teacher, I always carried a notebook to meetings, to other teachers' classrooms for observations, and to professional development. Taking on the role of instructional coach, I envisioned it as a place to track my meetings, observations, goals, and to-do lists. After two weeks of carrying my notebook, the principal called me in for a meeting to inquire, "What is with the notebook?" I was dumbfounded. I explained my notebook and the common practice in my former district. The principal then shared that many teachers felt threatened by what I was documenting and with whom I was sharing it. She asked me to consider making a change to assist in lowering the fear factor among the teachers. So, I began to use post-its. I kept them in my pocket out of sight. I wrote anecdotal notes on them and later placed them in my notebook, which stayed in my office. I also began to leave positive notes whenever I was in a classroom. I never expected my composition notebook to cause such controversy. Thanks to the principal, I was able to rectify this faux pas without causing any damage. Once the notebook was gone, my coaching conversations became more meaningful and I had better rapport with the teachers.

However, other difficult encounters with multiple teachers continued to plague me. Many teachers did not want me in their classrooms or want my help. So, I planned a community building activity for the teachers. On index cards, I wrote descriptions of myself and placed them in envelopes. I then gave groups of teachers an envelope and told them to pick out the words and phrases that described themselves. After roughly ten minutes, I asked teachers to share their descriptions. After most had shared, I asked them to look at the descriptions and told them that all described me. As I looked around the room, I explained that we all shared common ground. We were all individuals with commonalities working in the same building for a shared purpose: student success. It was the first time I felt like I did something right by showing my vulnerability and sharing personal information. This activity led to a shift in openness and assisted me with both rapport and the start of trusting relationships.

Trust takes time to develop. Rapport helps, and so does validation. During my second year, I began having teachers share their expertise at faculty meetings. Instead of me leading professional development or me doing the talking, I chose different teachers to do these things. I put teachers in the spotlight but provided the sometimes-needed back up. One example was having the special educator for severe disabilities share visual cues that she used with her students. After she presented, I posed the question, how can we use these ideas with our growing English learner population? This conversation led to much collaboration among the teachers about using more visuals in their teaching.

In addition to the faculty spotlights, I worked with teachers to present their work at a state conference, collaborating also with my former district and colleagues. After a planning meeting, one teacher looked at me and said, "You all talk different." I was confused. She elaborated stating that my former colleagues and I could cite the research and reference the foundation behind the teaching strategies we planned to present. She told me, "I want to do that!" I went home and reflected, realizing that I had stopped citing research when I took the instructional coaching job. I had stopped sharing articles and books. This teacher reminded me that these things were necessary.

I began sharing research with this teacher, and she began spreading the word. I also began putting articles in all teachers' mailboxes for us to discuss together and for their individual reference. During my final year as their instructional coach, a textbook company presented to the faculty. During the presentation, the teachers began questioning the textbook's use of key researchers' work and eventually told the textbook representative that the book was not presenting the concepts accurately. I was smiling ear to ear. Over three years' time, I had provided these teachers with instructional power. They could now see through a watered-down version of research-based practices and cared enough to speak up. I knew that I had empowered them!

## Lost Voices

*Francisco J. Ocasio*

Paterson Public Schools in Paterson, New Jersey, recommends that each school have a Parent and Teacher Organization (PTO) that will facilitate communication between parents and their school. The PTO in my middle school was created in 2010 to create cohesion and involve parents with their children's education and the school's activities. Our PTO was led by only a few parents. At first, the main challenge they faced was lack of participation from the other parents, teachers, and community. The next obstacles were growing their organization and taking leadership for it.

In September 2015, I assisted the PTO in the capacity of teacher support. Other teachers and I came up with different ideas to try to grow the organization. One idea was to designate homeroom parents for each class. One parent from each homeroom would try to create a parent calling/ message tree. Optimistically, it would create a structured web that would enable the PTO to contact parents efficiently. However, it was not successful. Teachers were asked to assist with the effort, but most teachers did not make the attempt to assist. I reached out to several parents, but they were not cooperative. They were too busy with their jobs, and many had night shift occupations. Additionally, many parents were extremely young. They were rarely available or provided the school staff with excuses. Next, we tried Google to connect the PTO executive leaders with constant communication, including agendas, sign-in sheets, parent/ teacher information, etc. They seemed to agree with the plan, and so a team of teachers and I created folders, documents, and flyers for the PTO. But then they did not want to learn how to use the Google platform. It was very frustrating.

I still wanted to make sure that the PTO could move forward in a structured and accessible manner, but the meetings were filled with over ten teachers and only five parents. The teachers felt disappointed again because parents were not involving themselves with their children's education. We continued to try to get parents and teachers to be more involved, but the organization dwindled after a while. Meanwhile, the PTO executive leaders grew very dependent on me. Due to this dependence, a meeting was held to discuss my supportive role within the organization. I had to clarify that I was not allowed to run it. After that, the PTO lost momentum because of lack of leadership. Currently, it is not as active as before.

For me, this experience has provided an example of how important leaders are in successful organizations. It also illustrates the importance of participation within an organization. It is the responsibility of all stakeholders – teachers and parents – to assist with the development of students. The teaching staff can only do so much during the school day. Parents need to be involved with the educational decisions that are being made for their children, and the PTO gives parents a voice. The parents in our middle school could hold a lot of influence if they only participated in the PTO meetings. However, some parents are not native speakers of English, do not understand their rights, have no interest, or work several jobs in order to provide for their families. Maybe we can try again next year.

## Questions for Further Reflection

*Jana Hunzicker*

1. In the first two reflections, instructional coaches Mark and Stefanie describe themselves as outsiders and emphasize the necessity of rapport and trust in working effectively with practicing teachers. In your experience, is it common for teacher leaders to meet with resistance from those they are trying to help? What underlying factors may cause teachers – and sometimes principals – to distrust teacher leaders? In what situations might such distrust be justified?
2. In "Lost Voices," Francisco describes how he and other teachers in his middle school worked together with parents to increase parent and community involvement through the school's PTO. Although their efforts were not successful, is it possible that Francisco will look back on this experience as significant to his development as a teacher leader? What challenging experiences in your own teaching career have shaped your teacher leadership skills and identity?
3. All three reflections describe at least one obstacle or challenge faced by teacher leaders as they engaged in their assigned leadership roles and responsibilities. Do you think obstacles and challenges are more common in PDSs and other school–university partnerships due to higher expectations and continuous innovation? Or, are obstacles and challenges more common in non-PDS or nonpartnered schools due to fewer resources and less support?

4. While each of these reflections suggests or describes various pathways from classroom teacher to teacher leader, none directly addresses teacher leader preparation. Based on the reflections and chapters in this section, do you think intentional and systematic teacher leader preparation is necessary to the development of teacher leadership, or do the best teacher leaders emerge naturally? If teacher leader preparation is necessary, what should it entail and who should participate? If teacher leaders emerge naturally, how can aspiring teacher leaders be encouraged and supported?
5. What are your personal and professional reflections on the topic of teacher leadership in PDSs and other school–university partnerships? Do you have teacher leader experiences and insights to share? As you finish reading this book, consider writing your own teacher leader reflection to share with others.

Chapter 18

# Teacher Leader Preparation and Development in PDS: Themes and Recommendations

*Rebecca West Burns*

### Abstract

This chapter synthesizes Chapters 13–17. After distinguishing teacher leaders as individuals who enact various functions of teacher leadership in today's schools, the chapter describes three themes related to teacher leader preparation and development in professional development schools (PDSs): (1) teacher leaders are made not born, (2) school–university partnerships create the conditions for developing high-quality teacher leaders, and (3) PDSs have the potential to develop teacher leaders as teacher educators. The chapter concludes with recommendations on how teacher leadership in PDSs can be strengthened.

*Keywords:* Informal teacher leaders; teacher leadership; professional development schools; school–university partnerships; teacher leadership functions; leadership capacity

Although politicians, practitioners, and scholars do not always agree on much, they do agree that educational reform is essential. However, they differ on mechanisms for actualizing reform. Unfortunately, the burden of educational change has been (mis) placed on individuals, namely teachers. Change cannot be the sole responsibility of teachers or schools. Rather, it must be a shared endeavor between those currently working with K-12 students and those preparing the next generation of educational professionals.

For decades, scholars have visualized that educational renewal could occur when schools and universities united around the common goal of improving student achievement, and their vision for unification was realized through a construct called professional development schools (PDSs; Rutter, 2011). PDSs are defined as "...innovative institutions formed through partnerships between professional education programs and P-12 schools." (National Council for the Accreditation of Teacher Education [NCATE], 2001, p. 2). To foster real change, both schools and universities would need to renew simultaneously rather than individually. Across the United States, there are few examples of strong, robust PDSs that have been able to actualize this vision, and one of their secret ingredients seems to be their focus on and integration of teacher leadership. However, what those few PDSs do exceptionally well has yet to be thoughtfully conceptualized, systematically embedded, and comprehensively enacted in the nature, understanding, and practice of what it means to be a PDS.

Perhaps one of the most exciting aspects of this contributed book is its focus on teacher leadership as the hidden gem of successful PDSs. The four chapters and teacher leader stories captured in the teacher leader preparation and development section offer concrete examples of teacher leadership in action. I was honored and humbled to read these chapters and offer insight into how we can successfully prepare and develop teacher leaders in PDSs to actualize educational renewal. The purpose of this chapter is to describe themes from across the chapters in this section on teacher leader preparation and development and to offer some recommendations on how teacher leadership in PDS can be strengthened.

## Defining Terms

It seems probable that some of the issues surrounding the comprehensive integration of teacher leadership into PDSs are rooted in the lack of common understanding of what teacher leadership is. Therefore, it is imperative that educational terms be regularly defined to develop shared understanding. Throughout this chapter, I will use the terms teacher leadership and teacher leader, but I will not use them interchangeably because the two are not synonymous. Teacher leadership is a function; it is a process of teachers' ability to influence and change peers' teaching practice to improve student learning and increase student achievement (York-Barr & Duke, 2004). Teacher leader, on the other hand, is the individual who enacts the function of teacher leadership. There are many roles that ask or require teachers to enact teacher leadership but they are often referred to by names other than teacher leader. Instructional coach, team leader, lead teacher, teacher-on-special assignment, and peer mentor are just a few examples of roles where teachers are enacting the function of teacher leadership. These kinds of formal roles where teachers are being asked to influence their peers' teaching practice to improve student achievement fall under the construct of teacher leadership, which means that the individuals in those formal roles should be considered teacher leaders even though their titles do not indicate "teacher leader." All teachers, though, can enact the function of teacher leadership without necessarily assuming a formal role. These informal teacher leaders are very similar to their peers who are in formal roles in that they can successfully work with and influence their peers to improve teaching for students' benefits, but the difference is that they are not formally recognized with an official title.

Many excellent, experienced teachers reach a stage in their careers where they desire more. They know that they do not want to become administrators but they do not know what they want to do. Teacher leadership can fill that professional void by rejuvenating their careers while keeping quality teachers connected to students. Interestingly, teacher leadership in PDSs may provide additional opportunities and benefits not found in other contexts to support teacher leadership development. As previously defined, PDSs are a unique innovation formed through intentional partnerships between schools and colleges of education. All PDSs have nine essentials (National Association for Professional Development Schools, 2008), which are paraphrased here as follows:

1. A comprehensive mission beyond either institution.
2. A professional culture that embraces teacher candidates as active participants in the school community.
3. Needs-based professional learning for all stakeholders.
4. A commitment to reflection and innovation.
5. Deliberate dissemination of investigations of practice.
6. A formal articulated agreement regarding roles and responsibilities.
7. Governance structures to provide reflection, collaboration, and direction.
8. Formal boundary-spanning roles.
9. Dedicated resources and formal recognition structures.

PDSs can be situated in various pathways to partnership development: partner sites, clinical practice sites, and collaborative inquiry sites according to Parker, Parsons, Groth, and Levine-Brown (2016) or in four stages of PDS development: beginning, developing, at standard, and leading according to the NCATE PDS Standards (2001). Interestingly, nowhere in either of these documents is teacher leadership mentioned, and yet as illustrated in the chapters in this section, teacher leadership in PDS is a powerful entity to support professional learning in teacher preparation, teacher induction, and throughout a teacher's career. Intentionally attending to the preparation and development of teachers as leaders in PDSs could be a thread that seamlessly weaves together teacher education as a coherent continuum of lifelong learning.

## Themes

This section on teacher leadership preparation and development in PDS features four chapters describing innovative programs as teacher leadership initiatives in PDSs and one chapter illustrating three reflective stories from teacher leaders living the trials and tribulations associated with teacher leadership in PDSs. Three themes emerged from the chapters:

1. Teacher leaders are made, not born.
2. School–university partnerships create the conditions for developing high-quality teacher leaders.
3. PDSs have the potential to develop teacher leaders as teacher educators.

In this section, I summarize the chapters and then describe in more detail each of the themes.

### *Chapter Summaries*

In Chapter 13, Matsumoto, Yoshioka, and Fulton describe the paradigmatic shift of how they conceptualized teacher candidates in their PDS. Rather than simply being students in a preparation program, their teacher candidates were imagined and treated as emerging teacher leaders and they describe how that shift in mindset positively influenced their teacher candidates.

In Chapter 14, Morettini, Luet, Vernon-Dotson, Nagib, and Krishnamurthy describe a program in their PDS called The Beginning Teacher Project designed to develop teacher leaders to support beginning teachers. They identify five key features in the successful preparation of teacher leaders. Those key features are targeted professional development, ongoing dialog, turnkey training, instructional decision-making, and community engagement.

In Chapter 15, Rahman, Munakata, Klein, Taylor, and Trabona describe how they partnered with five school districts to develop science teachers as leaders through developing professional learning communities that brought together vertical teams of elementary, middle, and secondary teachers focused on teaching science. Through dialog in this unique professional learning community, teachers' preconceptions about the conceptual rigor of elementary science instruction were challenged, which caused teachers to reexamine their expectations of student performance.

In Chapter 16, Lewis, Dikkers, Sikma, and Fink describe the outcomes of a teacher leadership program in their PDS called the Master Teacher Program, designed to develop their partnership teachers as constructivist leaders. Master teachers participated in a variety of leadership activities including mentoring interns, providing lesson demonstrations in university coursework, and serving as guest speakers, panelists, and advisory board members in their PDS. Interestingly, they were the only authors to include representation from both university and school partners as chapter authors.

In Chapter 17, three teacher leaders in PDSs reflect on their experiences. Interestingly, all of them focused on challenges resulting from the transformative process of transitioning from a teacher to teacher leader in formalized teacher leader roles. The first teacher leader, Mark Meacham, described the challenges he faced as he transitioned from teacher to instructional coach. He began his story with the principal's perception of instructional coach as a nuisance to her teachers. His reflections reinforced the importance of relationships in influencing change in teachers' instructional practice. The second teacher leader, Stefanie Livers, reflected on the transformational nature of the transition from teacher to instructional coach and identified tools to support teacher leaders as instructional coaches. Like Meacham, Livers noted that establishing trust and rapport in relationships was imperative to her success as a teacher leader. Finally, Francisco Ocasio described the importance of perseverance as a characteristic of teacher leaders. Oscasio argued that teacher leaders make mistakes but successful teacher leaders reflect on those mistakes, get back up, and try again.

### *Theme 1: Teacher Leaders Are Made, Not Born*

It is evident from the chapters that becoming a teacher leader is difficult and requires support. Teacher leaders are not born with the skills to influence instructional change in their peers. Instead, the preparation and development of teacher leaders must be systematically designed and include developmentally appropriate professional learning opportunities.

All three teacher leaders in their reflections in Chapter 17 describe the tensions they experienced and how reflection on those experiences helped them grow. What these teachers were describing was the transformative nature of becoming a teacher leader. Transformational learning occurs when an individual experiences cognitive dissonance, reflects on that dissonance, and ultimately alters his or her way of being. This process is usually highly emotional (Mezirow et al., 2000). For the teacher leaders in Chapter 17, they experienced a plethora of issues and tensions of becoming a teacher leader in PDS, but it was their reflective nature and desire to improve that resulted in transformational learning.

Morettini and colleagues (Chapter 14) reiterated the struggles in becoming a teacher leader as they chronicled the issues and tensions their teacher leaders faced in The Beginning Teacher Project. In their chapter, the authors describe how the teacher leaders were effective teachers of children but as they transitioned to working with adult learners, they struggled. Loughran (2006) argued that supporting the professional learning of teachers requires a specific knowledge base and skillset that must be learned and he deemed this concept a pedagogy of teacher education. Morettini and colleagues' struggles in The Beginning Teacher Project affirmed the notion of a pedagogy of teacher education, and they argued that teacher leader professional learning required signature pedagogies like targeted professional development, ongoing dialog, turnkey training, instructional decision-making, and community engagement. Drawing upon Yendol-Hoppey and Franco's (2014) concepts of signature pedagogies in PDS to support teacher candidate growth and development, signature pedagogies for developing teacher leaders in PDSs could be defined as systematically and intentionally designed routines that facilitate teacher leader learning that (1) engage the teacher as leader, (2) help the teacher recognize the complexity and uncertainty of teaching adult learners, and (3) potentially influence the teacher's professional habits and dispositions associated with distributive leadership. Morettini and colleagues may be the beginning of unearthing signature pedagogies for developing the professional learning of teacher leaders in PDSs.

Rahman and colleagues' (Chapter 15) discovery of the unique needs of teacher leaders as adult learners also reiterates the theme that teacher leaders are made and not born. In the mid-1980s, Knowles (1984) noted that adult learners were unique in their growth and developmental needs and argued for specific strategies geared toward these unique needs. They called this approach andragogy. When supporting the professional learning of teachers, Glickman, Gordon, and Ross-Gordon (2014) claimed that professional learning for teachers needs to meet them where they are developmentally, and they outlined several continuums of development like conceptual, emotional, cognitive, and psychological to name of a few. Teacher leader preparation and development should reflect these concepts and meet the unique, developmental needs of teacher leaders as adult learners.

Perhaps the most illustrative of this theme that teacher leaders are made and not born was Matsumoto, Yoshioka, and Fulton's chapter (Chapter 13) because they showed how teacher leadership must begin with teacher preparation. By shifting the mindset of prospective teacher to emerging teacher leader in their PDS, their teacher candidates changed their perspective of self – they began to imagine themselves as active, engaged members of the community. The authors wrote, "…(the teacher candidates) began seeing themselves not as novice teachers but as teacher leaders who actively contribute to a PDS–university–community partnership." (p. 202). Adopting this mindset of teacher candidate as emerging teacher leader is an imperative shift to move PDSs forward.

### Theme 2: School–University Partnerships Create the Conditions for Developing High-Quality Teacher Leaders

In this theme, I intentionally use the term "school–university partnership" rather than PDS because PDSs are a specific kind of school–university partnership; all PDSs should at least be school–university partnerships, but not all school–university partnerships are necessarily PDSs. Much like the Nine Essentials of PDSs, school–university partnerships have seven core ingredients that distinguish them from informal collaboration or a conglomerate of disjointed projects or initiatives between a school or school district and a university, and they include the following:

1. A shared, comprehensive mission dedicated to equity for improved PK-12 student learning and educational renewal
2. Designated partnership sites with articulated agreements
3. Shared governance with dedicated resources to foster sustainability and renewal
4. Clinical practice at the core of teaching and learning
5. Active engagement in the school and local community
6. Intentional and explicit commitment to professional learning of all stakeholders
7. Shared commitment to research and innovation through deliberate investigation and dissemination. (Burns, Jacobs, Baker, & Donahue, 2016, pp. 86–87)

As I read the chapters, it occurred to me that almost all of the initiatives described in the chapters could have occurred in school–university partnerships broadly. For that reason, I made this theme broader to indicate that when schools and universities intentionally partner on initiatives, as illustrated in these chapters, they can create the necessary conditions to facilitate teacher leader professional learning. I say almost all because Matsumoto, Yoshioka, and Fulton's (Chapter 13) description of a mindset shift in teacher candidates may be the exception. A partner school might politely welcome teacher candidates as professional educators, but PDSs both welcome teacher candidates and treat them as professional educators. PDSs embrace teacher candidates as members of their instructional staff, and they are committed to developing them as emerging teacher leaders. To foster such a paradigmatic shift is monumental and requires deep relationships to create such transformational change. These kinds of deep relationships are found or, at least, should be found in all PDSs. I am not certain that such a change could happen in a school–university partnership more broadly without the presence of deep relationships.

While all of the chapters were excellent illustrations of how school–university partnerships can create the conditions for developing high-quality teacher leaders, I was particularly drawn to Rahman and colleagues' (Chapter 15) description of their program that was designed to develop teacher leaders in a particular content area. To accomplish their goals of promoting teacher leadership and improving science instructional practice to impact student learning, they skillfully created the conditions to bring together different professionals to create hybrid professional learning communities. Their chapter is an excellent example of collaboration among colleges within a university (e.g., science and education) while also collaborating across the school–university borders. Their mindset was to bring together university faculty and school-based practitioners to foster a strong learning community. They shared, "While we could not prescribe a community of practice, genuine inquiry with similarly motivated teachers around issues of practice would support the growth of a strong learning community." (p. 240). Developing high-quality teacher leaders will require the creation of hybrid professional learning communities that traverse intra-institutional boundaries and inter-institutional boundaries. It will require university faculty who are genuinely interested in solving problems hand in hand with teachers and other school-based practitioners.

## Theme 3: PDSs Have the Potential to Develop Teacher Leaders as Teacher Educators

The chapters in this section highlight the fact that PDSs may be able to accomplish something unique in teacher leadership preparation and development that may not be possible in broader school–university partnerships. With the development of deep relationships and the attention placed on the professional learning of all stakeholders (NAPDS, 2008), PDSs are uniquely poised not only to develop teachers as leaders but also to develop teacher leaders as teacher educators. According to the Association of Teacher Educators Standards for Teacher Educators (2008), teacher educators are defined as "…those educators who provide formal instruction or conduct research and development for educating prospective and practicing teachers." (p. 5). What distinguishes a teacher educator from someone who facilitates the professional learning of teachers is the connection to "formal instruction" or professional study. Teacher educators can be university- or school-based as they can be faculty in higher education or they can be personnel in schools who, "…provide instruction or supervision of clinical experiences of prospective teachers…or who administer or conduct instructional activities designed to provide advanced professional study for teachers." (p. 5). High-quality school-based teacher educators are desperately needed to prepare high-quality educators. As I explained in Theme 1, developing teacher leaders requires thoughtful preparation and developing teacher leaders as teacher educators is no different.

To enact the mindset of teacher candidates as emerging teacher leaders found in Chapter 13, to mentor beginning teachers found in Chapter 14, and to influence the instructional practices of other teachers found in Chapter 15 requires skillful teacher educators (both university- and school-based) to develop teachers as leaders, but little attention has been paid as to how we should develop those teacher educators who will educate teacher leaders. Lewis and colleagues' description (Chapter 16) of their Master Teachers Program is one illustration of how teacher leaders can be developed as teacher educators. This program not only prepares teachers as leaders to influence their peers' practice, but also intentionally engages teacher leaders in learning how to better serve as mentor teachers in more intensive field experiences, provide demonstration lessons in university coursework, and design and lead professional workshops and trainings for other teachers. The authors also described how university teacher education researchers diminished power and positionality, embraced teacher leaders as co-researchers, and developed them as practitioner researchers. In their chapter, a teacher leader shared, "I never saw myself as an equal to a professor, but he quickly made me realize that we are partners in this research." (p. 265). While they do not use the term "teacher educator," their descriptions of how they are engaging teacher leaders as practitioner researchers, and how they are developing teacher leaders to facilitate the professional study of prospective teachers in clinical experiences and university methods coursework could be categorized as developing teacher educators.

## Recommendations

The chapters in this section demonstrate the powerful results when schools and universities collaborate to design meaningful, developmentally appropriate, job-embedded professional learning opportunities that empower teachers to develop their leadership capacity. However, we cannot be tempted to be satisfied with just partnering. Instead, we must continue to challenge ourselves to develop the kinds of deep relationships found in PDSs. After all, PDSs are living laboratories that generate authentic problems with which all stakeholders (e.g., teacher candidates, mentor teachers, university faculty, doctoral students, school administrators) can wrestle together. They are ideal contexts not only for preparing teachers but also for preparing teacher leaders and teacher leaders as teacher educators (Burns & Badiali, 2013).

The field of teacher education has been challenged to rethink how teachers are prepared. High-quality educator preparation involves scaffolded clinical preparation throughout the teacher education curriculum and intentional school–university partnerships that share the common purpose of improved student achievement (American Association of Colleges for Teacher Education, 2010; NCATE, 2010). But I contend that actualizing these calls require more than just school–university collaboration; it will require the kinds of deep, committed relationships and shared agenda of supporting PK-12 student learning found in PDSs. Forming, sustaining, and renewing PDSs involves work. Much like a successful marriage, they require ongoing communication, sustained resources, willing participants, and thoughtful structures to outlast transience. Some critics would argue that PDSs have not been able to actualize educational renewal beyond a few boutique programs. However, I contend that PDSs are well poised to address the calls for transforming educator preparation as the field of teacher education can learn from the successful and unsuccessful stories of how PDSs across the United States have struggled or flourished.

To lead the charge, I have two recommendations. First, PDS scholars and other scholars publishing research situated in PDSs must clearly articulate how their context is uniquely situated in a PDS, even if that PDS is just beginning. Labels like beginning, developing, at standard, and leading found in the NCATE PDS Standards (2001) can be useful for understanding the PDS context. Indicating how the PDS aligns with the NAPDS (2008) Nine Essentials would also be important in distinguishing the context as a PDS. If the school–university partnership is just beginning and not necessarily even a beginning PDS, language found in the Parker et al. (2016) can be helpful in providing a common understanding of the emerging partnership context. Similarly, describing how the school–university partnership addresses the Burns et al. (2016) seven core ingredients can be useful for providing a common understanding of the school–university partnership.

Second, the field of teacher education must prepare scholars of teacher education to be scholarly practitioners who have the knowledge, skills, and dispositions not only to conduct rigorous methodological research but also have the knowledge, skills, dispositions, and abilities to value the practical knowledge of school partners and to diminish power and positionality to recognize practitioners as partners in a shared endeavor. University faculty must shift the focus from preparing teachers to recognizing classroom teachers as exceptional pedagogues. They must adjust the vision of their roles from preparing teachers to supporting classroom teachers in becoming teacher leaders and developing teachers' pedagogies of teacher education. This means that teacher leadership must become a priority and a goal for PDSs (Nolan et al., 2009). Likewise, schools and districts must recognize and value the time administrators and teachers invest in being school-based teacher educators, and universities must recognize and value the time, knowledge, and skillset required of university faculty to build, sustain, and renew partnerships. Now more than ever, we need PDSs to focus on teacher leadership if teacher education is going to be turned upside down and if we are really going to actualize large-scale educational renewal.

## References

American Association of Colleges for Teacher Education. (2010). *The clinical preparation of teachers: A policy brief*. Washington, DC. Retrieved from http://edwebsfiles.ed.uiuc.edu/transitions/AACTE-Policy-Brief-March-2010.pdf

Association of Teacher Educators. (2008). *The teacher educator standards*. Retrieved from http://www.ate1.org/pubs/uploads/materialstouse1.pdf

Burns, R. W., & Badiali, B. (2013). Preparing teacher educators in the professional development school context. In J. Perry & D. L. Carlson (Eds.), *In their own words: A journey to the stewardship of the practice in education* (pp. 41–58). Charlotte, NC: Information Age Publishing.

Burns, R. W., Jacobs, J., Baker, W., & Donahue, D. (2016). Making muffins: Identifying core ingredients of school–university partnerships. *School–University Partnerships, 9*(3), 81–95.

Glickman, C., Gordon, S. P., & Ross-Gordon, J. M. (2014). *Supervision and instructional leadership: A developmental approach* (9th ed.). Boston, MA: Allyn and Bacon.

Knowles. (1984). *Andragogy in action: Applying modern principles of adult learning*. San Francisco, CA: Jossey Bass.

Loughran, J. J. (2006). *Developing a pedagogy of teacher education: Understanding teaching and learning about teaching*. Taylor & Francis.

Mezirow, J., & Associates. (2000). *Learning as transformation*. San Francisco, CA: Jossey-Bass.

National Association of Professional Development Schools. (2008). *What it means to be a professional development school*. South Carolina: The Executive Council and Board of Directors.

National Council for the Accreditation of Teacher Education. (2001). *Standards for professional development schools*. Washington, DC: NCATE.

National Council for the Accreditation of Teacher Education. (2010). *Transforming teacher education through clinical practice: A national strategy to prepare effective teachers. A report of the Blue Ribbon Panel on Clinical Preparation and Partnership for Improved Student Learning*. Washington, DC: NCATE.

Rutter, A. (2011). Purpose and vision in professional development schools. In J. Neopolitan (Ed.), *Yearbook for the National Society of the Study of Education* (Vol. 110, pp. 289–305). Columbia: Teachers College Press, Columbia University.

Parker, A. K., Parsons, S. A., Groth, L., & Levine-Brown, E. (2016). Pathways to partnership: A developmental framework for building PDS relationships. *School University Partnerships – Special Issue, "What is a PDS?" 9*(3), 34–48.

Yendol-Hoppey, D., & Franco, Y. (2014). In search of signature pedagogy for PDS teacher education: A review of articles published in school–university partnerships. *School–University Partnerships, 7*(1), 17–34.

York-Barr, J., & Duke, K. (2004). What do we know about teacher leadership? Findings from two decades of scholarship. *Review of Educational Research, 74*(3), 255–316.

# More Questions for Reflection and Discussion

## Introduction

1. Chapter 1 identifies four core purposes of professional development schools (PDSs) as envisioned by the Holmes Group in 1986: teacher preparation, professional development, inquiry and research, and student learning. Should all schools – PDS and non-PDS – pursue these core purposes? Why or why not?
2. One function of the four core purposes of professional development schools is to distinguish PDSs from other school–university partnerships. Do you believe such a distinction is necessary? If so, what are the defining characteristics of school–university partnerships?
3. Chapter 1 provides a brief history of professional development schools in the United States and Chapter 2 provides a brief history of teacher leadership in the United States. What historical parallels do you notice? In what ways are the two movements related, and in what ways are they unrelated?
4. In Chapter 2, Hunzicker defines teacher leadership in PDSs as "a strategic, process-oriented stance motivated by deep concern for students and activated through formal, informal, and hybrid leadership roles that span the boundaries of school, university, and community" (p. 24). Based on this definition, do you see yourself as a teacher leader? Please explain.
5. In Chapter 2, Hunzicker calls for more research focused on teacher leadership in PDSs and other school–university partnerships, and the contributors to this book have answered that call in a variety of ways. If you were to design a study on this topic, what research question would you ask? What data would you collect? What would you hope to learn?

## Section I: Teacher Leadership and Student Learning

1. Chapter 3 describes the collaborative efforts of three teacher leaders working to meet the needs of English learners (ELs). Are there

particular instructional approaches for ELs that you believe would be easy (or difficult) to implement in your school? Please explain.
2. The efforts to improve teaching practice described in Chapter 3 were applied for both preservice and practicing teachers. Identify one instructional improvement goal for your school and describe how teacher leaders might engage across preservice preparation and professional learning to meet this goal.
3. Chapter 3 highlights examples of teacher leader functions that are aligned with the Teacher Leader Model Standards. Which function of teacher leadership would you most like to address in your practice, and why?
4. In what ways are teacher leadership and student learning closely related? Can you think of any situation where the two are not closely related?
5. Chapter 4 describes a teacher-initiated de-tracking effort for ninth grade algebra students that began with a pilot project to establish instructional need followed by numerous meetings to garner collegial support. How might this start up process be replicated at your school, perhaps in a different academic discipline?
6. The de-tracking initiative described in Chapter 4 was sustained primarily through teacher buy-in based on social justice. If equity pedagogy is not part of a school's common practice, what strategies and supports might teacher leaders rely upon during the early stages of disbelief and the middle stages of delayed results?
7. The success of any student-focused initiative must be validated with evidence. In your school or district, what counts as evidence of improved teaching practice? What counts as evidence of increased student learning? What additional sources of evidence should be considered?
8. Chapter 5 presents four stories of collaborative inquiry through Project Teacher Leadership. Reflect on teacher leadership experiences in which you have been involved. What similarities and differences do you see between your own experiences and the processes described in Chapter 5?
9. Which aspects of the Project Teacher Leadership intensive workshop for cross-institutional teams would be most difficult to implement in your school or district? How could your school–university partnership overcome these challenges and/or modify the process to accommodate specific needs or conditions?
10. What does an inquiry stance look like? How does such a stance play a role in the educational settings where you work? How might an inquiry stance lead to increased opportunities for teacher leadership on behalf of students?

11. If you were to initiate a student-centered teacher leadership project in your own learning community or school–university partnership, what would it be? What core members would be crucial to your planning team, and why?
12. In Chapter 7, Badiali asserts that, rather than standards, Goodlad, Mantle-Bromley, and Goodlad's Agenda for Education in a Democracy may impart greater meaning to teacher leaders' contributions to the PDS movement (p. 107). In what ways might an agenda support teacher leadership more so than a set of standards? In what ways are standards superior? How might the two be combined to maximize support for teacher leadership in professional development schools and other school–university partnerships?
13. Just as schools must look beyond test scores to recognize student learning, schools must also look beyond formal leadership roles and responsibilities to recognize teacher leadership. If you were to create a list of informal teacher leader actions that directly and indirectly support student learning, what would be the top three on your list?

## Section II: Definitions, Structures, and Cultures that Promote Teacher Leadership

1. Chapter 8 reports on the perceptions and experiences of teacher leader liaisons-in-residence. How might the felt challenges and successes described in Chapter 8 be used to better understand teacher leadership in school–university partnership contexts?
2. Do you believe it is more important for teachers in field experience coordination roles to maintain a classroom teacher identity or a teacher leader identity?
3. What types of professional spaces could best cultivate and sustain formal, informal, and hybrid teacher leadership in school–university partnerships? Consider who, what, when, where, why, and how.
4. Chapter 9 describes a school–university partnership that views all teachers as learners and as leaders. How does school culture encourage and support (or discourage and impede) teachers who are interested in taking on teacher leadership roles and responsibilities?
5. What role does distributed leadership play in effective professional learning communities (PLCs)? How can PLCs be used to develop teacher leadership capacity?
6. How might learning walks enhance the culture and instructional practices in your school setting? What areas of focus would you target?

7. In what ways could co-teaching support both mentors and preservice teachers during field experiences at all levels?
8. What professional development opportunities exist (or could be designed) to ensure that common definitions and structures of teacher leadership support theory to practice transitions?
9. Chapter 10 asserts that National Board Certified Teachers (NBCTs) are highly accomplished teachers and effective mentors. From a teacher candidate's perspective, what might be the advantages/disadvantages of having an NBCT for a mentor teacher?
10. When mentoring teacher candidates, what does effective feedback look like? How can mentors provide feedback that deepens teacher candidates' understanding of effective teaching practice?
11. What connection do you see between preservice education and effective in-service teaching? How can school–university partnerships address the conflict that sometimes arises between the idealism of the university and the reality of the P-12 school?
12. When trying to understand teacher leadership, which is more useful to you: commonly agreed upon standards such as the Teacher Leader Model Standards or descriptive research and personal reflections such as those presented in this book?
13. In Chapter 12, Cosenza asserts that avoiding a common definition of teacher leadership may allow the concept to remain open to various roles and responsibilities. Do you agree or disagree?

## Section III: Teacher Leader Preparation and Development

1. Chapter 13 describes how one school–university partnership develops teacher candidates' leadership skills as a part of the teacher preparation process. Is requiring teacher leadership during teacher preparation likely to elevate the teaching profession over time? Why or why not?
2. Ideally, what percentage of a teacher preparation program should be devoted to candidates' development of teacher leadership skills?
3. Every teacher has the potential to be a teacher leader. Do you agree or disagree with this statement? Please explain.
4. Chapter 14 describes The Beginning Teacher Project, which encountered challenges when teacher leaders engaged in turnkey training of their peers. How can school–university partnerships better equip teacher leaders to teach adult learners?

5. Why is it important to engage teacher leaders with the community and vice versa? How can teacher leaders' engagement with the community counteract any deficit-based perspectives of students and their families?
6. What are the implications of using a sociocultural approach to create a distributed leadership model for the preparation and development of teacher leaders? How can school–university partnerships build programs that respond directly to participants' needs and provide developmentally appropriate learning opportunities?
7. Chapter 15 describes a two-year fellowship program designed to develop teacher leaders in the sciences. How might teacher leadership development differ for teachers in various content areas?
8. When differences emerge between teacher leaders and administrators, whose agenda should be prioritized? How can such differences be successfully navigated and/or resolved?
9. Extra supports and structures are a central benefit of school–university partnerships. If teacher leader autonomy is the eventual goal, should scaffolds designed to make teacher leadership part of the district culture eventually be retracted? Is it ideal to remove all teacher leader supports and structures, or should some scaffolds remain?
10. How do you typically respond to opportunities or requests to lead in your department or school? What motivations or priorities guide your decision-making?
11. Chapter 16 describes a Master Teacher Program designed to develop and promote teacher leadership within a school–university partnership. How can school–university partnerships support leadership development in teachers who may not yet see themselves as leaders?
12. When resources are limited, how can school–university partners generate buy-in for teacher leader development? Once teacher leader development programs are established, how can such programs be made sustainable and scalable?
13. In Chapter 18, Burns asserts that PDSs have the potential to develop teacher leaders as teacher educators. In your opinion, what responsibility should veteran teachers have for preparing the next generation of teachers?
14. How does (or could) your school–university partnership encourage and support teacher leader development?

Author's note: Thank you to all 49 contributors for helping to craft the questions for reflection and discussion posed in this section.

# Tables, Illustrations, and Figures

**Chapter 2**
Figure 1    Teacher Leader Model Standards Seven Domains.
Figure 2    Teacher Leadership Competencies.

**Chapter 3**
Table 1     2016 and 2017 NYSESLAT Results: Averages by Grade and Modality.

**Chapter 4**
Table 1     Algebra I CP End-of-Course Passing Rates.
Figure 1    Project Implementation Timeline.
Figure 2    Algebra 1 CP Math Team Format.

**Chapter 5**
Appendix A  Project Teacher Leadership Completed Action Plan.

**Chapter 6**   None.

**Chapter 7**   None.

**Chapter 8**   None.

**Chapter 9**
Figure 1    Standards-Referenced Report Card Overview.
Figure 2    Seventh Grade Math Report Card.
Figure 3    UW Lab School Learning Walk Agenda.
Figure 4    Learning Walk Observation Form: Math.
Figure 5    Co-Teaching/Traditional Mentoring Continuum.
Figure 6    Elements of Successful Co-teaching.
Figure 7    UW Lab School MAP Data: 2015–2016.

**Chapter 10**
Table 1     Crosswalk of Teacher Leadership Standards.

**Chapter 11**  None.

**Chapter 14**
Table 1   Data Sources and Findings.
Figure 1  Signature Features of Sociocultural Approach to Teacher Leader Development.

**Chapter 16**
Figure 1  Master Teacher Program Design.
Table 1   Master Teacher Timeline.

**Chapter 17**  None.

# About the Contributors

**Sarah Anderson** is a Clinical Instructor in the Department of Curriculum, Instruction, and Foundational Studies at Boise State University in Boise, ID, USA.

**Bernard J. Badiali** is an Associate Professor of Education and Program Coordinator for Curriculum and Supervision in the Department of Curriculum and Instruction at Pennsylvania State University in University Park, PA, USA.

**Ashley Bennett** is a Third Grade Teacher and Principal Designee at Davis Park Elementary School in Terre Haute, IN, USA.

**Rebecca West Burns** is an Assistant Professor in the Department of Teaching and Learning at the University of South Florida in Tampa, FL, USA.

**Carolyn Cort** is a Clinical Instructor in the Department of Literacy, Language, and Culture at Boise State University in Boise, ID, USA.

**Michael N. Cosenza** is an Associate Professor and Director of the Professional Development School Program for the Graduate School of Education at California Lutheran University in Thousand Oaks, CA, USA.

**Azaria Cunningham** is an Eighth Grade Science Teacher at New Roberto Clemente Middle School in Paterson, NJ, USA.

**Amy Garrett Dikkers** is an Associate Professor in the Department of Educational Leadership at the Watson College of Education at the University of North Carolina Wilmington in Wilmington, NC, USA.

**Sherry Dismuke** is an Assistant Clinical Professor in the Department of Curriculum, Instruction, and Foundational Studies at Boise State University in Boise, ID, USA.

## About the Contributors

**Nancy Dubetz** is a Professor in the Department of Early Childhood and Childhood Education at Lehman College, City University of New York in the borough of the Bronx in New York City, USA.

**Bruce E. Field** is the Department Chair and a Professor in the Department of Teaching and Learning at Georgia Southern University in Statesboro, GA, USA.

**Katie Fink** is a Social Studies Teacher at Trask Middle School in New Hanover County Schools, Wilmington, NC, USA.

**Maria Fella** is the English as a New Language (ENL) Coordinator at Public School 291 in the borough of the Bronx in New York City, USA.

**Lori Fulton** is an Associate Professor of Elementary Education in the Institute for Teacher Education at the University of Hawai'i at Mānoa, Honolulu, HI, USA.

**Keri Haley** is an Assistant Professor of Special Education at the University of West Florida in Pensacola, FL, USA.

**Jayne Hellenberg** is a Partner School District Facilitator and Adjunct Professor for the College of Education at the University of Wyoming in Laramie, WY, USA.

**Margaret Hudson** is Principal at the UW Lab School in Albany County School District #1 and an Adjunct Professor for Educational Leadership at the University of Wyoming in Laramie, WY, USA.

**Jana Hunzicker** is an Associate Professor in the Department of Teacher Education and Associate Dean for the College of Education and Health Sciences at Bradley University in Peoria, IL, USA.

**Rhonda Baynes Jeffries** is an Associate Professor in the Department of Instruction and Teacher Education and Program Coordinator for the Curriculum Studies Program at the University of South Carolina in Columbia, SC, USA.

**Nancy Cryder Jones**, a Retired First Grade Teacher, is a University Clinical Educator for the Child Development Associate of Applied Science Practicum at Ohio University in Chillicothe, OH, USA.

## About the Contributors

**Emily Klein** is a Professor of Secondary and Special Education at Montclair State University in Montclair, NJ, USA.

**Sharada Krishnamurthy** is a Doctoral Student in the College of Education at Rowan University in Glassboro, NJ, USA.

**Clare Kruft** is an Educator in the Department of Organization Development, Baltimore County Public Schools in Baltimore, MD, USA.

**Yokaira LaChapell** is an English as a New Language (ENL) Kindergarten Teacher at Public School 291 in the borough of the Bronx in New York City, USA.

**Somer Lewis** is the Director of the Professional Development System in the Office of Teacher Education and Outreach at the Watson College of Education at the University of North Carolina Wilmington in Wilmington, NC, USA.

**P. Erin Lichtenstein** was recently named Associate Principal of Highville Charter School in New Haven, CT, USA.

**Stefanie D. Livers** is an Assistant Professor in the Department of Childhood Education and Family Studies at Missouri State University in Springfield, MO, USA.

**Kathryn McGinn Luet** is an Assistant Professor in the Department of Language, Literacy, and Sociocultural Education for the College of Education at Rowan University in Glassboro, NJ, USA.

**Vail Matsumoto** is an Assistant Professor in the Institute for Teacher Education at the University of Hawai'i at Mānoa, Honolulu, HI, USA.

**Mark Meacham** is an Instructional Coach for Beginning Teachers at the North Carolina New Teacher Support Program and a Lecturer in the School of Education at the University of North Carolina at Greensboro in North Carolina, USA.

**Brianne W. Morettini** is an Assistant Professor in the Department of Interdisciplinary and Inclusive Education for the College of Education at University in Glassboro, NJ, USA.

**Mika Munakata** is a Professor of Mathematics Education at Montclair State University in Montclair, NJ, USA.

**Nina Nagib** is a Doctoral Student in the College of Education at Rowan University in Glassboro, NJ, USA.

**Suzanna Nelson** is a Seventh Grade Reading Teacher at John C. Fremont Professional Development Middle School in Las Vegas, NV, USA.

**Francisco J. Ocasio** is an Eighth Grade English Language Teacher at New Roberto Clemente Middle School in Paterson, NJ, USA.

**Anna M. Quinzio-Zafran** is an Instructor in the Department of Curriculum and Instruction at Northern Illinois University in DeKalb, IL, USA.

**Zareen G. Rahman** is a Doctoral Candidate in the Mathematics Education Ph.D. Program at Montclair State University in Montclair, NJ, USA.

**Jennifer Rivera** is a Universal Literacy Reading Coach at Public School 291 in the borough of the Bronx in New York City, USA.

**Lynn Sikma** is an Assistant Professor in the Department of Early Childhood, Elementary, Middle Grades, Literacy, and Special Education at the Watson College of Education at the University of North Carolina Wilmington in Wilmington, NC, USA.

**Jamie Silverman** is a Full-time Lecturer in the Department of Secondary and Middle School Education at Towson University in Baltimore, MD, USA.

**Jennifer L. Snow** is Associate Dean for Teacher Education and Professor in the College of Education at Boise State University in Boise, ID, USA.

**Monica Taylor** is a Professor of Secondary and Special Education at Montclair State University in Montclair, NJ, USA.

**Kristen Trabona** is a Doctoral Candidate in the Teacher Education and Teacher Development Ph.D. Program at Montclair State University in Montclair, NJ, USA.

**Christopher Urquhart** is a Special Education Varying Exceptionalities Teacher for Hillsborough County Public Schools in Riverview, FL, USA.

**Lisa J. Vernon-Dotson** is a Professor in the Department of Interdisciplinary and Inclusive Education for the College of Education at Rowan University in Glassboro, NJ, USA.

**Elizabeth A. Wilkins** is a Professor in the Department of Curriculum and Instruction and Co-coordinator of Graduate Career and Professional Development at Northern Illinois University in DeKalb, IL, USA.

**Diane Wood** is a Professor at Towson University in Baltimore, MD, USA.

**Jon Yoshioka** is a Professor and Chair of the Master of Education in Teaching Program in the Institute for Teacher Education at the University of Hawai'i at Mānoa, Honolulu, HI, USA.

**A. J. Zenkert** is an Assistant Clinical Professor in the Department of Curriculum, Instruction, and Foundational Studies at Boise State University in Boise, ID, USA.

# Index

Advanced learning, 169–170
Algebra I College Prep (CP)
   de-tracking
   democracy-driven professional development, 60
   educational tracking, 60
   Foundations of Algebra, 63
   inquiry-based learning, 61
   instructional leadership
      guidance department assistance, 65
      mastery learning design, 66–67
      math team format, 65, 66
      student learning outcomes, 67
      theories, 61
   pilot project research, 71
   project implementation timeline, 64
   research methods, 64–65
   school–university partnerships, 61
   self-assessment, 61–62
   self-fulfilling prophecy theory, 61, 62, 70–71
   student learning outcomes, 62, 69–70
   teacher buy-in, 67–68
   teacher collaboration model, 64, 70
   theoretical frameworks, 61
American Association of Colleges for Teacher Education (AACTE), 14, 219
American Federation of Teachers (AFT), 9
Architecture of Accomplished Teaching (AAT), 175
Association for Supervision and Curriculum Development (ASCD), 30

Baltimore County Public Schools (BCPS), 80
   context, 81
   funding and implementation, 84
   information meeting, 81–82
   reflections to improve, 84–85
   weekend workshop, 82–84
Beginning Teacher Project, 217–218, 231, 282
Blue Ribbon Panel, 13, 14
Boundary spanners, 22–23

Carnegie Task Force, 8
Center for Teaching Quality (CTQ), 29
Certification process, 162
Citizen leaders, 4
Classroom-based evidence, 54–55
Classroom teachers, 1
Clinical practice supervision course, 167–168
Clinical Preparation and Partnerships for Improved Student Learning, 13
Collaborative inquiry, project teacher leadership "centers of inquiry," 79

grade level team, 78
institutional and cultural barriers, 79
knowledge-making, 79
local knowledge, 91
principles, 78
school and university bureaucracies, 80
Collaborative partnership, 193
College of Education faculty, 157
Common Core State Standards, 60
Community advisory board (CAB), 225
Community contributions, 210–211
Community engagement, 230
Community leaders, 4
Conceptual diversity, 21
Constructivist leadership, 258
Continuous Improvement Plan (CIP) Committee, 102, 103
Co-teaching models, 176, 195
Co-teaching strategies, 145
  classroom management, 153
  College of Education faculty, 157
  elements, 154, 156
  Measures of Academic Progress (MAP) data, 157, 158
  mentoring skills, 152
  pedagogical and assessment strategies, 153–154
  professional relationships, 153
  traditional mentoring continuum, 154, 155
  train-the-trainer workshop, 154
Council for the Accreditation of Educator Preparation (CAEP), 14, 162
Common Core State Standards (CCSS), 60

Council of Chief State School Officers (CCSSO) report, 164

Decision-making, 23–24
Democracy-driven professional development, 60
Developmental Reading Assessment (DRA), 54
Direct and oversee learning, 171–172
Distributed leadership theory, 24, 220–221
  functions, 24
  grade-level teams, 25, 26
  mentor teacher, 25
  social and situational factors, 25, 26

Educational policy, 20
Elementary and Secondary Education Act, 109
Elementary school (intermediate), 88
Elementary school (primary), 87–88
English Language Arts Standards (ELAS), 51
English language learners (ELLs), 111
English language proficiency, 55, 56
English learners (ELs)
  communities, types, 41
  educational needs, 41–42
  grade level content, 42
  learning facilitators
    classroom, 52
    professional learning series, 49–52
  skill set, 49
  Lehman/Public School 291, 43

pre-service candidate learning
   adult learning, 46
   factors, 47
   gradual release model, 47–48
preservice teacher education curriculum, 48–49
professional learning opportunities, 42
research-based teaching practice, 43–44
student learning
   classroom-based evidence, 54–55
   English language proficiency, 55, 56
   language proficiency, 53
   long-term effects, 55
   quality, 44
   Teacher Leader Model Standards (TLMS), 45–46
   teacher learning, 52–53
   urban school districts, 42
Enhancement Partnership Grant program, 15
Every teacher a leader model, 21

Field and learning
   elementary school (intermediate), 88
   elementary school (primary), 87–88
   high school, 89–90
   middle school, 88–89
   team inquiry projects, 86
Formal leadership, 193
Formal teacher leadership, 21–22, 28
Foundations of Algebra, 63

Grade-level teams, 25, 26
Gradual release model, 47–48

High school, 89–90
Hillside Public Schools, 218, 222
Holmes Group, 7, 8, 10
Hybrid learning environment, 257
Hybrid teacher leadership, 21–22, 136–138

Informal leadership, 193
Informal teacher leadership, 21–22
Inquiry-based learning, 61
In-service teaching, 174
Institutional leaders, 4
Instructional decision-making, 229–230
Instructional leadership, 21, 26, 28–29, 31
   guidance department assistance, 65
   mastery learning design, 66–67
   math team format, 65, 66
   student learning outcomes, 67
   theories, 61

Knowledge-of-practice, 92
K-12 science teachers
   features
      curriculum development, 246
      horizontal and vertical learning, 239–241
      mentoring, teacher leadership, 244–246
      mini-grants, 246
      monthly professional development workshops, 241–243
      teacher leadership projects, 243–244
      teaching practice, 247
   goal of, 236
   STEM professional development center, 237

teacher leadership, 237–238
Wipro Science Education Fellowship (SEF), 236
    change agents, 248
    education reform, 238
    elementary science teachers, 249
    Montclair State University Network for Educational Renewal (MSUNER), 238
    ownership, 248
    selection, 239
    supports, 249
    themes, 247
K-8 university laboratory school, 194

Laboratory schools, 6
Lab school teacher
    opportunities for
        co-teaching strategies, 145, 152–157
        National Staff Development Council, 144
        professional development experiences, 145
        professional learning communities (PLCs), 145–148
        school learning walks, 145, 147–152
    professional development practices, 142
    school–university partnership, 142
        College of Education, 143
        elementary classroom teachers, 143
        leadership roles, 143–144
        positive learning community, 143
        Wyoming schools, 143
    student learning and school improvement, 141
    sustainable schoolwide reform, 142
Leadership competencies, 31
Learning accountability, 4
Learning communities, 172–173
Learning facilitators
    classroom, 52
    professional learning series, 49–52
        core teaching practices, 49
        experience and professional knowledge, 50
        New York State English as a Second Language Achievement Test (NYSESLAT), 50–52
        professional learning opportunities, 52
    skill set, 49
Learning walks, 195
Lehman/Public School 291, 43
Liaisons-in-residence, 193–194
    democratic leadership, 124–125
    hybrid teacher leadership, 136–138
    informal teacher leaders, 122
    leadership structure, 123
    mentor teachers, 122
    professional/leadership identity, 125–126
    research design
        data analysis, 127
        data sources, 127
        phenomenological case study, 126–127

school-based teacher educators, 122
school–university partnership, 123
servant learning
  "coach in the copy room," 129–130
  explicit tensions, 133
  participants feelings, 132
  prioritizing roles, tensions, 134
  professional growth, 128
  professional learning, 127–128
  roles and responsibilities, 128
  self-development, 130–132
  service and equity, 135–136
  teaching professional practice, 124

Master of Education in Teaching (MEdT) program, 202
  alumni Pipeline, 205–206
  assignments, 206–208
  innovative practices
    community contributions, 210–211
    open-door policy, 210
    personalized learning, 209–210
  iterations of, 204
  placements, 205
Master teacher associates (MTAs), 258, 260–262
Master teachers
  evolution of
    constructivist leadership, 258
    growth opportunities, 259
    hybrid learning environment, 257
    inspiration and encouragement, 257
    instructional practice, 258
  master teacher associates (MTAs), 258, 260–262
  Promise of Leadership (POL) Award recipients, 259
  timeline, 259, 260
  organizational structures, 255
  program redesign reflections, 264–266
  P-12 schools, 255
  school–university partnership, 256
  story of, 262–264
  teacher education programs, 255
  Watson College of Education (WCE), 256
Mastery learning design, 66–67
Measures of Academic Progress (MAP), 157, 158, 176
Mentoring, 196. *See also* Pre-service candidate learning
Middle school, 88–89
Montclair State University Network for Educational Renewal (MSUNER), 238
Multidimensional inter-organizational settings, 33
Multiple leadership roles model, 21

National Assessment of Educational Progress results, 108
National Association for Professional Development Schools (NAPDS), 2, 12, 111, 165, 219, 279
National Board Certified Teachers (NBCTs), 27

advanced learning, 169–170
Architecture of Accomplished Teaching (AAT), 175
certification process, 162
clinical faculty members, 165
clinical practice supervision course, 167–168
content and pedagogical knowledge, 170–171
co-teaching models, 176
Council for the Accreditation of Educator Preparation (CAEP), 162
Council of Chief State School Officers (CCSSO) report, 164
data collection and analysis, 168–169
direct and oversee learning, 171–172
feedback, 173, 174
in-service teaching, 174
leadership qualities, 177
learning communities, 172–173
Measure of Academic Progress, 176
mentoring and communication skills, 174
National Association for Professional Development Schools, 165
National Board for Professional Teaching Standards (NBPTS), 162
National Council for Accreditation of Teacher Education (NCATE), 163
participants, 167
positive professional relationships, 176
pre-service teachers, 175
P-12 school clinical educators, 163
Teacher Leadership Exploratory Consortium (TLEC), 163
teacher leadership roles, 165
teacher leadership standards crosswalk, 165, 166
university-based teacher educators, 175
National Board for Professional Teaching Standards (NBPTS), 27, 162
National Commission on Excellence in Education, 26
National Council for the Accreditation of Teacher Education (NCATE), 11, 116, 163, 278
National Education Association (NEA), 9
National Network for Educational Renewal (NNER), 2, 9
National professional network, 12
National Staff Development Council, 144
New York State English as a Second Language Achievement Test (NYSESLAT), 50–52
Nine PDS Essentials, 12, 111, 116, 165, 202, 219, 279, 283, 287
No Child Left Behind (NCLB), 109 legislation, 28

Open-door policy, 210
Organizational culture, 29
Organizational leadership, 24
Organizational skills, 185
Organizational structures, 255
Overarching competencies, 31

Parallel leadership, 24
Parent and Teacher Organization (PTO), 274–275
Participative leadership, 24
Performance-based compensation systems, 27
Personalized learning, 209–210
Policy leadership, 31
Political leaders, 4
Pre-service candidate learning
  adult learning, 46
  factors, 47
  gradual release model, 47–48
Preservice teacher education curriculum, 48–49
Pre-service teachers, 175
Professional learning communities (PLCs), 282–283
  collaborative process, 145
  faculty benefit, 146–147
  implementation, 146
  learner-centered education, 146
  seventh grade math report card, 147, 148
  staff-based training, 146
  standards-referenced report card, 146, 147
Professional learning opportunities, 42, 52
Professional learning series
  core teaching practices, 49
  experience and professional knowledge, 50
  New York State English as a Second Language Achievement Test (NYSESLAT), 50–52
  professional learning opportunities, 52
Project teacher leadership
  Baltimore County Public Schools (BCPS), 80
  context, 81
  funding and implementation, 84
  information meeting, 81–82
  reflections to improve, 84–85
  weekend workshop, 82–84
  chain-of-command structures, 77
  collaborative inquiry
    "centers of inquiry," 79
    grade level team, 78
    institutional and cultural barriers, 79
    knowledge-making, 79
    local knowledge, 91
    principles, 78
    school and university bureaucracies, 80
  conceptualization of, 76
  data analysis protocols, 85
  field and new learning
    elementary school (intermediate), 88
    elementary school (primary), 87–88
    high school, 89–90
    middle school, 88–89
    team inquiry projects, 86
  knowledge-of-practice, 92
  problem-solving teachers, 90
  "reality checks" teachers, 75–76
  "stance of inquiry," 91
  teacher-centered professional development, 77
  Teacher Leader Model Standards (TLMS), 77
  teacher–professor–intern collaboration, 86

top-down professional cultures, 92
Towson University (TU), 80
  context, 80–81
  funding and implementation, 84
  information meeting, 81–82
  reflections to improve, 84–85
  weekend workshop, 82–84
Promise of Leadership (POL)
  Award recipients, 259
P-12 schools, 255
  clinical educators, 163
Pygmalion Effect, 61

Quality teacher preparation, 4

Reflective feedback, 185
Research-based teaching practice, 5, 43–44, 53

School learning walks, 145
  agenda, 150
  classroom visits, 150, 151
  collaborative leadership, 147
  complex and dynamic process, 152
  education program, 149
  instructional strategy, 149
  observation form, 151
School–university–community partnerships, 30
School–university partnership, 2, 5, 9, 24, 32, 61, 142, 283–284
  American Association of Colleges for Teacher Education, 219
  Beginning Teacher Project, 217–218, 231
  College of Education, 143
  Council for the Accreditation of Teacher Preparation (CATP), 219
  distributed leadership, 220–221
  elementary classroom teachers, 143
  empirical evidence, 223–224
  features, 227
    community engagement, 230
    dialog and feedback, 228
    instructional decision-making, 229–230
    sociocultural theoretical framework, 226
    targeted professional development, 226–228
    turnkey training, 228–229
  Hillside Public Schools, 218, 222
  initial findings and resources, 225–226
  K-12 science teachers. See K-12 science teachers
  leadership roles, 143–144
  master teachers, 256
  National Association for Professional Development Schools, 219
  positive learning community, 143
  research context, 222–223
  sociocultural theoretical framework, 218
  teacher leadership, 220
    sociocultural approach, 221
  teacher preparation, 219
  Wyoming schools, 143
Self-fulfilling prophecy theory, 61, 62, 70–71

Index  311

Servant learning
  "coach in the copy room," 129–130
  explicit tensions, 133
  participants feelings, 132
  prioritizing roles, tensions, 134
  professional growth, 128
  professional learning, 127–128
  roles and responsibilities, 128
  self-development, 130–132
  service and equity, 135–136
Service practices, 3
Side by Side (SBS) Charter School, 184
Site-based decision-making, 27
Sociocultural theoretical framework, 226
Sputnik, 7
Stakeholders, 3–4
Student learning, 20, 53
  and achievement, 7–8
  agenda, 116
  authentic community, 114
  beyond test scores
    Elementary and Secondary Education Act, 109
    English language learners (ELLs), 111
    National Assessment of Educational Progress results, 108
    No Child Left Behind (NCLB), 109
    P-12 achievement, 108
    zero-tolerance discipline policies, 110
  classroom-based evidence, 54–55
  Continuous Improvement Plan (CIP) Committee, 102, 103
  courageous, collegial partnership, 99–102
  educational experiences, 107–108
  English language proficiency, 55, 56
  exercise, significant and responsible, 114
  formal organizations, 112
  grade level and team-based collaborations, 113
  inquiry-based teaching and learning, 112
  institutional barriers, teacher leadership, 111
  learning and collaboration, 104–106
  long-term effects, 55
  National Association for Professional Development Schools (NAPDS), 111
  National Council for the Accreditation of Teacher Education (NCATE), 116
  organizational constraints and pressures, 113
  outcomes, 62, 67, 69–70
  quality, 44
  Teacher Leader Model Standards, 115
  Teacher Leadership Exploratory Consortium, 115
  Zane Trace Elementary School, 102

Targeted professional development, 226–228
Targets of Measurement (ToMs), 51

Teacher candidates (TCs)
  passions, 211–214. *See also* Teacher preparation program (TPP)
Teacher-centered professional development, 77
Teacher collaboration model, 64, 70
Teacher education programs, 6, 13
Teacher-in-residence program, 23
Teacher Leader Model Standards (TLMS), 29, 30, 45–46, 77, 115, 192
Teacher leader preparation and development
  formal roles, 279
  National Association for Professional Development Schools, 279
  National Council for the Accreditation of Teacher Education (NCATE), 278
  partnership development pathways, 279–280
  themes
    Beginning Teacher Project, 282
    professional learning, 282–283
    reflective stories, 280
    school–university partnerships, 283–284
    teacher educators, 285–286
    transformational learning, 282
Teacher leader reflections, 196–197
  Continuous Improvement Plan (CIP) Committee, 102, 103
  courageous, collegial partnership, 99–102
  empowerment and leadership, 187
  free educational workshops, 188
  instructional coaching, 269–271
  learning and collaboration, 104–106
  organizational skills, 185
  Parent and Teacher Organization (PTO), 274–275
  professional development program, 187
  professionalization, 183
  reflective feedback, 185
  residency model, 184
  school-based professional development, 189
  Side by Side (SBS) Charter School, 184
  teaching and learning experiences, 186
  time management, 185
  tools for, 272–274
  total teacher leaders, 181–183
  traditional student teaching model, 184
  William Paterson University (WPU) PDS Network, 188
  Zane Trace Elementary School, 102
Teacher Leadership Exploratory Consortium (TLEC), 29, 115, 163, 192
Teacher leadership model, 19, 21
Teacher learning, 45–46, 52–53
Teacher mentoring programs, 27
Teacher preparation program (TPP)
  distributed leadership perspective, 203–204
  "grow your own" philosophy, 215

Master of Education in
    Teaching (MEdT)
    program, 202
  alumni Pipeline, 205–206
  assignments, 206–208
  innovative practices, 209–211
  iterations of, 204
  placements, 205
  partnership level, 214–215
  school–university partnership,
    201
  teacher leadership, 202–203
Teacher–professor–intern
    collaboration, 86
Teacher Quality Enhancement
    Partnership Grant
    program, 11
Teacher Quality Partnership
    (TQP), 15
Teaching and learning practices,
    23
Teaching/learning cycle, 3
Time management, 185
"Tomorrow's Schools of
    Education," 10–11
Top-down leadership, 197
Towson University (TU), 80
  context, 80–81
  funding and implementation,
    84

information meeting, 81–82
reflections to improve, 84–85
weekend workshop, 82–84
Traditional mentoring continuum,
    154, 155
Transformational learning, 282
Turnkey training, 228–229

Watson College of Education
    (WCE), 256
William Paterson University
    (WPU) PDS Network,
    188
Wipro Science Education
    Fellowship (SEF), 236
  change agents, 248
  education reform, 238
  elementary science teachers,
    249
  Montclair State University
    Network for Educational
    Renewal (MSUNER),
    238
  ownership, 248
  selection, 239
  supports, 249
  themes, 247

Zane Trace Elementary School,
    102

www.ingramcontent.com/pod-product-compliance
Lightning Source LLC
Chambersburg PA
CBHW052132010526
44113CB00035B/1993